THE S

AND E

OF HORACE

THE SATIRES

AND EPISTLES

OF HORACE

A Modern English Verse Translation
by
SMITH PALMER BOVIE

THE UNIVERSITY OF CHICAGO PRESS

CHICAGO & LONDON

THE UNIVERSITY OF CHICAGO PRESS, CHICAGO 60637
The University of Chicago Press, Ltd., London

International Standard Book Number: 0-226-06776-9
  (clothbound); 0-226-06777-7 (paperbound)
Library of Congress Catalog Card Number: 59-16413

CONTENTS

EPISTLES

GENERAL INTRODUCTION

The *Satires* and *Epistles* of Horace show us the life and mind of a renowned artist and citizen of Augustan Rome. From these hexameter poems, which constitute nearly one-half of Horace's entire literary production, there emerges a more complete view of the man and poet than can be derived from any other body of professional work by a Greek or Roman writer known to us today. The *saturae* or *sermones*, "little talks on random subjects" or "conversation pieces," are the first works Horace published. The "letters," personal but deftly versified communications to a dozen or more friends, are among the last of Horace's works, brought out some years subsequent to the eighty-eight lyric poems comprising the first three books of famous *Odes*. The whole list of Horace's writings would also include the *Epodes*, seventeen poems probably collected and published the year after the second book of *Satires*, modeled on the savage Greek "lyric" poems of Archilochus, and composed in a variety of iambic couplet rhythms; the stately *Carmen saeculare*, written to commemorate the festival of national thanksgiving in 17 B.C.; and a fourth book of fifteen *Odes* produced soon thereafter, contemporary with the second book of *Epistles*. A mere chronological review of Horace's lifework shows how consistently he lived as a man of letters keeping pace with his times, as commentator and critic, as citizen and artist.

In the *Satires* and *Epistles* we find ourselves most completely in the presence of this man, and I have chosen to translate the eighteen "talks" and the twenty-three letters into English verse partly out of eagerness to recall to the modern reader's mind the very modernity and lifelikeness of Horace's portrait of himself and his world. Ushering in the career of a modest man who was destined to scale the heights of lyric poetry and whose Roman achievement was to be "the gradual conquest of one poetic genre after another through continuous adaptation of such Greek models as had not been Latinized before,"[1] the *Satires* seem to me as strong as a Roman aqueduct and as purposeful in their design. The hexameter form that Horace began with and was to revert to at the other end of his poetic career is a kind of masonry, capable of carrying a steady flow of thought, a stream of vigorous intelligence moving on like a river: *vehemens et liquidus puroque simillimus amni.*[2]

By the time of the *Epistles*, Horace's hexameter style is perhaps better compared with the appurtenances of a stylish Roman villa. Some of the letters are like slender columns supplying perfect support and graceful proportions to a well-planned portico. Others are like inner rooms to read, rest, or grumble in; still others like central courts, awash with sunshine and clear air. The longer letters of the second book spread out like gardens and walks where the owner might stroll to view his property at a distance and consider its worth, speculating about its future while deriving pleasure from its evidently real present. Whatever analogies may come to mind, the fact remains that Horace wrought individual and lasting effects with the form of the *Satires* and *Epistles*. In so doing, he established a style serviceable to his Latin successors and re-established a genre that was to thrive again, particularly in the European literature of the Middle Ages and the seven-

[1] Eduard Fraenkel, *Horace* (Oxford, 1957), p. 47. Throughout my analysis I am indebted to Professor Fraenkel's incomparable discussion of the relevant texts.

[2] Horace *Epistles* ii. 2. 120.

teenth and eighteenth centuries, and to prove highly adaptable to the purposes of prose satire at large, both then and now.

In 4,000-plus hexameter lines Horace combines self-revelation and literary production to create a quite distinctive species of the satirical genre. Wryly admitting his kinship with serious-minded poets, close to the *genus irritabile vatum* but clearly diffident toward the epic style which served others as the medium for heroic adventure, philosophic speculation, historical or patriotic narration, Horace made of the form a kind of documentary film, candidly picturing his own conduct, voicing quiet opinions riveted to experience and common sense, focusing on a variety of scenes, most of them far from complimentary to the Roman way of life. The form made it possible for him to walk abroad among his fellow men, to talk with them and about them: he repeatedly reminds us of the pedestrian nature of the muse who attends the lines that unreel casually along scenes of Roman life and landscape. But these "talks" that wind their way onward, always on solid ground, *sermones . . . repentis per humum,* are not only a confession of curiosity on Horace's part. They result from a style, a way of dealing with men and manners. The portraits, documents, anecdotes, scenes, and colloquial exchanges he produces result from his craftsmanship and are animated and illuminated by his art. As poems, they deserve to stand alongside the *Odes,* complementary to the shapely perfection of the lyric poetry by virtue of their own sustained, vibrant, and durable hexameter measures.

Born in the small town of Venusia in the southern province of Apulia on November 8, 65 B.C., Horace grew up under the watchful care of his father. In the decades that immediately preceded and set in motion momentous changes, virtual "rev-

olutions" in the government of Rome through successive con-
flicts of power from republic to empire, Horace's father, a
simple freedman, managed to provide his son with a good education and a fair seedtime of youthful leisure. He brought
the boy to Rome for early schooling beside the favored sons
of the wealthy, under the best teachers available, and ulti-
mately sent him to "the university," i.e., Athens, to complete
his studies. Horace was in Athens by the time he was twenty,
continuing his study of philosophy, rhetoric, and mathematics
(and perhaps delving into volumes of Greek lyric verse with
special if unsuspecting interest), when the course of his life
was abruptly turned in another direction. The conspirator
Brutus journeyed to Athens in the late summer of 44 B.C. on
his way to assume the governorship of Macedonia and Asia
Minor, and Horace, together with other angry young Romans
among his enthusiastic fellow students (notably, Cicero's son),
rallied to the banner of the patriotic assassin. Horace left
Athens in the retinue of Brutus and sometime during the next
year or so was appointed to the rank of field-grade officer as
tribunus militum on Brutus' staff. He saw action at Philippi
and shared in the final rout of the republican army by the
forces of Antony and Octavian at the second battle.[3]

Presumably, sometime during this disastrous period Horace's father had died; certainly the property in Venusia, farm-
land and town house, had been confiscated by the victorious
Caesarians,[4] and Horace returned to Rome in hopelessly reduced circumstances. He had abandoned the lost cause of the
republicans after Philippi—unlike the young Cicero, for ex-

[3] Eighty-five years later, at Philippi, Paul first preached the gospel in Eu-
rope. Two passages from Horace's *Epistles*, i. 14. 36 and ii. 2. 141–42, suggest
to me that Paul may have known them. Two others recur to the same image:
i. 1. 10. and ii. 1. 99–100.

[4] Either in 43 B.C. or a few months after Philippi. Cf. Fraenkel, p. 13.

ample, who kept on with the resistance formed under Sextus Pompey until it was finally dispersed by Octavian and Antony in 35 B.C.—and in return was granted a pardon for his role in the rebellion. With further address, he now managed to pull away from difficulty by investing what remained of his financial resources in the acquisition of a good administrative post in the "treasury department."[5]

And so, curiously enough, in his twenty-fifth or twenty-sixth year, Horace's life turned back in the right direction as he assumed the duties of an official scribe and simultaneously began to test his strength as unofficial writer, or artist. Some twenty years later, in a letter to Julius Florus, Horace summed up the whole sequence with the declaration that poverty drove him to literature:

> Romae nutriri mihi contigit, atque doceri
> iratus Grais quantum nocuisset Achilles.
> adiecere bonae paulo plus artis Athenae,
> scilicet ut vellem curvo dinoscere rectum,
> atque inter silvas Academi quaerere verum.
> dura sed emovere loco me tempora grato,
> civilisque rudem belli tulit aestus in arma
> Caesaris Augusti non responsura lacertis.
> unde simul primum dimisere Philippi,
> decisis humilem pennis inopemque paterni
> et laris et fundi, paupertas impulit audax
> ut versus facerem.[6]

The context within which this passage occurs is ironic ("a man has to be angry, if not plundered and penniless, before

[5] From the Suetonian *Vita:* bello Philippensi excitus a M. Bruto imperatore tribunus militum meruit; victisque partibus venia impetrata scriptum quaestorium comparavit.

[6] *Epistles* ii. 2. 41–52.

he'll do anything unusual . . . my back was to the wall . . . now that I'm well fixed, I'd be out of my mind to go on writing . . ."—all this in excellent hexameters!). And Professor Fraenkel has judiciously interpreted the remarks:

He does not want his reader to infer from his words that it was solely *paupertas audax* that impelled him to write his early poems. But he does mean to say that, had it not been for the ruin of his former expectations and the loss of his property he would not have become a "professional" poet although, like many educated Romans, he might have written some verses in his spare time. Finally, it could not occur to any of Horace's contemporaries to take his words as indicating that after Philippi he hoped to make a living out of the work of his pen. Such a hope would have been absurd. And as for the chance of finding a wealthy patron who might support him, that was, at best, a very remote one.[7]

But, remote as the possibility was, it materialized for Horace fairly soon. And it is interesting to see how he responded to this crisis: *paupertas*, assuredly, was not the main blow but rather the last in a series—as Horace himself places it in the account given above—the culmination of events that were to leave indelible impressions on his poetry and his thought. A sound education, leading to preoccupation with philosophy and the need to tell the crooked from the straight; "hard times"—an impetuous youthful allegiance to the wrong side and a brief hour of military glory ending in ignominious defeat and clipped wings; the loss of his father's estate (and of his father); the grinding need to acquire some kind of status —these things *did* impel Horace to assert himself, and self-realization came about by means of his first poetry.

He wrote a few satires, and possibly some epodes. The poems attracted the interest of friends and acquaintances,

[7] Fraenkel, p. 14.

among whom were Vergil and Varius. And Vergil, who now because of his *Eclogues* (published in 40 B.C.) enjoyed the friendship of Maecenas and Octavian, introduced Horace into the privileged circle. The presentation was seconded by Varius, and from sometime around 38 B.C. on, Horace was to be assured for the rest of his life of the recognition and support of an influential patron. Our classical dictionaries used to say of Maecenas that his fame rests on his patronage of Horace and Vergil, but it is only just to add that the fame of Horace and Vergil owes a great deal to the patrician Maecenas, who saw to it that these men had the leisure and independence to devote their lives to the proper ends. Certainly, when he first accepted Horace into his circle of friends, Maecenas could not have foreseen the *Odes*, the *Epistles*, the *Carmen saeculare*, or even the bulk of the *Satires* and *Epodes*. For him, it was a case of recognizing talent and betting on its future. For Horace, it was a case of thanking his lucky stars[8] for a connection with a powerful figure, highly placed in the social and political sphere, who took a direct interest in his literary career and made possible the concentration on writing that his life had been evolving toward.

By 35 B.C. Horace had produced the first book of the *Satires;* five years later he brought out the second book and shortly thereafter the *Epodes*. Maecenas made Horace a present of the Sabine Farm, probably in 33 B.C., and as the troubled decade of the "thirties" drew to an end Horace's prospects were serene. His first artistic efforts had won the recognition of men whose opinion he valued;[9] he was acquiring craftsmanship and confidence; he could feel secure. Octavian's

[8] Cf. *Odes* ii. 17. 21–22: utrumque nostrum incredibili modo / consentit astrum.

[9] Cf. *Satires* i. 10, end.

conquest of Antony at Actium in 31 ended the struggle for power that had gone on in one form or another since 44 and established the princeps in complete control of the Roman government.[10] Through the good offices of Maecenas, Vergil, and others, Horace was to enjoy the friendship of the future emperor and was to become, perhaps more definitely than Vergil, the poet laureate of the Augustan Age. And somehow this first prestige and success did not spoil the writer, now in his thirties, who had come from Venusia to Rome for an education, plowed through the course of his early years with a certain steady resourcefulness, and conducted himself in the early campaigns of his life as something of a free lance.

He proceeded with his art, going on to compose the most enchanting and most splendidly versatile lyric poetry the world had yet known. He lived on quietly, with that utter naturalness and freedom of mind he may well have inherited from his foursquare father, and aimed primarily, it seems to me, at keeping on good terms with himself and with his fellow men, from the foreman on the Sabine Farm to the princeps on the Palatine. In the hexameter poems, adhering to this aim meant being critical of other's shortcomings while still mindful of one's own, confessing to and pleading for good standards of human behavior. It meant being inquisitive and striving for clarity of thought in an effort to make conduct square with experience. It meant setting the gyroscope of morality spinning gaily on its well-balanced course.

On the literary side, Horace's purpose in both the *Satires* and the *Epistles*[11] was to rejuvenate and improve an artistic

10 Octavian assumed the title "Augustus" in 27 B.C. In the *Satires* Horace refers to him by name, "Caesar," whereas in the *Odes* and *Epistles* he uses the title.

11 I follow Fraenkel in classifying all the poems in one genre, as *sermones*. Horace uses the term twenty-four times, evenly divided between the *Satires* and *Epistles*.

genre invented for Romans by Lucilius, who, more than a century earlier, had enjoyed somewhat the same relationship with Scipio Africanus and his circle that Horace enjoyed with Maecenas and Octavian, and whose *life*, furthermore, Horace reminds us, was an *open book*.[12] Horace set out to improve the shape and durability of Roman satire, to form it into a thing of wit to annoy forever those who would cling to second-rate lives and be content with inaccurate guesses in place of self-knowledge. Satire was to be quick-moving, uncluttered, funny and fiendish in its exposition of man, the complex variable. Its spirit was to be bright and energetic, its substance particular and apposite. *Un corps solide qui brille!*

Nowhere is Macaulay's doctrine of "the infinite superiority of the particular to the general" more manifest than in Horace's talks and letters, as the poet's lines lay bare the interconnected tissue of example. Every poem is a case in point. And the whole group forms a radiant body of solid sense.

The cascading hexameters of Horace, furthermore, occupy a definite branch of "social" literature. The subject matter is simply Horace and his friends, Horace and his fellow men, the poet being determined to keep his head and use his mind while assiduously converting material and motives alike into literary substance. The result may seem at times to be wax rather than honey,[13] but Horace's sorties into the world of men have as their unmistakable purpose to add to the store of social good. Satire in general seems to persist in serving soci-

---

[12] *Satires* ii. 1. 30–34.

[13] It is the *Odes* that are the honey. Cf. *Odes* iv. 2. 27–32:

> ego apis Matinae
> more modoque
>
> grata carpentis thyma per laborem
> plurimum circa nemus uvidique
> Tiburis ripas operosa parvus
> carmina fingo.

ety in this way, bringing criticism to bear on human conduct, irradiating the sluggish waters of self-concern with the pure air of the human condition, a social atmosphere. Horatian satire is at one with the whole art when it arouses friends and disarms enemies, describes the pitfalls and obstacles in the way of the good life cheerfully enough to enable us to avoid them.

The *Epistles* are eminently, and obviously, social—another of Horace's many means of keeping in touch with people and with his art at the same time. The quality of satire is not lacking, however, for criticism and objectivity play an important role in the later poems, as in the earlier. The very last lines of the *Letter to the Pisos* (or the *Art of Poetry*) serve as a howling indictment of poetic delusion and personality delusion. The letters and the talks like to keep us laughing, and also to keep bringing us back to our senses.

What we encounter along the length and breadth of this work is not only literary skill and social sensibility but the image of a goodhearted, painstaking man who is companionable because he is self-understanding. It has often been said that Horace is cheerful, that he befriends the reader, and this is as true as it is familiar. A certain largeness of soul and a genuine but open-minded concern for the sensitive flesh of human character (very much like the qualities Montaigne displays in the *Essays*) keep Horace from being in any ultimate sense offensive. For most readers he will remain the poet of fellowship, the laureate of men and manners. His *sermones,* together with his lyric poems, form a finished portrait of the artist as a grown man, welcome in the good company he kept, known, respected, even listened to, by his fellow men.

SATIRES

INTRODUCTION
TO BOOK ONE

The individual poems comprising each book of the *Satires* are not arranged chronologically in the order of their composition. Instead, Horace offers us a book with a table of contents as varied as the menu of a formal dinner or an exhibition of paintings or an evening of music in different styles and moods. The first satire is programmatic, unfolding the philosophical implications of Horatian satire as a whole. The tenth is "literary," a concluding speech in defense of the form used throughout the book. And as a seeming afterthought, the poet orders his slave to add this poem to the rest: *i, puer, atque meo citus haec subscribe libello.* But the structure of the whole group that begins with an appeal to Maecenas for social sensibility and ends with a summons to the "copy boy" and a responsible commitment to the book is based on thematic considerations.

As in the *Odes* and *Epistles,* a dedicatory address to Maecenas inaugurates the work and establishes the tone on an ethical and dignified level. The first satire is philosophical and argumentative, "with a moral view designed / To cure the vices of mankind" by subjecting them to analysis. Both the ethical inquiry and the analysis of misconduct are complementary sides of Horace's philosophy, a philosophy of *life,* as conventional as it is true. He thinks that a moderation of desire, according to a reasonable standard of attainment, is the best and happiest direction for human energy to take:

> est modus in rebus, sunt certi denique fines,
> quos ultra citraque nequit consistere rectum.[1]

[1] Cf. also *Epistles* i. 18. 9:
   virtus est medium vitiorum et utrimque reductum.

In the analysis of greed which forms the main part of Horace's first satire, Aristotle's view of ethical progress as the habit of arriving at the central point equidistant from the extremes of deficiency and excess is appropriated for Roman purposes. Avarice, furthermore, well epitomizes the doctrine of the mean, for it shows us man gripped simultaneously by both extremes, morally confused by mistaking "too much" for "too little," and blind to the fact of "enough." As avarice in general mirrors inconsistency in action, so Horace's miser Ummidius, who had so much money he had to measure, not count, it, is correspondingly insecure and fearful, impoverished and nerve-racked by his rampant compulsion.

The main body of the poem follows expertly on the introductory lines which probe into that formidable inconsistency in the directing of their energies to which all men are prey. It is inconsistent, Horace argues, to want more than we need, inconsistent to want to be what we are not. The drive to acquire more than we have carries us swiftly past the point of what we need into the region of excess, and the only reasonable solution is provided in the doctrine of the mean: we must skilfully, reasonably, and wilfully discern the point at which we can make optimum use of what we have. This counsel, furthermore, holds good for spiritual resources as well as for material: our inconsistency oscillates so violently as to shatter our peace of mind when we fail to recognize and enforce the proper use of ourselves. The arc of human action, when it describes a course from nothing to everything, is more like a falling star than like a measurable sine wave. As for the idea that unlimited acquisitions or the boundless exertion of undirected energy can confer happiness or satisfaction on man, Horace would say that this is the sort of idea that needs to be cured, not refuted. The skinflint gazing in bittersweet solitude on the gold pieces in his strongbox is a miserable miser. Tantalus will *always* be thirsty, and Horace intends us to take the story to heart: *mutato nomine de te / fabula narratur.*

Horace's first satire dwells on the folly of excess, on the spectacle, played over day after day, of men carried beyond themselves by the acquisitive instinct. It leads into the main doctrine with some crisp words on the "Concept of Interchangeability" (as Thomas Mann ironically labels it in his comic novel on a similar theme, *The Confessions of Felix Krull, Confidence Man*). Why is it, Horace asks Maecenas, that no one can see his way through the delusion but keeps hankering to be otherwise? Because, he explains, by arraying examples before us to observe and judge, everyone who illustrates this delusion passes beyond the point of no return in the use of his moral energies and beyond the boundary lines of his material needs. Men *can* drive themselves, or be driven, beyond their limits, and Horace makes the point with his cases of inconsistency and greed.

Then, deliberately returning to the point of departure, after having rounded up his many relevant examples, Horace reiterates it, and the poem tapers off with a congenial counter-image cast in a familiar Epicurean mold: Life *was* meant to bring pleasure into the world! I don't mean to deny men the privilege of satisfying their desires. But the end depends upon the means by which you pursue it, and I have tried to show you men not pursuing their desires but pursued by them, routed, in fact running wild.[2] Life is probably not a "race" at all. It is a kind of banquet to which we have all been invited,

[2] Tolstoy, in *How Much Land Does a Man Require?* sets his main character running on too wide a course. He will be entitled to all the land he can "cover" in a day's journey, but he arrives back at the starting point at sundown, after encircling the largest area (of all the contestants), to drop dead of physical exhaustion at the judges' feet.

the seating arrangements being taken care of by our solicitous hostess, nature. Our welfare is spread plain before us. Why not fall to with a relish and, after the banquet is over, rise to depart, nourished, sustained, well satisfied, perhaps even grateful?

The second satire follows the theme of conduct in another direction, fastening on the sensational subject of adultery and love pangs at large. Here too, deficiency can lead straight off the cliff and plunge us into excess, and for Horace there is no more amusing sight than the male animal "falling" in love. Lovers are liable to wild distortions of the problem of truth and beauty and are prone to assume the most compromising positions, Horace discovers, and he posts warnings against such absurdities. Nor is self-control the least of the matters at issue, as is made clear in an imaginary exchange of remarks between the amorous male and his *membrum virile*, the "slave" in this case proving to be more instinctively reasonable than his master. And as in the first satire, after a scandalous review of typical excesses, Horace opposes to them his well-tempered and moderate solution. Make love, by all means! But if you go at it stupidly or dishonestly, there'll be hell to pay.

Hermogenes Tigellius, whose recent obsequies get the second satire off to a gay start and whose disappearance from the poem is as marked as his disappearance from life, is not merely a person, or two persons. Tigellius, like others whom Horace ridicules by name, is a handy type of the malfunctioning *homo insipiens*. Fabius at the end of the second satire and Crispinus at the end of the first are two more, and so it goes through the whole spectrum of foolishness, names without number. Individual subjects stay near enough the context for Horace to be able to lay hands on them quickly. The names are pegs to hang more particulars on. Embodying statements about misconduct, the persons in Horace's morality plays add the third dimension to the poet's art by animating it.

The names of persons, unnamed persons ("the bore" of the ninth satire), giveaway names ("Porcius," or "Nomentanus and Pantolabus"—out of Lucilius by Parasitus)—these all strengthen the structure, like knots in a net, by making us mindful of real people. They often provide a starting point for the poem, and its terminus. But the whole problem of the structure of the *Satires* is too large to be solved in terms of any one feature. Horace is less the calculating architect here than he is in the *Odes*. He lets someone or something set the subject in motion and follows that motion where the mind leads. Given an occasion or a horrible example, *Orazio satiro*, whom Dante found still walking calmly about Limbo, follows the kindly light of his hexameter torch amid the encircling gloom. In the mobile form of the *satura*, he finds opportunities for pausing long enough to register protests, post warnings, and paint images, but then he moves on in search of the right words for the wrong things, testing the strength of his form, careful not to tax its conversational powers. Usually, he plunges *in medias res*, then lets his *stilus* trace the contours of the Terrabil Terrain. He is reading a map, not rendering a blueprint.

And yet there emerges from a given poem a general unity, reinforced by the particular cases in point, as the unchanging laws of rhetoric require. There is often a remarkable "return," as the original theme is heard again in the concluding chords. A satire of Horace builds its case. The truth of the matter gradually evolves out of the inquiry being made into it. The aberrance in question is given a local habitation, the offender a name, the structure a durable life.

In the third satire Horace starts off again making fun by name. Tigellius, the Great Virtuoso, was, it seems, more "o so" than "virtuous." The fact is, he was just a bundle of nerves, psychologically never on the level: *nil aequale homini fuit illi.* Inconsistent, unpredictable, "uneven": *nil fuit umquam / sic impar sibi.* But Horace refuses to pound his victim to pieces. The point of departure leads surprisingly into an elaborate plea for indulgence, for toleration of other people's shortcomings and recognition of our own, which takes on a lapidary luster halfway along in the poem by the recollection that "No man is born free of faults / The best man has simply the fewest": *nam vitiis nemo nascitur: optimus ille est / qui minimis urgetur.* For all the criticism and complaint welling up in our hearts at the follies of our fellow men, we are better advised to make allowances, to be excessively forgiving rather than deficiently disdainful. What offends us may actually derive from an eager compulsion to *please,* to be thought worthy of our attention. *De Horatio haec fabula narratur:* what a simple-minded chatterbox he is to break in on Maecenas the way he does, to invade his privacy with some impromptu *sermo!* How tactless! Fortunately, Maecenas makes the necessary allowances.

As the satire proceeds, it winds downward toward the negative again and stumbles across a sociological rationale for this "offensiveness" of which we are so critical. An excellent passage, evocative of Lucretian dogma and tinged with empirical truth, states the case for moral evolution. Men have, Horace writes, at last learned to make better use of their primitive instincts, have thought their way out of the jungle. They have learned to stop fighting and live together, to fence off their world from the predatory instincts that threaten it by building up towns and laying down laws.

Cum prorepserunt primis animalia terris
mutum et turpe pecus, glandem atque cubilia propter
unguibus et pugnis, dein fustibus, atque ita porro
pugnabat armis, quae post fabricaverat usus,
donec verba, quibus voces sensusque notarent,
nominaque invenere. dehinc absistere bello
oppida coeperunt munire et ponere leges,
ne quis fur esset, neu latro, neu quis adulter.

Long before Helen, the war between men and women had raged perpetually, signifying that the state of nature was the state of every man against every man and, no doubt, a form of existence to be thought of as solitary, poor, nasty, brutish, and short:

nam fuit ante Helenam cunnus taeterrima belli
causa, sed ignotis perierunt mortibus illi
quos venerem incertam rapientis more ferarum
viribus editior caedebat ut in grege taurus.

Horace's blistering indictment of the predatory male spun along by sexual instinct on an endless cycle of aggression is a negative blow, but leads to the positive counterstroke. It has proved more human and less bestial in the long run for man to establish conventions and abide by them. Expedience and "utility," the parent of law and order, have made this truth perfectly plain. Justice derives from the fear of injustice. "Civilization" has evolved from its "discontents." Primitive man *was* offensive, and nature has no way of distinguishing right from wrong. Social conventions, human equability, and levelheadedness have taken over the job from nature. A useful mother brings us to the point where ethical conduct begins to be a rational function.

In the latter part of this satire Horace seems to be siding with the Epicurean view of moral development against the

Stoic insistence upon an absolute duality of good and evil. Adopting the view that our own natural history shows how we have made use of ourselves and developed the capacity for social behavior and law and order, Horace seems to be warning against the tyranny of the absolute, whereby justice becomes little more than revenge and punishment a terror inflicted on the weak by the strong. As with the Stoic exaggeration of rational prerogatives in the form of the wise man's monopoly on reason, and other inconsistencies which he ridicules at the end of the poem, Horace finds no room in Stoic psychology for the adjustment of differences, for toleration and distinctions of degree in wrongdoing. Stoic righteousness is a barricade behind which the philosopher-king retires in fanatical seclusion. Horace prefers the company of his friends, the status of a private citizen in the real realm of sensitive, reflective, fellow men.

Next, literary criticism. If the first theme of Horace's book was social, the second is the writer's role as literary sheepdog. Like a good working dog,[3] the satirist needs breeding, instinct, and form, and all these must be harnessed to method if he is to keep constantly alert to the vagaries of the lonely crowd. In the fourth satire Horace aligns himself with those poets whose work has been critical in intent, mentioning several authors of Greek comedy including Aristophanes and turning in particular to the Roman satirist Lucilius. More than a century earlier (*ca.* 180–102 B.C.) Lucilius' thirty books of *saturae* had come into being to establish a formidable

---

[3] Cf. *Epodes* vi. 5–8:

> nam qualis aut Molossus aut fulvus Lacon
> amica vis pastoribus
> agam per altas aure sublata nives,
> quaecumque praecedet fera.

precedent for any future incumbent. Horace is clearly conscious of the mass and energy evident in the work of his
literary relative (of which some thirteen hundred lines of
fragments are all that remain today) and plans to meet the
challenge of this multitudinous array of salty sayings in the
following way: he will write fewer lines, in a better style. The
style, Horace admits, is hardly to be called "poetic"—let such
a title be reserved for the grand authors, in whose ranks he
is not to be numbered. This is the tenor of Horace's colloquy
with an imaginary critic in the early part of the fourth satire,
with "someone" who objects to satire as a *form:*

> primum ego me illorum dederim quibus esse poetas
> excerpam numero: neque enim concludere versum
> dixeris esse satis; neque si qui scribat uti nos
> sermoni propriora, putes hunc esse poetam.
> ingenium cui sit, cui mens divinior atque os
> magna sonaturum, des nominis huius honorem.

Take away the meter, arrange the words in a different order,
Horace argues, and you'll find there is no poetry left. But
if you break apart the epic speech of Ennius, you'll still find
the fractured limbs of a poet: *invenias etiam disiecti membra
poetae.*

In the first part of the fourth satire Horace's rippling and
resounding verses, with their shattering climax, *disiecti membra poetae,* take on an almost Orphic resonance. Starting out
by admitting that he follows in the path of Lucilius but intends to step along somewhat more gracefully, he then pauses
to comment on two cases of literary delusion: Crispinus
thinks the best writer is the fastest, and Fannius goes in for
publicity. The real trouble is, Horace continues, that satire
provokes people, keeps running into opposition, and so poetry

gets a bad name: *omnes hi metuunt versus, odere poetas.* People resent the artist who takes them to task because they are afraid he will put them in his book.[4] So Horace retreats to the level ground of prose; but the retreat, like the rout at Philippi, has strategic advantages, for it gives him the occasion to label and characterize the "pure prose," the *sermo merus,* the "plain talk," that comprises this conversational genre. He maneuvers nimbly around the point: plain words . . . simple talk, ordinary talk . . . except for the rhythm, meter, and word order, utterly unpoetic. None of the grandeur of epic. I surrender.

And the second part wanders off into social considerations, literary criticism apparently having dissolved, the problem of form having gone by default. Horace now hears himself being asked about content rather than form. Why do you have to keep picking on people? He answers in two ways, first innocently: *"What* people? When I said so-and-so thought of himself as a conversationalist and raconteur but was in reality a windbag and a bore, I wasn't referring to *you,* was I? Why take it personally? ('What individual could resent / When thousands equally were meant?') The satirist, you must admit, speaks out frankly and publicly. He doesn't talk behind your back, never indulges in character assassination at private parties. He doesn't gossip and he never HINTS. Talk about your 'smooth and sophisticated' man about town—*comis et urbanus*—dishing out the dirt at a dinner party! I'd say the man was better described as drunk and disorderly. You won't find the satirist guilty of such treachery."

---

[4] Proust says, "People in society are too apt to think of a book as a sort of cube one side of which has been removed, so that the author can at once 'put in' the people he meets. This is obviously disloyal, and authors are a pretty low class."

Second, Horace answers his critics by citing from experience, his own experience. "The content of this form is corroborated by the truths I once learned from my father, a judicious mentor and critic. He taught me to recognize good and bad forms of conduct by pointing out both. As he took me about Rome, he singled out examples of both sorts of men, describing for me the consequences of this action and that one. In so doing, he said, he was keeping me afloat until such time as I knew how to swim along by myself. The fact is, he formed me with his words: *sic me / formabat puerum dictis*. And I am only continuing to shape and manage my existence according to this life-preserving method of precept by example. I intend to go right on picking out the good from the bad to the end of my days. My life is often a kind of soliloquy on virtue, a monologue on self-conduct. Better do it this way . . . *that* will make me happier . . . my friends will approve, surely. . . . Let's hope I never pull a trick like *that*."

And by the end of the satire, social criticism has fallen neatly into place alongside literary criticism, as Horace joins the two parts of the poem with a concluding view of himself the artist and critic in a characteristic pose, silently reflecting on human nature and conduct and then when he has a few moments just jotting something down on paper: *ubi quid datur oti / illudo chartis*. It's his main weakness, this minor vice of being a POET—and if we don't concede it to him, it may be our position that is endangered. The retreat was merely feigned, for "poetry" has not, after all, evaporated in the heat of battle. Unless we assent and allow poets their rightful place, they'll descend en masse and convert us to their point of view.

Having now introduced both themes, Horace will proceed for the rest of the hexameter poems with variations of one sort or another. Social criticism will dominate the *Satires*, literary criticism the *Epistles*, although the one will seldom be heard to the exclusion of the other. The *Satires* will of course abound in gaucherie, caricature, horrible examples, the *Epistles* offer matter more strictly germane to belles-lettres. But a sustained contrapuntal treatment of the artist-in-society distinguishes Horace's hexameter music from beginning to end. The fifth satire of Book I, for instance, seems to be sheer satire, a medley of minor misfortunes. The poet undergoes a journey from Rome to Brindisi and the concomitant torments of travel. But this *sermo* has at least two distinctly literary sides—not to mention its embarrassingly candid rendering. For one thing, it rivals a similar piece by Lucilius and thus forms a literary link to the conventional mode of the old master. For another, placed midway in the course of Book I, the fifth satire gathers up both the poet and his reader from the bivouac and marches them off in physical transition from the first half of the book to the last. In the ninth satire, Horace will take us on another jaunt before coming to a halt in the last poem of the book—this time merely across the city (and again in literary parallel with Lucilius), and even more of an experiment in slow motion.

In the sixth satire Horace is protecting himself and Maecenas against envy and gossip. His defense is real and plain enough: "Maecenas chose to accept me into his circle, which proves that he's no snob. And who am I? No one important, the son of a freedman, who once commanded a legion. I'm lucky to enjoy Maecenas' company, and have Vergil and Varius to thank for that. My father brought me to Rome from Venusia when I was a boy and watched over me. . . . I'll be everlastingly grateful to him. And what have I amounted to? Nothing much, only myself. I travel light, respect my diet, live as I please. I roam about the city at will, I read and write a bit. I'm perfectly happy. Of course, some people are never happy unless. . . ." From defense, Horace goes over to the attack, enumerating some typical deviations from the standard of good sense.

The seventh and eighth satires form a pair of variations on the theme of conduct, an anecdote and a diatribe: look on this portrait of social misfits, and on this. The subject matter may be coarse, the tone harsh and bitter, but the rendering is subtly swift and forceful.[5] In the seventh poem Mr. Rex of Praeneste rolls darkling down the torrent of his fate, while the sophisticated Mr. Persius outclasses him in a lawsuit. The scene is Clazomenae in Asia Minor, the time 43 or early 42 B.C. Persius' triumph consists of a well-placed pun,[6] whereby he implores Brutus, descendant of regicides and regicide in his own right, to kill this Rex.

If Brutus the liberator moderates curiously between the extremes of Persius and Rex in the seventh satire, that patron saint of primitive Rome, Priapus, rules just as curiously over the two woeful witches in the eighth. The mechanical operation of Sir Fertility's spirit blasts Canidia and Sagana out of their wits, while their "Hexen Extase"—a more gruesome ritual than the legal rigmarole of King and the Persian— invites a fiendish and flatulent *fiat nox. Et erat* obnoxious. Priapus is the pungent master of these revels. Yet, for all its ribaldry, the eighth satire is carefully wrought. Lucilian echoes

---

[5] We are advised not to take these poems as specimens of "early Horace." Fraenkel is perfectly definite on the point and shows that the second and third satires are more likely candidates.

[6] "When Caesar, on 26 Jan. of 44 B.C., returned to Rome from the celebration of the *feriae Latinae*, some among the populace greeted him as king. He protested with good-natured humor . . . 'my cognomen is not Rex but Caesar' " (Fraenkel, p. 120).

are audible, as are foretastes and overtones of epodes 5 and 17. Mock-heroic quotations from Homer are worked in, as they were for the Wrath of Wrecks and the Persian. The "garden imagery" is deftly disposed and firmly ensconced. Priapus traces his origins back to a fig tree: the carpenter, in doubt as to whether to make the wood into a bench or into a garden image, decided in favor of the fellow. And so Priapus presides over the handsome new Esquiline Gardens in Rome, the former site of a ghastly potter's field where slaves, riffraff, and the nondescript poor were buried by whoever was left of their number to provide for their removal (in a cheap wooden box) from the temporary crowded cells they had lived in to the ultimate hole in the ground. The former graveyard property, which was of course public and not for sale, has become the "Gardens of Maecenas," a landscaped promenade for Imperial Romans to enjoy. The area has been developed and improved so that people can now live, not just lie, here:

> nunc licet Esquiliis habitare salubribus atque
> aggere in aprico spatiari, quo modo tristes
> albis informem spectabant ossibus agrum.

The tempo of the first part swings back and forth, balancing "then" with "now." Then I was fig wood, now I am a big god; then this was a burial ground for the poor, now it is a residential quarter for the rich, with a beautiful view out over what used to be a field filled with bleached bones. The second part merges "then" into "now," as Priapus witnesses the frantic liturgy enacted by the witches over the souls of the departed and their spectral efforts to unnerve the living and unearth the dead, to revive "then" and destroy "now." Presto! Priapus hits on a handy argument a posteriori to put an end to the festivities. Canidia and Sagana are routed, "now" is restored, "then" vanishes as Horace's dissonant tone poem ends not

with a ping but a scamper. If the seventh satire was a brisk
two-part invention ending on a joke in the major, the eighth
is an evocation of an undulant *danse macabre* in the minor,
les Indences.

One still-wandering ghost of this poem will always haunt
the later reader. Horace himself was buried in this Esquiline
Park, alongside Maecenas, on Nov. 27, 8 B.C., only a few
weeks after the death of his patron and friend.[7] And yet, to
the goodhearted glory of the poet and of his aristocratic
companion, let it be remembered and recorded forever that,
from Horace's point of view, one could *not* do worse than be
a singer of dirges:

> absint inani funere neniae
> luctusque turpes et querimoniae;
>   compesce clamorem ac sepulcri
>   mitte supervacuous honores.[8]

The ninth satire is a conversation piece to end all conversation pieces. The social sorrow inflicted on Horace by the bore
is the counterpart of the literary mayhem inflicted by the
writer at the end of the *Ars poetica* who reads his listener to
distraction and bleeds him to death like a leech. Even Dante
may have smiled to think of *Orazio satiro* in this plight, for
Dante heard himself urged firmly by Vergil:

> Però pur va, ed in andando ascolta!

---

[7] Cf. *Odes* ii. 17:

> a! te meae si partem animae rapit
> maturior vis, quid moror altera
> nec carus aeque nec superstes
> integer? ille dies utramque
> ducet ruinam.

[8] *Odes* ii. 20. 21–24: "Let dirges be absent from what you falsely deem my
death, and unseemly show of grief and lamentation! Restrain all clamor and
forego the idle tribute of a tomb."

Would that Horace could keep walking, and not have to listen to that man talking. But that man won't stop; wanting to make an impression on Horace, he succeeds at least in leaving a depression in what had promised to be a fine day in the city. Horace's bore is a kind of cloud gatherer, rumbling and sputtering, making everything look black. He misjudges Horace and misinterprets his "connections," name-drops his own name, which falls so far that we never learn what it is. When Aristius Fuscus meets the two "friends" walking and talking, instead of rescuing Horace he leaves him excellently obfuscated, and Horace abandons all hope. But happily, Apollo is standing by, and when the persistent bore is hauled off to court and Horace goes along as a willing witness, the light shines again.

Like the seventh and eighth satires, the ninth has its Lucilian whispers, notably at the beginning, *ibam forte*—"I happened to be going"—and at the end, *sic me servavit Apollo* —which Lucilius had quoted directly from Homer in the Greek. Yet Horace improves on the coarse-grained hostility of the master's model by making the ninth conversation piece a lighter, more agile complaint than Lucilius seems to have been capable of. Images, dialogue, setting, all have a bright descriptive air, the very fact of dialogue perhaps pointing ahead to the double style of the second book. Here Horace counterposes himself against the social insect: his interest flags as the other's quickens, his plight darkens as the other's brightens. The poem is not so much about the bore as about Horace-and-the-bore, oneupmanship being perfectly matched by onedownmanship. The agony is prolonged; the action seems to grind to a halt and then is resolved and relieved all at once. As Horace saunters along the Sacred Way, he just by chance meets his doom in the form of the persistent bore. It's more than a man can bear, and Horace feels like an overloaded donkey (his *ears* droop: *demitto auriculas*). Farther on in the death march he feels like a captive chained to the victor's chariot (*cum victore sequor*). At the last hour he feels like a sacrificial victim whom Fuscus has deserted with the knife at his throat (*sub cultro*). But then, the bore's own fate suddenly comes round the corner. Horace gladly offers his ear to the touch (*oppono auriculam*—a legal gesture, signifying his assent to serve as a witness in the case against the bore). The captive is no longer being dragged but the conqueror being hustled off to court (*rapit in ius*), and Apollo has spared the innocent victim. The god of literature has provided his loyal subject with a social collision and in so doing has replenished his literary ammunition.

The tenth satire balances with the first and complements the fourth in further developing the literary theme, and it serves to round the whole book into final shape. The first poem had looked out over the field of satire, making its choice of terrain, planning the moves. The second and third measured lines and computed angles in Horace's moral geometry, not without reference to the logarithmic tables of love. All three worked at the social problem by means of axioms, hypotheses, formulas, examples. In the third satire we may even discern a kind of Pythagorean theory of inconsistency wherein the human compulsion to find fault, squared, is equal to the sum of ignorance and self-satisfaction, squared. The fourth satire introduced literature, brought up "the problem of Lucilius," and leaned at the end on a certain autobiographical justification for the artist's mission. In the tenth satire Horace returns to the literary basis, makes further progess with the problem of Lucilius, clarifies his choice of literary form, leans on literary history, and briefly reviews his intellectual biography.

The intervening satires strengthen the social fabric with inter-woven patterns of conduct.

What morality is to the first, literature is to the tenth satire. Just as the first delineates first principles, voices sensible sayings, and portrays characteristic images of human behavior, the tenth also has its declarations of principle, its firmly phrased aphorisms, its literary portraits. "Why is it, Maecenas, that no one is ever quite happy with . . . my estimate of Lucilius? I may point out his shortcomings, but right on the same page I also point out that his satire is salty and keen. The truth is that when I praise a writer I don't canonize him. For what after all are the requirements of good satire? It needs to be brief, so that the meaning can proceed unencumbered:

> est brevitate opus ut currat sententia neu se
> impediat verbis lassas onerantibus auris.[9]

It needs variety of tone and a change of pace as the writer plays the roles appropriate to different/ scenes. It should be sophisticated, restrained, economical. A provocative smile can often do more with a tough problem than sober disdain." This whole passage, with its flicker of good-humored truth at the end,[10] is a kind of literary reprise of the opening of the first satire, with its apology for gladness whereby Horace checks himself and brings his discussion around again to the actual seriousness inherent in the subject.[11]

[9] *Satires* i. 10. 9–10.

[10] *Satires* i. 10. 14–15:

> ridiculum acri
> fortius et melius magnas plerumque secat res.

[11] *Satires* i. 1. 23–25:

> praeterea ne sic ut qui iocularia ridens
> percurram: quamquam ridentem dicere verum
> quid vetat?

Horace goes on to single out some literary aberrations: "modern" poets who prate only of Calvus and Catullus, "modern" critics who admire Roman poetry most when it is sprinkled with Greek words. Then, too, there are the epic poets, who sprawl all over their long books. Meanwhile, Horace assures us, I will stay with my minor genre, which I have chosen by the following simple process of elimination: Fundanius writes the best comedy nowadays; Pollio can handle tragedy; Varius' province is epic; and Vergil is the pastoral poet beyond compare (even the muses admit it). Others have tried satire, but I seem to get along rather better with it. Of course, I didn't invent the form, but not being a creative writer shouldn't prevent me from becoming a productive one.

Incidentally, I'm not out for Lucilius' crown: he deserves it, despite the flaws in his work. He needed an editor—even Homer needed an editor, apparently. Lucilius himself "edited" Accius and drew attention to Ennius' lapses without crowing over his predecessors. And so I believe that Lucilius' work could stand shortening, shaping, unwrinkling. Nevertheless, he was by nature and genius "smooth and sophisticated." *Comis et urbanus:* affable and refined, congenial and clever. Horace has deliberately saved up the phrase for emphatic reiteration at the end of his book. In the fourth satire (at line 90) he has shown how we can mistake loose talk for free speech. We were wrong to think of the string of remarks unleashed by a liquorous tongue as "devastating, uninhibited, cosmopolitan," wrong to disregard the drunken woolgatherer as *comis et urbanus.* The conscious and articulate Lucilius alone possessed the true satiric sensibility. His work has established him as *comis et urbanus,* a man of the world, and humane.

Lucilius was, finally, an adventurer in this new non-Greek form that appeals to the Roman temperament. If he were still alive, he'd be enough of a person to want to improve on and edit his own work. And this is, after all, the writer's main job, REWRITING! He is a slave to self-improvement and is perfectly happy if he can win a few appreciative readers.

> saepe stilum vertas iterum quae digna legi sint
> scripturus, neque te ut miretur turba labores,
> contentus paucis lectoribus.

Contentus paucis lectoribus: "and fit audience find, though few," as Milton was one day to hear himself declare. It is the exact idea on the literary side of the scale to balance the weight of Horace's human aspiration, *contentus parvo.* And the substance of the tenth satire draws even with the social discourse of the first, as Horace's first book draws to its close. He is interested, this poet, in the ways in which literature and life touch upon each other; he is concerned to distinguish and to relate, without confusing the two. Throughout the book he shows himself to be at home in the world. In the world of his friends and appreciative readers Horace shows himself to be at home in his art.

I · 1

DON'T GO OVERBOARD

Qui fit, Maecenas, ut nemo, quam sibi sortem

Why is it, Maecenas, that no one is ever quite happy
With the life he has chosen or stumbled upon, and never
Abides by it happily, but loves to praise instead
All who do something else? "Now, take businessmen:
They're really well off," says an old army man, weighed down
By years of service, his frame bruised and blunted with
      · work.
But the businessman says, as he rides out a perilous squall
On his ship, "The army's the thing. And why? Well, look:
There's a fight, and in no time at all you've got your results.
You win or you lose—death or success—and it's over!"
The man versed in legal procedure, waked up at dawn
When a client raps at his door, envies the farmer,
While the latter, dragged into town to appear in a case,
Loudly admires the life city dwellers lead.
And so it goes. To rehearse the string of examples
Would tire even garrulous Fabius. Not to detain you,
Here's how I see it. Suppose some god were to say:
"I shall grant whatever you wish. You, now a soldier—
Be a businessman. You, now a lawyer, are free to become
The rural type. You've changed your roles: you can *go* now,
And you two, too. Well! What are you waiting for?"
      Naturally,
When they could be happy, they wouldn't take the chance.

33

Isn't this why Jove quite rightly might puff out both cheeks
And declare that in future he will not again lend so easy
An ear to their prayers?
                         I shouldn't make fun of the subject,
And yet—there's no law against telling the truth with a smile.
Smart teachers, for instance, give crunchy sweets to children
To make them learn their letters. But joking aside,
Let's continue.
              The man who turns the heavy earth
With his unyielding plow or the rascally sharp innkeeper
Or the soldier or undaunted sailors who set out across
Any old sea, all say they put up with such work
To retire safe and sure in old age when they've scraped up
     enough
To subsist on: just as their model, the miniature ant
Who works like a giant, drags up whatever he can
In his mouth to add to the heap he is busily building,
By no means unconscious of or out of touch with the future.
The ant, when watery winter has turned the year round,
No longer creeps out, but wisely makes use of supplies
Laid by months before. But nothing will stand in your way,
Not blistering summer, not winter, not fire, flood, or sword,
So long as someone remains even richer than you.
Just what is the good of your furtively, fearfully digging
A hole in the ground for a great weight of silver and gold?
"Well, if I touch it, the sum dwindles right down to nothing."
But if you don't use it, what charm adheres to the pile
You've constructed? You've threshed a hundred thousand
     bushels
Of wheat, but your stomach accommodates no more than
     mine.

Just as, if you among other slaves carried a basket
Of bread on your bowed shoulders, you would receive the
    same rations
As the man with no load. Tell me, if you please, what's the
    difference
To the man who knows how to live within nature's true limits,
Between plowing a good hundred acres and plowing a
    thousand?
"Well, it's nice to draw from a big pile." But you're perfectly
    willing
To permit us to draw exactly as much from our small pile,
So why do you praise your silos above our grain boxes?
It's as if you needed a jar, or a cupful, of water
And said, "I'd much rather drink from a great big river
Than draw the same amount from this trickling spring."
And so it happens that those who delight in having
A more than moderate share the flood-raging Aufidus
Sweeps away with its crumbling bank, but he
Who wants only what he needs neither drinks water
Churned up with mud nor loses his life in the waves.
    Mankind for the most part, fooled by its own false desires,
Says, "There's no such thing as enough. You are worth
Only as much as you have." And what can you do
With a person like this? Oh, well! Wish him hell and
    farewell,
Since he's headed that way by choice. Like the man they
    tell of
In Athens, filthy but rich, who despised the voice
Of the people and kept saying, "So! The citizens hiss at me!
Ah! But I applaud myself alone at home
When I gaze on the coins in my strongbox." Thirsty Tantalus

Makes for the water that always recedes from his lips.
You laugh? Well, just change the name and you'll find
      that this story,
As a matter of fact, means YOU. You sleep on the sacks
Of money you've scraped up and raked in from everywhere
And, gazing with greed, are still forced to keep your hands
      off,
As if they were sacred or simply pictures to look at.
Don't you know what money can do, or just why we want it?
It's to buy bread and greens and a pint of wine
And the things that we, being human, can't do without.
Would you rather stand guard, half-dead with fright, and
      tremble
Day and night over sneak thieves, fire, or slaves
Running off with your loot? If this craven type seems to lead
The more abundant life, I prefer to be poor.

    And suppose your body begins to ache, when malaria
Offers her chilly touch, or that some other mishap
Pins you in bed. Have you someone to sit by your side
And fuss with your bandage, call the doctor in to fix you,
And hand you back to your children and precious relations?
The truth is that neither your wife nor your son wants you
      back:
Your neighbors and "friends," man, woman, and child, all
      despise you.
Are you so amazed, who have always put money first,
That no one extends you the love you have not tried to
      earn?
Or do you feel that to try to hold on to your family,
To make friends of those whom nature has given you gratis,
Would be just a waste of time and effort, like trying
To teach a donkey to run on the Campus like a race horse

And respond to the reins?
                    Let your grasping for money cease, now
That you have so much more and should fear want so much
        the less.
You've got what you craved: begin to end up your work,
So that you don't end up as Ummidius did. It's not a long
        story.
So rich he had to measure, not count, his money,
So stingy he never dressed better than a slave, he still feared
Right up to the end, that a shortage of food would destroy
        him.
His freedwoman, actually, the brave Clytemnestra type,
Divided him squarely in two with an axe. "And so,
What would you persuade me to do? Live like Nomentanus
Or Naevius?" But you proceed to oppose one extreme
To another, like matched gladiators! I say don't be close, I
        don't say
Be a sap or a cloudbrain. There is still room for us in
        between
Tanais the eunuch and Visellius' ruptured beau-père.
There is a moderate measure in things, there are definite
        limits
Which sensible conduct should neither exceed nor fall short
        of.
    I return to my first point. How is it that no greedy person
Ever approves of what he is doing, but likes
To praise those who do something else? Why does he turn
        green
If another man's goat gives more milk? Why fail to compare
Himself with the throng of people poorer than he is,
And strain to outdo first this man, then that one? Someone
        richer

Always stands in the way of his drive, as the charioteer
Lashes his horses on after the chariots in front of him,
When they're off at a hoof-thudding pace with a lunge from
    the starting line,
And forgets about those also running behind him. So it is
That you rarely find someone who admits to having been
    happy
With the time allotted him, who admits that he has lived
    well
And lived right and is ready to leave, like one who gets up
From a banquet.
                    This is all: I won't add a word, for fear
You will think I've ransacked the lecture material and notes
That Crispinus Conjunctivitis keeps in his file.

I · 2

ADULTERY IS CHILDISH

Ambubaiarum collegia, pharmacopolae

The Syrian Society of Fastidious Feminine Flutists
And Dancers, the Neighborhood Druggists, the Mendicant
     Priests
Organized for Cybele, Strip-Teasers United, the Pitchmen—
Everyone of this sort is quite downhearted and worried
By the death of Tigellius (a singer, not a dessert).
He was so openhanded! The opposite type of person,
Afraid to be labeled a liberal, begrudges the little
He might give a friend to help ward off cold and starvation.
If you ask still another, a spendthrift, why he runs through
His father's and grandfather's fine estate to appease
His insatiable appetite, buying all sorts of rare foodstuffs
And borrowing money to do it, he answers you back
That he never would wish to be thought of as mean or stingy.
For this he is praised by some and blamed by others.
Fufidius, rolling in real estate, lush with the loans
He has out at interest, worries for fear he'll be labeled
Pushover or dimwit, so when he lends money he carves out
Five times the usual interest, to safeguard his capital,
And the direr the borrower's straits, the higher his price.
He hunts up accounts among young men just come of age
Whose fathers have budgeted them strictly. "My God, what
     a tightwad!"
Everyone says who hears about this. "But he spends

39

Heavily on himself, with that income?" Oh, no! You
  wouldn't
Believe how hard a man like Fufidius can be
On himself: the father described in Terence's play
Who forced his son to leave home, and so lived unhappily
Ever after, didn't treat himself worse than does our hero.
  But if someone now asks, "Just what is your point?"
    I reply:
Fools, in avoiding one vice, run into its opposite.
Malthinus ambles along with his tunic at half-mast:
Another stalks by with it drawn right up to his censored.
Rufillus reeks of pastilles, Gargonius of he-goats.
There seem to be no middle courses, but only extremes.
  Some men won't go near a woman unless she's married;
Another will only go on when the light is red.
When a certain notorious fellow was seen coming out
From a certain hole-in-the-corner, our godlike Cato
Is said to have said, "May your tribe increase! To be sure,
When loathsome lust fills the veins, it's right for our young
  bloods
To drop down the social scale, not grind to a pulp
Other men's wives." "Well, I wouldn't want to be praised
In this way," pipes up a man named Desire, well known
As a great connoisseur of family jewels—other families'.
  It is well worth while for all who do not wish well
To the pursuit of happiness on the part of adulterers
To hear how rare is their pleasure, how often attended
By fear and trembling, how prone to end up in real trouble.
One fellow jumped off the roof. Another was flogged
To pieces, nearly. Another in flight fell into
The clutches of roughnecks. Another had to hand over
The money to ransom himself. Another got hosed down

By the kitchen help when they made water: they went even
    farther
And sliced off some pieces—his works were cut out for him!
"Served him right," as everyone said, except good old Galba.
    It's safer to go second class, that is, go abroad
With freedwomen only. Sallustius, of course, is as mad
In pursuit of this sort as the man who goes after matrons.
If he wanted to be nice and openhanded, insofar as his means
And good sense indicated, insofar as a modestly liberal
Fellow might be, he would tip the girls just enough,
Not so much as to go bankrupt or get himself talked about.
But he hugs himself with this one great thought, and
    congratulates
And loves himself for it: "I never lay hands on a matron."
Just as, only a few years ago, that fellow Marsaeus,
The actress Origo's lover, who lavished upon her
His family's farm and estate, was quoted as saying,
"It will never be said that *I* seduced other men's wives."
But—when you go in for actresses, or for fast women,
Your good name fares even worse than your goods. Is it smart
To avoid the adulterer's role, but not keep clear
Of the troubles it brings in its train? You're no adulterer—
But to lose your good name, to mess up your father's estate,
Is bad, however you do it. So what does it matter
Whether you slip with a matron or a slave who has put on the
    toga?
    The "son-in-law" of Sulla (how the name took him in!)
Kept getting it right on the chin in that Fausta affair;
He took more than he should have, poor Villius—got slugged,
    slashed,
Kicked out of the house, while Longarenus had access
To the interior. Now, what if his mind had spoken

As follows, taking the form of his own mellow instrument,
Familiar with such a wide range of pathetic phallacies:
"What *is it* you're after? Did I ever ask you to furnish me,
Even when my dander was up, with a morsel of flesh
Descended from a mightly consul, arrayed as a highborn
Matron?" What could Villius say but, "This girl
Was born of a powerful father."

                            How much better off
You would be to lay off what shouldn't be touched, as nature,
Rich in her own resources, advises. MANAGE
Your life: don't mix what's worth having up with what isn't.
Do you think it makes no difference whether your trouble
Is your own fault or simply inheres in the nature of things?
Therefore, to save yourself grief, stop chasing matrons:
Plucking this fruit is a much too troublesome task.
The matron, even though sheathed in pearls and emeralds,
Does not, for all that, have a thigh soft as yours, Cerinthus,
Nor a straighter leg than her servant, who's often much
    better.
Besides, *she* offers her wares without faking, who's open
And aboveboard. She displays what's for sale, and if she *has*
    charm
She won't flaunt it or flout it in order to muffle her weak
    points.
After all, this is how the big shots buy horses: the beasts
Are kept under wraps while they look them over; in this way
A good shape cannot take the buyer's eye off a weak hoof
While he drinks in the handsome back, short head, and
    arched neck.
It's a good way, isn't it? For your part then, don't look
At the good parts with Lynceus' keen eyes and then be as
    blind

As Hypsaea when it comes to observing defects. "What legs!
What arms!" But what a splay foot, big nose, small behind,
And high hips she's graced with! The matron has nothing on
View but her face: her full-flowing robe veils the rest
(Unless, of course, she's like Catia). If you seek this
        forbidden
Fruit, so well barricaded—and of course this is why
You crave it so madly—some things intervene: (1)
        attendants,
(2) a litter, with bearers, (3) beauticians, with curlers, (4)
        and scroungers
At each meal, (5) a dress reaching down to the ankles, (6)
        a cloak
Circumscribing the whole, (7) and lots else, to keep you
        from having
A real view. The loose woman, now, doesn't make things so
        hard.
Through her silk dress you can see what she's like in the raw,
        that her legs
Are all right, and her feet. You can measure her flanks with
        your eye.
You prefer to be taken in first? Be relieved of your money
Before you've been shown the goods? Our bird watcher
        carols:

   "Just as the hunter tracks down the hare in deep snow
   But if it is laid out before him just lets it go—
   So my love is ever a rover and likes least to cling
   To a sitting duck and likes more to soar after things on
        the wing."

   How poetic! You don't think such jingles will drive out
      the grief,

The fever, the anxious concern, from your heart? Or do you?
Would you not profit more from shrewdly inquiring of nature
What limits she sets to desire, what she goes without,
What she can't go without without suffering, and profit by
    learning
To distinguish between romance and mere sexistentialism?
Thirsty, throat-parched, you insist on a gold-covered cup?
Hungry, turn up your nose at everything but
Peacock and flounder? Your passionate part on the rise,
A young servant girl or a nice boy standing right by,
At your service, you choose to explode with your impulse?
    Not me!
I'll take the pleasure that's easy to get, and accessible.
To quote Philodemus:

                "Matrons that say 'Bye and bye'
    Or, 'Yes, but more money,' or, 'Wait 'til my husband is
        out'
    Are for castrated priests, not for the sensible guy.
    Give me the freedwoman: the issue is never in doubt.
    The tariff? *Prix fixe*, and never impossibly high."

    Let my girl be fair and straight, and made up to look
Simply as tall and as fair as nature has made her.
When her left flank gives in to my right, Alba Long to her!
She's Ilia, she's my Egeria: she's all the nymphs
I can name. And when we make love I don't have to worry
About her husband just dropping in from the country, the
    door
Splitting open, the dog yapping, house in an uproar of
    crashing
And pounding on all sides, my girl tumbling head over heels
Out of bed, as white as a sheet, while her maid (and
    accomplice)

Shrieks it's not *her* fault—deathly afraid of her legs
Being broken as punishment—the wife, thinking now to
    herself
"There goes my dowry," while I eye myself sprinting off
In a panic, my tunic undone, and trying to salvage
My money, to safeguard my future and save my behind.
       IT'S BAD TO GET CAUGHT. The stock Stoic view I
         begrudge,
       And I'd win my case even if Fabius sat as the judge.

I · 3

BUT NO ONE ASKED YOU TO SING

Omnibus hoc vitium est cantoribus, inter amicos

The trouble with all singers is, when you want them to sing,
They're not in the mood, but when you just wish they
    wouldn't,
They can't refrain. Tigellius (a Sardine, not a dessert)
Was just like that. Even Caesar, who could have compelled
    him,
Got nowhere by pleading friendship, his own or his father's;
But if Tigellius felt in the mood, he would RENDER
"Yo, Bacchus!" complete, from soup to nuts, letting fly
With the high notes first and then rolling out the barreltones.
There was no *consistency* in him. He dashed about
At times, like a soldier running from the enemy, but
Just as often you'd see him inching along like a priest
Bearing offerings to Juno. Sometimes he had two hundred
Slaves, other times just ten. He'd be all agog
With big talk—mentions of high life, kings, court, and
    sultans—
Then he'd say: "I'll just have a plain deal table, some salt,
Plain salt, in a sea shell, a toga course and thick,
To keep out the cold." If you gave a million dollars
To this frugal chap, so glad to live on a shoestring,
In five days you'd find he hadn't a cent to his name.
He'd stay up all night until dawn, then snore out the day.
No one has ever been so thoroughly inconsistent.
    Now if someone says, "Well, Horace, what about you?

Don't you have shortcomings?" Yes, but they're different,
and perhaps
They're more trivial. When Novius was out of the room,
Maenius
Criticized him, and somebody said "Hey you, don't you know
Yourself? You ignore the fact that we're not so ignorant."
"Oh, I don't ab-use, I exc-use myself," he replied. *Amour-
propre*
Like this is improper and silly—good subject for satire.

Why glance at your glaring faults like a man with sore eyes
Whose eyelids are greasy with salve, but, as for your friends,
Look piercingly at their mistakes, eagle-eyed or possessed of
The vision of marvelous reptiles? This works against you
When your friends train their eyes on you and examine your
faults.
So-and-so's touchy, a bit too quick-tempered, and not quite
the man
For our nose-in-the-air modern critics. After all, he's a laugh,
With his hair country style and his "flowing" toga and shoes
Too big for his feet. But in fact he's a very fine fellow—
As good as they come—and your friend, whose rough exterior
Cloaks a man of powerful parts. So SHAKE YOURSELF OUT:
See if perhaps any seeds of vice have been sown
In you by nature or habit. If the field is neglected,
It has to be burned right over to clear out the weeds.

On the other hand, playing down faults may mean being
blind to them.
Lovers overlook the mistress' defects, love to praise them
As beauty spots: thus Balbinus *enjoys* Hagna's wart.
But I wish that we in the name of friendship might so err
And that teachers of ethics might see their way clear to
bestowing

A charitable name on our wish to make allowances.
Why find fault with our friends when we could indulge them
As the father indulges the son? If the son is born cross-eyed,
Papa proudly proclaims him as "Blinker," or if he's a runt
(Like the dwarf Sisyphus Mark Antony kept), he's called
      "Chick."
If he's bowlegged, "cowboy"; if he wobbles, awkwardly
      propped
On his swollen ankles, in baby talk he's "Eddie Puss."
If a man is too tight, call him frugal. Someone who shows off
And shows himself up in the process acts this way
To make an impression on friends: he wants to befriend them.
Someone is rude, too outspoken? He's brave and sincere.
Hot-headed? Let him be numbered among the eager.
This is how, in my view, friends are made and retained.
Yet even their good points we turn upside down; we keep
      wanting
To smudge the clean bowl. A fellow we know is a good sort,
But very retiring: we call him slowpoke, thick-witted.
Another avoids every trap set for him and never
Lays himself open to scoundrels. But this world of ours
Revolves around people whom pitiless envy and slander
Inspire: instead of calling him prudent or sound,
We call him guileful, or "deep." The ingenuous soul—
How often, Maecenas, your Horace must seem just that sort,
Breaking in with some chatter when you'd rather read or be
      quiet—
"Clearly lacks social grace," we decide.

                  How rash we are
To pass a law that punishes, chiefly, ourselves!
For no man is born free of faults: the best man has simply
The fewest. My friend with all due justice should weigh

My good points against my faults and tip the scale
In favor of the good (if they actually weigh more) if he
Expects to be loved in return. And I will weigh his
On the very same scale. The man who expects his friend
Not to grimace at his swellings must himself overlook
His friend's warts. It's only fair play: if you ask indulgence
For your foibles, you have to be indulgent in turn.
Finally, since it's unthinkable that we poor sinners
Should ever have anger, and those other failings that cling to
        us,
Cut out by some libid-ectomy, why shouldn't reason,
Or at least the Few Gifted Thinkers, take logical measures,
In fact, set up a sound bureau of weights and measures,
And punish offenses just as the facts require?
If you caught your slave finishing off a half-eaten plate
Of fish he'd been told to remove and guzzling the cold sauce,
And you threatened to crucify him, sensible people
Would regard you as madder than Labeo. But how much
        wilder,
How much more grave, is the following offense: your friend
Makes a slight slip, the sort of thing it's uncouth to resent;
You hate him for it, avoid him, as Ruso's debtor
Steers clear of him, knowing that on the inevitable first
Of the month when he still isn't able to dig up from anywhere
Either principal or interest, he will have to sit still and listen
To Ruso recite his grim "histories," like a captive,
With outstretched neck. A friend of mine gets drunk
And wets my couch or knocks off the table a vase—
An antique that got its first wear at the hands of Evander—
Or, ravenous, snitches some chicken from my side of the dish.
Is he therefore less dear to me? What would I do if he stole,
Betrayed a confidence, or went back on his word?

Those who hold that all faults are practically equal
Have trouble when they come down to cases: our behavior,
   our feelings,
Or the utilitarian standard—virtually the mother
Of law and justice—all work against this view.
   When living creatures first crawled forth on the earth,
They were a mute inglorious tribe who fought over acorns
And lairs to sleep in, with nails and fists, and then sticks,
And then weapons forged by experience. They discovered
   words
At last, verbs to express their feelings, nouns for ideas.
Then they began to leave off warring, and instead
To build, build towns and lay down laws against theft,
Against robbery and adultery. Oh yes, the lecherous life
Was lived long before fair Helen—the revolting cause
Of many a war was the crotch—but those who lived it
Perished, we know not how, when more manly males,
Like bulls in the herd, caught them and cut them down
In the act of their random rape taking animal form.
   If you look at historical facts, the records will show
That justice evolved from the fear of injustice, that nature
Cannot distinguish the right from the wrong in the same way
She contrasts the good with the bad, that is, the desirable
With the undesirable. Nor can reason affirm,
For her part, that he sins as gravely who plucks a ripe
   cabbage
From his neighbor's garden as he who, thief in the night,
Steals from the gods. There must be a sliding scale
By which crimes can be punished in the degree they deserve,
So that what should be whipped is not fanatically flayed.
I'm not worried about your letting off with a few light taps
The culprit who rates severer blows, when you say

All crimes are equal, that theft is the same as robbery,
And you threaten to weed out big and small alike
With the same ruthless scythe, if men make you king.
   If the allegedly real philosopher alone is king,
Alone really handsome, wealthy, and a good shoemaker
To boot, why then wish for what you already have?
"You don't understand the words of our father Chrysippus:
   The philosopher never makes sandals or shoes for himself,
But is still the last's past master." What's that? "I mean,
Tigellius is still the best warbler even when he's silent,
As Alfenus was still the best cobbler, sole master craftsman,
In spite of abandoning his tools and shutting up shop.
So your sage, who knows all the know-how, best deserves to
      be king."
Fresh kids will pull your beard, wise man, crowd around you
And taunt you unless you beat them off with your stick,
And you will stand helplessly by, fuming and moaning,
O King of Kings.
                  To put the case briefly, O King,
You may make your way to the threepenny public baths,
Escorted by no one except that absurd Crispinus.
My generous friends will surely forgive me my faults,
As I in turn will cheerfully put up with theirs.
So I'll play the role of the fool, not that of the king,
And be happier on my private shelf than Your Royal Self.

AND WHEN I HAVE TIME, I PUT
SOMETHING DOWN ON PAPER

Eupolis atque Cratinus Aristophanesque poetae

The poets Cratinus, Eupolis, and Aristophanes,
And the others who wrote Old Comedy, used to name names:
They felt perfectly free to describe the rascal and thief
As a rascally thief, the lecher as lecher, the cutthroat,
Or anyone with a bad name, as deserving his real
Reputation. Lucilius' satire distinctly derives
From these writers; he followed them closely, only in meter
And form differing from them. Fastidious, clever, and caustic,
He set down rugged verses. I would say that Lucilius
In fact wrote a bit too much: as a feat, he would dictate
Two hundred lines in an hour while standing on one foot.
He flowed—but the stream is muddy and needs dredging out.
He was wordy, too lazy to take the pains to write well;
Write well, I say. He could turn out the stuff, I admit.
    Now here comes Crispinus wanting to make me a bet
And offering good odds. "You take my tablet, Horace;
I'll take yours. We'll fix a place and a time,
And appoint referees. Let's see who can write the most!"
Thank heaven, the gods were good enough to make me weak-
Minded, uninventive, chary of, wary in, speech.
But you go ahead and blow, as you seem to prefer,
Like the air locked inside a goatskin bellows that labors
Till the fire has softened the iron. That lucky stiff Fannius

Hands out his books and cases to hold them and his picture.
No one reads my stuff, and I'm rather worried about reading
It in public because, well, satire can give offense,
You know—it applies so widely. Pick someone out,
Anyone, from the crowd: he's struggling along out of greed
Or miserable ambition. Here's someone frantic with love
For married women, someone else who's in love with boys.
This man has taken a shine to fine silver, but Albius
Is ga-ga for bronzes. The next is a slave to the market,
Trading in goods from all over the map, from the land
Of the rising sun to the land the sunset warms:
He is swept through cycles of crisis like a column of dust
In a whirlwind, fearing to lose his investment or anxious
To add to it. These people all dread verses and loathe
The poets. "There's hay on his horns. Keep out of his way!
He doesn't care if the laughs are on him or his friends,
As long as they're laughs. And what he's once smeared on the
    page,
He's only too glad to have bandied about by some slave-kids
Or old women on their way back from bakery or fountain."
    But wait: why not look at it briefly this way? I insist
On excluding myself from the number of those I would call
The true poets. You will admit that a poem requires
Something more than just meter. You can't call a man who
    writes TALK,
As I like to do, a real poet. If someone has genius,
An inspired way of thinking, a sublime way of voicing ideas,
Let him have the fame of the name. Literary critics
Inquire whether New Comedy is, or is not, poetic:
Its diction, its subjects, lack the force and the fire of great
    thought,
And, except for the meter, it's no different from pure prose.

You may argue, there's energy here: "A furious father
Raves at his son, who is mad for the love of a woman
Of ill repute and refuses the wife father picked
For him (a wife with a big dowry) and, still more—
This *is* awful—reels out in daylight drunk, behind
    torchbearers."
But wouldn't Pomponius get told off in similar terms
If his father were living? Therefore, you see, it won't do
To write down a verse of plain words of the sort that,
    transposed,
Any father would use, as the one in the play does. Take these
I transcribe, or that Lucilius used to compose, and remove
The rhythm and meter, shuffle their order, changing
The first word for the last: it wouldn't be like breaking up

> "After foul discordant Fate
> Broke down War's brazen pillars and her gate. . . ."

For in these lines you'll find, though dismembered, the limbs
    of a poet.
    Enough of that! For the present I waive discussion
Of whether this form is poetic. I now would consider
The problem of whether it really deserves your suspicion.
The private detectives, keen Mr. Sulcius and Caprius,
Make their rounds, gravel-throated, armed with their
    notebooks,
An absolute terror to robbers. But if a man lives right
And his hands are clean, he despises them both. Your being
Like Caelius and Birrus, the confidence men, doesn't mean
That I'm like Sulcius and Caprius, so why quake at me?
No drugstore or bookstore will show off my work for the mob
To thumb through, for the sweating palms of Tigellius to
    maul.
I recite to friends alone, and only when asked,

Not in public, and not to just anyone. Some poets like
To declaim in the middle of the Forum, many at the Baths,
Where the resonant vault makes the voice ring. That kind of
    thing
Soothes the vanity of men themselves incapable of knowing
That what they are doing is done in bad taste and comes
At the wrong time. "You revel in hurting people," I hear,
"And you do it with malice aforethought." *Where* did you find
That charge to hurl at me? Is the author among
My close friends? One who nibbles away at an absent friend,
Not coming to his defense when someone attacks,
Who provokes guffaws at a friend's expense, to gain
Renown as a wit, who makes things up he could not
Have seen, the sort of man who can't keep a secret,
This is the blackened soul: men of Rome, beware!
    At a big party, seating four guests at each three-man couch,
You will often find one quite ready to cast aspersions
On everyone present but the host who provides the
    diversion—
And even on him, soon enough, when the tattler is drunk
And the god of truth has disclosed his innermost thoughts.
This man you find oh, so charming, urbane, uninhibited—
You who detest the blackguard. If I laugh because
The silly Rufillus reeks of mouthwash, or Gargonius
Stinks like a goat, do I seem to you spiteful and snappish?
If reference is made, in your presence, to the alleged
    embezzler,
Petillius Capitolinus, your defense goes as follows:

    "Well, he's been my friend and my patron, ever since
        childhood,
      And he's done me many good turns, and, frankly, I'm
        glad

He lives unmolested in town. But still, I must say,
It's a wonder he's managed to escape conviction
    entirely."

Why, this is the squid's black-ink technique: soul erosion!
Such malice, I promise you, if I can promise you anything,
Will always be farthest from me, first of all from my mind,
And then from my pages.
                If I speak too freely, too gaily,
Won't you please make allowances? The best of all fathers
    trained me
To avoid all sorts of mistakes, by forming the habit
Of pointing them out one by one, with examples. His advice
To me about living frugally, thriftily, happy
With what he himself had provided, used to go like this:
"Don't you see what a mess Albius' son's life is, and how
    hard-pressed
Baius is? Let that be a lesson to you not to squander
The money you get from your father." To deter me from
    having
A sordid affair, he'd say, "Now, Horace, don't BE
Like Scetanus." To keep me from adultery, when
I could form a decent liaison, he'd argue: "Trebonius
Was caught in the act and acquired a bad reputation.
Philosophers may give you reasons about what is best
To pursue and best to avoid. For me, it's enough
If I keep within the bounds of tradition handed down
By my parents to me and, as long as you need a protector,
Keep your life and your name safe and sound. When time
    makes you strong
In body and spirit, you'll swim without needing the cork."
So, with his words he formed me. And whenever he told
Me to do something, "Here's your authority, here," he'd say,

And point to a judge on the bench. Or again, when he told
Me what not to do, he would say, "Can you doubt it's
     unseemly,
Or has misfired completely, when so-and-so stands in the
     glare
Of a bad reputation?"
                     And just as a neighbor's funeral
Makes gluttons feel suddenly sick, and, deathly afraid,
They are forced to take better care of themselves, so disgraces
That happen to others often turn young minds from mistakes.
And because of my father's influence I am now free
Of the vices that prove ruinous, and only at fault
In certain minor matters you may well forgive.
Even these perhaps may well be materially reduced
By maturer age, an outspoken friend, and second thoughts.
For when I withdraw to my couch or go off for a walk
Through the colonnade, I never neglect myself:
"This is better . . . I'll be happier if I do that . . . my friends
Will like me for this . . . that was NOT nice; will I
Ever act like that, caught off guard some day?" Lips sealed,
I ponder it all to myself.
                    And when I have time
I sit down and jot something down—a minor vice
Among those I mentioned just now. If you can't abide it,
A large group of poets—for we number, you know,
More than half the world—will come to my rescue, and then,
Like the Jews, we'll make you join us and join in our views!

I · 5

FROM ROME TO BRINDISI, WITH STOPS

Egressum magna me accepit Aricia Roma

I left lofty Rome on a trip, stopping first at Aricia,
At a quiet little inn. My companion was Heliodorus,
By far the best Greek rhetorician alive. From Aricia
We pushed on to Forum Appi, a place jammed with boatmen
And sharp innkeepers. This forty miles took us two days—
Took us slowpokes two days: real travelers make it in one.
The Appian Way is less rough if you take it in stages.
At Forum Appi I found the water so foul
I made war on my stomach and waited fuming while friends
Finished their dinner.

               Now night was preparing to spread
Her darkness on earth, to station her stars in the heavens.
And boatmen and slaves began cursing each other to pieces.
"In here with that sieve!" yells a porter. "OH, NO!" shouts a
    slave,
"You've already got three hundred on board! Call it quits!"
Never take a night boat, reader. You spend the first hour
Paying fares and hitching up the mule. Then fearless
    mosquitoes
And resonant swamp frogs keep sleep safely at bay.
A sailor and passenger, soused with cheap wine, compete
In songs to their absent girl friends. The mule driver finally
Drops off to sleep: the lazy driver lets the mule browse,

Fastens the rope to a rock, stretches out, and snores.
    Dawn was already at hand before we observed
That the boat hadn't budged an inch. Then a hot-tempered
        tourist
Leaped ashore, cut a switch from a willow, lit into the mule
And the driver, drumming on their domes and their bones.
Even so, it was ten when we finally got through the canal
And washed our faces and hands in your sacred spring,
Feronia, goddess of groves.
                            And then, after breakfast,
We wormed our way onward, taking the rest of the day
To arrive at the village of Anxur, loftily posed
On its limestone cliffs. Here was the rendezvous
With noble Maecenas and Nerva, on a mission of state,
Men deft at settling the quarrels of sensitive allies.
And here I treated my poor inflamed eyes with black salve.
Then Maecenas arrived, and Nerva, and Fonteius Capito,
A perfectly turned-out person, and close friend of Antony.
    At Fondi we gladly took leave of His Honor Aufidius
And laughed at this Special Assistant, the so-protocolorful
Erstwhile slave, clad in purple and broad-striped toga,
With his charcoal burner of a thurifer.
                                    Next, Formiae,
Mamurra's town, of course, where we stayed for a while
Resting up, at the villa of L. L. T. V. Murena,
But took our meals with Capito. The next day's dawn
Shone forth most auspiciously, for Vergil, you see,
And Plotius and Varius joined our group at Sinuessa.
These men are surely the finest the world has to offer,
And no one is more indebted to them than am I.
We embraced and rejoiced at being together again!
As long as I'm in my right mind, I'll never prefer

Anything in the world to a delightful friend.

Our next roof
Was a small farmhouse near the bridge as you enter
    Campania,
Where the *padrone* is always required, according to law,
To supply you with food and fuel. We went on to Capua,
Where the mules laid aside their packsaddles early in the day.
Maecenas went off to play ball, but Vergil and I
Went to sleep. Playing ball is hard on a man with sore eyes
And a man with a weak digestion.

The farm of Cocceius,
Lying north of the taverns of Caudium, next took us in
And into its well-stocked larder.

Now, Muse, I'll recite
Quite briefly, the battle of wits between that jackass-
Of-all-trades, Sarmentus, and Messius, named Cock-of-the-
    Walk.
I'll review the lineage of each combatant: good Messius
Derives from the Oscan yokels. Sarmentus belonged to
His owner, still living. From these progenitors our heroes
Came to do battle. Sarmentus struck first: "I say you,
You eunuch horn!" That brought the house down; even
    Messius
Laughed. "*Touché!*" he agreed, and brandished his forehead.
"Lucky for us," Sarmentus kept on, "your one horn
Was cut off; you're bad enough as it is, as you are,
In your amputated state." (Shaggy Messius' scar
Cut an ugly line through his forehead.) And Sarmentus kept
    after him,
Making cracks about his face and allusions to Naples disease.
"Hey, you play the part of Cyclops the Shepherd: you won't
    need

A mask, or boots, or anything." Cock-of-the-Walk
Had a few things to say of his own. "Have you hung up your
    chains
To the *lares, ex voto?*" he asked. "You're a white-collar
    worker,
Of course, but your owner has property rights, you know.
And why run away in the first place? A thin little thing
Like you could live nicely on one pound of flour." Such
    horseplay
Made supper a festive occasion.
                           Next stop, Benevento.
Here our painstaking host set his house afire while basting
Some skinny little thrushes. The fire slipped out of the grate,
Took a nonchalant stroll around the old kitchen, then rushed
Toward the roof, soaring upward and beginning to lick at the
    beams.
You should have seen the starved guests and the quavering
    slaves
Grab their food, and all trying to put out the fire at once.
  Next, the familiar hills of my native Apulia
Showed their sirocco-scorched features. We just wriggled
    through
By the grace of a farmhouse near Trivicus that took us in
For the night. The green branches, leaves and all, in the
    fireplace
Brought tears to our eyes. Here, like a fool, I was tricked
By a girl who had said she'd drop in. I waited till midnight,
When sleep overcame my desire, and my pique at the cheek
Of such flagrant nocturnal omission. Even so, my dreams,
Composed of improper views, drenched my stomach and
    nightgown.
  We next rolled downhill in carriages twenty-four miles

61

To stay at a town whose name just won't scan, but whose
    nature
It's easy to describe. They *sell* water here, but the bread
Is marvelous, so good that the smart tourist loads up his
    slaves
(For Canusium, formerly founded by brave Diomedes,
Has bread made of gravel and owns not a jug more of water).
Here, Varius sadly took leave of his sorrowful friends.
    Then, weary, we came into Rubi—the stretch was a
        long one
And made worse by the rain. The next day's weather was
    better,
But the road was worse, to the walls of fish-fertile Bari.
    Gnatia, a town clearly built when the fresh water nymphs
Were at odds with the natives, gave us some jokes and some
    laughs.
They want you to think that the incense flares on the altars
Without any flame. LET APELLA THE JEW BELIEVE IT—
I WON'T. I've been taught that the gods live a carefree life;
That if nature produces a miracle, it is *not* the gods
In their anger who send it on down from high heaven.
                              Brindisi
Marked the long journey's end, and at this point I ran out
    of paper.

I AM ONLY A FREEDMAN'S SON

Non quia, Maecenas, Lydorum quidquid Etruscos

None of your fellow Etruscans, of Lydian stock,
Maecenas, is nobler by birth than you: in time past,
Your grandparents on both sides commanded large armies.
But you do not, as many do, look down your nose at
     nobodies
Like me, born the son of a freedman. Refusing to count
As important a man's parentage, you show your belief
That, many times, many fine men appeared out of nowhere,
Before the power and rule of that commoner Servius,
And gained their country's respect; but a man like Laevinus,
Of the Valerians who drove out Tarquin, is not worth a
     cent more
Because of his parents, at least in the eyes of the people—
And you know what judges they are, how quick to honor
The undeserving, what slaves they are to mere rumor,
How terribly impressed by titles and family portraits.
    What are people like me, who are far, far removed
From the public eye, meant to do? Let' suppose that the
     crowd
Would elect a Laevinus to office, rather than a Decius,
Whom nobody knows; that Appius the Censor would strike
My name from the senators' lists if I couldn't claim
A freeborn man as my father; and that I'd deserve
Exactly this treatment if, like the donkey in Aesop,

I refused to accept as my lot the skin I was born with.
But ambition pulls everyone forward, chained to the wheels
Of her gleaming chariot: nobodies, somebodies, everybody.
What else caused you, good Tillius, to run for the office
Of tribune again, to try for the purple you lost?
You're more envied now than you would have been had you
        remained
In private life. When someone is crazy enough
To wind the black leather laces half up the calf,
As senators do, and angle the broad-striped toga
Across his chest, you can hear people say "WHO'S THAT?
Who was his father?" It's as if you had Barrus' disease,
Who wished to be thought of as handsome and wherever he
        went
Inspired the ladies to question and study his good points—
His face, his ankles, his feet, his teeth, and his hair.
Thus, when a man promises voters he will take charge
Of the city, the empire, of Italy and the gods' holy shrines,
He makes every one of them worry and want to find out
Who his father was, whether his mother's descent was lowly.
"Do you, son of Syrian Dama, or Dionysius,
Dare sentence citizens and turn them over to the hangman?"
"My associate, Newman, sits one seat behind me: you see,
He is only just now what my father was." So, you think
        you're Messalla
Plus Paulus? Newman could drown out the noise of three
        funerals
And two hundred carriages if they met in the Forum, blowing
        horns
And trumpets. This show at least makes some impression
        on us.
    Now I come back to myself, the son of a freedman.
Everyone rides me for being the son of a freedman

And for having dinner with you, Maecenas, and for having
Commanded as tribune a legion, not so very long ago.
The last point is not like the former, of course: anyone
Might legitimately envy my office, but not so my being
A friend of yours who are careful to choose worthwhile
    people,
Devoid of political ambition. It was NOT just by luck or by
    chance
That I happened onto your friendship. The excellent Vergil
First, and Varius next, recommended me to you.
The first time I met you I managed a few awkward words,
But bewildered and bashful, I balked at blurting out more.
I did *not* say my father was highborn, that I liked to ride
Around my estate on my thoroughbred nag; I just frankly
Said what I was. You answered, quite briefly as usual,
And I went away. After nine months you called me back
And asked me to join your circle of friends. I take pride
In thinking that I suited you, who distinguish the trues
From the fakes on the basis of conduct and character, not
Of their ancestry.
               Graced as I am with a few modest faults,
A bit crooked here and there, I admit—these flaws
Are the sort you would normally find disfiguring somewhat,
Like birthmarks, an otherwise perfectly good-looking body.
If there is something quite straightforward in my behavior,
If no one can rightly accuse me of greed or vulgarity
Or cheap self-indulgence, if my friends all find me decent,
Conscientious, and dear (as they say they do), then the
    CAUSE
Of all this was my father. He was poor, he had a small farm
But refused to send me to Flavius' school, which, in my
    town,
The prominent sons of centurions all went trudging off to,

Satchels and slates slung across their shoulders, and clutching
On pay day the fee of eight cents. He had the nerve
To bring his boy right to Rome, to be taught the subjects
Senators and big businessmen want their children to learn.
If anyone noticed my clothes and the slaves in attendance
In the midst of the crowd, he would think such expenses
    derived
From inherited wealth. My father himself watched over me
In the presence of my teachers, an incorruptible guard.
What more shall I add? He adhered to the primary virtue
And kept me decent, free not only from vice
But from scandal. He wasn't afraid to be criticized
For lavishing money on me, even if I turned out
As a low-salaried salesman, or tax collector, as he was.
I wouldn't complain if I had, for that matter. Now,
As things have turned out, I owe him thanks all the more.
I'll never forget him, never regret what he did.
And I'll never fall back on the line that some people take
Who say, "It wasn't my fault my father failed
To be famous, or freeborn." I say, and I think,
Otherwise. For instance, if nature arranged for us all
After a specified time to begin life all over,
Choosing parents who suited our fancy, I'd stick with mine
And not go for persons distinguished in public life.
The mob would think me insane, but you, perhaps, wouldn't,
For being unwilling to shoulder a load I'm not used to.
If I took on this role, I'd straightway need some more
    money,
Need to receive more callers and endure more visits,
Take this friend along or the other, and never go out
By myself or get out to the country. I'd maintain a stable
Of horses, and grooms, and need a few cars. As it is,
I can ride to Taranto if I want to, on my little old donkey,

The saddlebags chafing his flanks, the cowboy his back.
And no one will call me a cheapskate, as you are called,
My good Tillius, a judge who jogs out to Tivoli
With five slaves walking behind you carrying jugs
And chamberpots. In this, and in thousands of other respects,
I am much better off than you, my dear Public Figure.
   I go where I want, on foot and alone. I inquire
The price of vegetables and flour. In the late afternoon
I drop by the Circus and watch the confidence men,
Or nose around the Forum after hours, or stop and take in
The fortunetellers. Then home to dine on beans,
Scallions, and pancakes. My supper is served by three slaves;
The table is marble and features two drinking cups,
A ladle, a plain saltcellar, an earthenware saucer,
And oil jar. To bed, unworried by having to meet
Someone early at the statue of Marsyas, whose rolled-up eyes
Seem to register horror at Newman Junior, whose bank desk
Stands opposite. At ten I get up, go out for a stroll,
Or else do a little quiet reading or writing,
And rub down with oil of a much better kind than the stuff
Stinky old Natta steals from oil lamps. Around noon,
When the more and more merciless sun advises me to,
I push off, tired, to the Baths, being careful to miss
The Campus Martius, where they're all playing three-cornered
      catch.
I dine sparingly, just enough to not go all day
On an empty stomach, and busy myself about home.
   This is the life of people free of the weight
And the pain of ambition. With these things I comfort
      myself,
Knowing that I live more sweetly than ever I could
If my grandfather, father, and uncle had all been officials.

KING REX: OFF WITH HIS HEAD

Proscripti Regis Rupili pus atque venenum

One man's Mede is another man's Persian, which connects
With the story that's going the rounds, of Rupilius Rex,
The Proscribed Rex, the unkingdomed Prince of Pus
And Poison, who took his medicine from Persius.
Now this half-breed Persius was one of the very big wheels
In business at Clazomenae, with several big deals
On the fire, and some maddening lawsuits with Rex on as
        well.
The tough, conceited Persian knew how to raise hell
Even better than King, and ran such a fast line of talk
That, like a white horse, he finished the race in a walk.
    But to get back to King. They couldn't decide the case
Out of court. All heroes, it seems, have the right to face
One another whenever hostilities start to break out.
Take fiery Achilles and Priam's Hector, whose bout,
Based on fatal anger which only death could settle,
Was caused by this fact: BOTH MEN WERE MEN OF METTLE!
Of course, if two cowards fall out, or an unequal pair,
The weaker gives in and invites the other to share
In his goods, as Glaucus and Diomede did. This affair,
As I said, between King and the Persian, took place at court
When Brutus as praetor ruled the rich East, and the sport
Was as good as a heavyweight bout.
                        They rushed, all aglow,

Into court, each promising to put on a jolly good show.
Persius opened the case, making everyone laugh.
He lavished praises on Brutus and on his whole staff.
He called Brutus "the Sun of the East," his whole entourage
He referred to as "stars of good omen," except that mirage,
Rupilius King. That son of a bitch, he averred,
Was the Dog Star that comes to madden the farmer's herd.
The words rushed out in a flow of eloquent spleen,
Like a brook pouring down a far-distant mountain ravine.

In reply to the big stream of salt squeezed out by Persius,
The King of Praeneste turned on his own country curses,
Like a rough vinedresser pressing out wrath from his grapes
In his backwoods way, who is more than a match for the
            japes
The passer-by flings as he strolls past yelling "Cuckoo!"

The Greek in turn, now perfumed and soaked with the dew
Of Italian vinegar, shouted, "OH, GODS! ET TU!
I beseech you, Brutus—yes, and your ancestors too,
So brutal to kings in the past: MURDER THIS REX!
It's right down your line: first Tarquin, then Caesar . . . who's
            next?"

I · 8

A LITTLE WALPURGISNACHT
MUSIC

Olim truncus eram ficulnus, inutile lignum

I was once, long ago, the trunk of a wild fig tree.
This wood is no good, so a carpenter racked his brains
As to whether he ought to turn me into a stool
Or into Priapus, and plumped for the god. So I'm god,
And scare holy hell out of thieves and birds. The thieves
I coerce with the sickle my right hand holds and the THING
That projects long and red from my worst of all possible
        parts.
My crown of reeds chases off the persistent birds
And keeps them from settling down in the Esquiline Gardens.
    This place was once the last resting place for slaves,
A plebeian community sepulcher, "Parasites Lost"
(For guys like Pantolabus, or that fool Nomentanus),
Where a fellow slave paid for the corpse to be brought in a
        box,
Evicted at last from its cramped living quarters in town.
"A thousand-foot frontage, three hundred deep," the sign
        said,
"H.M.H.N.S.—this plot (and this marker)
Is not a private estate: no one can inherit it."
    Now it's the Esquiline Park, a salubrious spot
Where people reside and like to take promenades
Along the embankment that used to depress with its view

Of the hideous field and bleached bones down below. I just
    stand here,
And the wolves and the vultures that used to infest the place
Don't keep me worried and busy: it's haunted by witches
Who stir up the souls of the living with potions and chants.
I cannot prevent them, as soon as the wandering moon
Shows her full, fair face, from coming to gather up bones
And poisonous herbs.
                I have seen Canidia myself,
Waddle up barefoot, black cloak tucked over her knees,
Her hair undone, making mewsic with the elder sister,
Sagana. Their deathly hue made them both repulsive
To view. They dug at the ground with their nails, then began
To bite a black ewe lamb to pieces, then poured out the
    blood
In a ditch to evoke the dead souls and make them give
    answers.
They had two effigies, the larger one made out of wool
To punish the smaller wax image. The latter, submissive,
Stood still as a slave awaiting the sentence of death.
One called "Hecate!" the other "Tisiphone, DREADFUL
TISIPHONE!" Serpents writhed, hellhounds wandered,
The shamefaced moon withdrew behind the great tombs
To keep from witnessing such goings-on. If I lie
In the least, may the blackbirds splatter white turds on my
    head:
And let Julius, and that fairy named Boyer and that thief
    Voranus
Come out here and piss and do poops, at their pleasure, all
    over me.
    Shall I go into further detail and speak of the spooks
Squeaking sad antiphons with Sagana in high-pitched tones?

71

Tell how the witches so furtively hid in the ground
Spotted snake's tooth and hair from the beard of the wolf?
How the wax image flared into flame?
                            In horror, I witnessed
The mutterings and putterings around of this Furious Duo
But at last got revenge with a fart, when my fig butt split
With a noise like a bladder bursting apart.
                            WHAT A FARSE!
They raced back to town. Sagana's big wig fell down,
And Canidia's false teeth fell out. The magical herbs
And charms they had in their arms got lost in the rout.

BORED TO DISTRACTION

Ibam forte via Sacra, sicut meus est mos

I was walking down the Sacred Way, my usual route,
Turning over some lines in my head, completely absorbed.
A man I knew only by name ran up, seized my hand:
"How *are* you, my dear old fellow?" "Just fine," I answered,
"The way things are going. I hope *you* are getting on nicely."
When he kept up with me, I thought I'd forestall him by
  asking
"There's nothing I can do for you, is there?" "Oh, YES!" he
  shot back,
"Get to know me. I'm quite avant-garde." "Oh, good," I
  replied,
"I like you for that." Trying awfully hard to shake him,
I went on faster, then stopped in my tracks and whispered
Something in my slave's ear while sweat streamed down to
  my ankles.
"Bolanus," I thought to myself, "I envy the way
You blow your top. That would fix this fellow," who
  meanwhile
Kept yammering on, ga-ga with the big city sights.
When I failed to respond, he piped up, "I see how impatient
You are to be off. It's no use. I'm sticking with you—
I'll just tag along—where are you headed?" "Oh, NO,
Don't put yourself out! I'm going to see a sick friend,
Someone you don't know, way over in Trastevere

Near the Villa Aurelia." "Oh, well, I've got nothing to do,
And I'm not afraid of the walk, so I'll go along with you."
    My ears drooped down as a donkey's will do when he knows
He's loaded beyond his strength. Then he started in,
"If I know myself, you'll find me as good a friend
As Varius or Viscus. What author writes *more*, for example,
Or *faster* than I do? What dancer is more suggestive?
And sing? Why, Hermogenes [he meant Tigellius H.,
The singer, not the dessert] would envy my voice."
This was my chance to cut in, "And your poor old mother,
The relatives who care for you, won't they be worried if. . . ?"
"I haven't a soul in the world! I've buried them all."
"Lucky people," I sighed. "I seem to be all that's left.
Finish me off! For the hour is come the old gypsy
Foretold in my youth, as she shook the lots in an urn:

> 'This lad shall not be killed by malignant poison
> Nor by the enemy's sword, neither by pleurisy
> Nor pneumonia, nor gout that goes slow. But someday
>   someone
> Will simply talk him to death. When he comes of age,
> If he's smart let him keep his distance from Talkative
>   Persons.' "

    By now it was nine o'clock, and we had arrived
At the temple of Vesta. My companion, it seemed, was due
In court at nine, or would forfeit his case. "Won't you please
Stay around and lend me support?" he asked. "Hell, no!"
I answered. "I can't stand around, and I'm no good at law.
You know where I'm hurrying off to." "I just don't know
What to do," he mused, "leave you, or my case." "ME,
    please."
"I couldn't do that," he concluded, and started on ahead.

And I—well, you can't beat a winner—so I followed after
   him.
   "How are things with you and Maecenas?" he asked. I
      answered,
"He's a man of much sense and few friends." But he kept
   boring in,
"You've drawn good cards and played your hand right, you
   have.
Now if you wanted to do something more, you'd bring in
   myself,
The fellow who's talking to you. I'd be a help,
And I'm willing to play second fiddle. Damn it all, man,
You'd make them all knuckle under." "We don't carry on
Quite the way you think," I said icily; "there's no place so
   free
From intrigue as Maecenas', no place so thoroughly honest.
It just doesn't matter to them whether someone is richer
Or smarter than somebody else. Everyone gets along."
"A TALL one," he said, "hard to believe." "But it's true!"
"Well, it just makes me hotter than ever to be admitted."
"Keep wishing. Your talent is such that you'll storm his
   defenses.
He's a man one can conquer—for this is surely the reason
He makes the approaches so hard." "I bet I don't fail.
I'll bribe all his servants. I'll keep coming back, pick my
   times,
Meet him walking in town, join his escort. Nothing
In life comes to men without labor."
                                    While we were talking
Along comes my dear friend Aristius Fuscus, who knew,
Perfectly well, the man I was with. We stopped.

"Where are you coming from, where are you going?" got
    asked
And answered. I started pulling his sleeve and tugging
At his unfeeling arm. No response! I nodded, and winked
Fiercely at him to save me. No response but a laugh from
    the wag,
Who pretended to misunderstand. I was livid and spluttered
"Oh, Fuscus, you said you had something to say to me
    privately."
"Yes, I know, but let's save it for some other time. Today
Is the Thirtieth Sabbath. You wouldn't want to offend
The circumcised Jews, now would you?" "Oh, I'm not
    religious,"
I said. "Well, *I* am," he said, "it's a weakness I share
With most people. You forgive me? Some other time
I'll tell you what I had in mind to say." How black
Can things look? That best of all blackguards, Aristius
    Fuscus,
Ran off and left the knife at my throat.
                                        Just then
The plaintiff chanced to come by and see his opponent.
"You scoundrel, where are you off to?" he yelled. "Would you
[Turning to me] be a witness to this arrest?"
WOULD I! He dragged him to court, both of them shouting.
A crowd had formed. And thus I was saved by Apollo.

THE FINE ART OF CRITICISM

Nempe incomposito dixi pede currere versus / Lucili

Yes, I did say Lucilius' lines occasionally falter:
What fan of his is so stupid as to deny it?
But the same man is praised on the very same page of my
    poem
For the salty satirical way he rubs down the city.
To pay him this tribute is not to attribute all virtues
To him; if I did that, I'd have to admire, as poems,
Laberius' mimes.
              To make your audience grin
From ear to ear, though a fine thing, is not quite enough.
You need to compress if you want the meaning to flow
And not be held back by the words that weigh on, and tire,
Your hearers' ears. You need a change of pace,
Now tart, now smart; playing now the part of a speaker
Or poet, in serious, formal guise, and in turn
The role of the polished talker and man about town,
Who wisely saves up his strength for ironic thrusts.
A good witticism is often conclusive and forceful
Where a sober remark is not. Old Comedy authors
Stood their ground on this point, and deserve to be followed.
That smoothie Hermogenes simply never has read
The old boys, nor has that other monkey whose forte
Consists entirely in harping on Catullus and Calvus.
    "Lucilius was terribly clever to mingle in Greek

With his Latin." What New Criticism! You don't think it's
    hard
Or inventive to do what Pitholaus of Rhodes could manage?
"But when two languages blend, the flavor improves
As it does when you blend Falernian with Chian wine."
I ask you; does this apply to poetry only?
Or also to pleading a long and difficult lawsuit
Like "The Peculation of Petillius"? While talented jurists,
Corvinus and Pedius Publicola, to take two examples,
Sweat out their lengthy briefs, will you so forget
Your Father Latinus and your native land as to fish
For words from abroad to intertwine with your Latin,
Like bilingual Canucks?
                      I used to write Greek verses,
I who was born on this side, until Romulus
Spoke out against it as follows, appearing to me
After midnight, the time when dreams that come true are
    seen:

    "It's as crazy to transport timber into a forest
      As to make the swollen throng of the Greeks even
        morest."

So, while Furius the Frenzied apocalyptically features
His epic account of the Gallic Wars and dismembers
The head of the Rhine in the process, or furiously mangles
Poor Memnon, his victim in the New Aethiopian Epic,
I just play along with these trivial pieces of mine,
Which will never be heard in the Official Workshop of
    Drama,
Where Tarpa can judge them, nor time and again on the
    stage.
    Fundanius, you alone of the living can write

In your self-possessed way the crisp little lines that suit
The style of New Comedy: Watch the shrewd mistress—she
And Davus, the young man's slave-confidential-and-clerk,
Will fool the old father named Chremes. Pollio sings,
In his tragic trimeter rhythm, the sad death of kings.
Varius weaves the tough, strong fabric of epic
Better than anyone. Tenderly, playfully, Vergil
Has won the acclaim of the pastoral muses. But satire
Is mine: Varro Atacinus, and others, have tried it
In vain, while I have done better—though I still must yield
To Lucilius, who showed us the way. I'd never dare
To try to win from him the crown that clings to his brow
So gloriously.
                    I did say Lucilius' stream is muddy
And often washes down more you would like to take out
Than leave in. But really, as a man of taste and learning,
Don't you sometimes find Homer at fault? Friendly Lucilius
Saw things to change in the tragedies of Accius, didn't he?
He laughted, didn't he, at the verses where Ennius lapses
From dignity, meanwhile insisting that he, Lucilius,
Was not superior to those he criticized? So we,
As we read our Lucilius—what will keep us from asking
If the cause inhered in him or in his rugged themes,
That denied him smoothness beyond what a writer attains
By framing his thought in units of six, quite content
With the feet, and proud of having composed two hundred
Before dinnertime and two hundred more after dinner?
Such a gift was Cassius', the torrential Etruscan writer
Who made rapid rivers seem slow. At the end, you remember,
His funeral pyre was made of his books and bookcases.
I willingly grant to Lucilius wit and good temper,
His being more highly polished than you might expect

Of one inventing a form untouched by the Greeks
And more polished, too, than most of our senior poets.
Still, were he slated to be a poet today,
He would smooth out his work quite a lot and prune away all
That trailed on beyond proper limits, and while he was
    writing
Would scratch his head and chew his nails to the quick.
    You'll often have to erase if you mean to write something
Worth reading twice. And don't try to dazzle the mob—
Fit audience find, though few. You're not such a fool
That you want your works used as textbooks in second-rate
    schools?
Not I! As the actress, valiant Arbuscula, said
Good and loud, when the rest of the house started hissing,
"It's enough for me if the orchestra seats applaud."
    Should I let that louse Pantilius get under my skin?
Or be tortured if when I'm not there Demetrius needles me?
Or because that ass of a Fannius, who hangs around
With "Homogenes Jellyfish," tries to make me feel bad?
Let Plotius and Varius, Maecenas, Vergil, and Valgius
Approve, and Octavius and excellent Fuscus; and would that
The two brothers Viscus might praise me! Flattery aside,
Let me name you, Pollio, you, Messalla, your brother,
And Bibulus and Servius, also you, honest Furnius,
And many another scholar and friend, whom I
Leave out on purpose. With these men I want my poems,
Such as they are, to find favor, and I will regret
When they give less joy than I hoped for.
                        But you, Demetrius,
And you, Tigellius, I bid you: a-dew the soft seats
Of your female disciples with the stream of your tearful
    refrain.
HERE, BOY: ADD THESE LINKS TO THE REST OF THE CHAIN.

INTRODUCTION
TO BOOK TWO

By 30 B.C. Horace was ready with a second book of satires, and the firm grasp of form evident in this next group of eight poems shows a mastery of the medium. All eight are quite different from the first ten, and yet there are many links between the two groups. As in Book I, moralizing content supplies the main energy; but arguments about style are waived as Horace molds the subject matter into its ultimate form. A classical balance inheres in the predominant use of dialogue as the pendulum of talk ticks off cases in point one by one. And yet there is time to pause, to wind the mainspring back by means of deliberate monologue passages. The preachment of that stout original, the rustic Italian Ofellus, is a nourishing mouthful in the second satire; the prolix gospel of Stertinius, in the third, runs the stertorous risk of all long sermons. The sixth, most famous of all Horace's satires, distributes the weight of the discourse on: (1) two prayerful speeches of the author, (2) colloquial remarks flung at him by busy Roman city dwellers, (3) the quiet talk of country neighbors, (4) the dramatic dialogue of *mus rusticus* and *mus urbanus*. In the seventh satire Horace endures a monologue massage at the hands of his slave and temporary superior, and in the fourth he hears out the latest of a Brillat Savarin–style lecture relayed by Catius, who has been taking notes at the master's table. But in and out, over and under, the surface of the entire book, the double style insures an exchange of views, a comparing of notions, and a sifting of evidence. Horace not only decrees that the tournament of satire be held; he shows himself peerless in jousting with his fellow philosophers and in jesting with his fellow wits. He himself speaks with authority and writes with conviction, and even allows himself to be spoken to. The whole book could well be called "The Dialogues of Horace."

In structural outline the second book differs from the first. There is a pairing-off whereby the two "country" satires (2 and 6) can be taken together, and the two "food" satires (4 and 8) and the two "stoic discourse" satires (3 and 7), with the first satire forming a link to Book I and the fifth serving as a turning point, like the fifth satire of Book I. Or the moralizing element can be taken as a kind of orientation whereby we familiarize ourselves with the whole extent of the book: the solid insistence on the free prerogatives of criticism being announced in the first poem, and Ofellus' critique of loose living, Stertinius' of inconsistency, Horace's of metropolitan madness, Davus' of Horace, constituting patterns of conduct reinforced by the fabric of the absurd found in the other satires of this book. But such interrelated parts are no more than clues to the unity of the book. We should regard Horace's satire as a study in force and energy rather than search for the kind of unity of structure to be found in epic or dramatic poetry or within the narrower confines of the lyric. For one thing, satire tends toward prose, *prosa oratio,* or the straight-on-ahead type of discourse. For another, it includes the most heterogeneous contents and is as seldom formal as it is dignified. The eight items on Horace's agenda in the second book read like a "series" of essays by Montaigne, arbitrary in their order and choice of subject: (1) On Writing Satire, (2) On Native Intelligence, (3) On a Saying of the Stoics, (4) On the Menu, (5) Of Other Men's Wills, (6) My Chateau, (7) On Slaves and Masters, (8) On Dining Out. Horace's verse satire becomes here his art of portraying the examined life, and his ironic wit flows from the negative pole of "Que Sais-Je?" to the positive of "This I Perceive."

The rhythms change, the tonality darkens and brightens, the dynamics rise and fall, the length increases and diminishes. The first satire, for all its jokes jostling its judgments, conveys a serious message; the last is a mad takeoff on the banquet image, so dear to Epicurean hearts. The town mouse and country mouse poem, a perennial favorite, is still considered "the most accomplished of all Horace's satires."[1] Commentators agree in finding the fifth satire Horace's most vicious piece but differ as to the merits of the third, a 326-line excursion into Stoic dogmatics. Surely the seventh, wherein Horace's slave gives the master a piece of his mind, ranks among the most brilliant recitative passages in our literature. Ofellus, in the second poem, can sound the serious note convincingly, and the food satires show us what gluttons for punishment Roman trenchermen were.

Horace's talk with his lawyer Trebatius launches the book on its course. Like a doctor, Trebatius prescribes for the harried satirist the medicine of rest and silence, and good wholesome exercise. If the satiric style itself is at fault, Trebatius advises Horace to switch to epic and sing of Octavian's triumph, as Lucilius sang of Scipio. Horace is not so sure how this would *go over* and argues in defense of his form that it suits better what he wants to do. Even Castor and Pollux had different inclinations, although both were athletic, and Horace confesses to a certain pleasure in prosody:

> quot capitum vivunt, totidem studiorum
> milia: me pedibus delectat claudere verba
> Lucili ritu nostrum melioris utroque.

[1] Fraenkel, p. 140.

Here, and in the sixth satire, Horace cultivates his own garden for the last time in the *Satires* (although he will landscape it in the *Epistles*). The Lucilian "ritual" was to intrust one's life to one's books, for better or for worse, to paint one's whole life on a "votive tablet," as if to commemorate an escape from shipwreck:

> ille velut fidis arcana sodalibus olim
> credebat libris, neque si male cesserat usquam
> decurrens alio, neque si bene; quo fit ut omnis
> votiva pateat veluti descripta tabella
> vita senis.

And I follow his fine old example, Horace continues, being of frontier stock myself. My *stilus* is a weapon for defense, a sheathed sword, but, like an animal's horns or teeth, it will leave its mark on him who provokes me: he'll weep when he hears himself sung all over town. And I must insist on doing my work; whatever color my life turns, I will still write.

Trebatius has two more arguments in his briefcase: (1) You'll be abandoned by your friends. But, Horace counters, Lucilius wasn't, when he named names. His loyalty to virtue. and to virtue's friends proved to be the best policy. (2) You're liable to indite libelous verse, in which case you will be sued. Horace takes *mala carmina* in the aesthetic, not legal, sense and cheerfully agrees that if he writes badly, he deserves to be hounded for it. But suppose, he adds, I compose more felicitously, and Caesar likes what I write? That I bark at someone who really is a menace, when I'm in earnest and in the right? Oh, then, Trebatius admits, the court will cancel the proceedings and adjourn in a hail of laughter. The defense rests.

Enter Ofellus, Horace's neighbor somewhere in the Sabine

Hills. You wouldn't make much of his frugal disposition if you attended to his discourse after dinner, Horace begins, as he pushes the second satire off in the direction of some typical Epicurean whirlpools. You're a specialist in fine food? But whatever became of the idea of nourishment? When I say frugal, Horace reminds us, I don't mean sordid or niggardly. But the main point is that if you keep on stoking your stomach at the fashionable rate, you'll be a physical as well as a financial wreck.

Now wait . . . I can afford to live well, interrupts the puzzled interlocutor. But Horace stops him in his tracks with a serious and sobering CAN YOU?

> cur eget indignus quisquam, te divite? quare
> templa ruunt antiqua deum? cur, improbe, carae
> non aliquid patriae tanto emetiris acervo?

Social conscience joins the counsel of moderation as Horace's sense of values here assumes an impregnable form, and we are ready for the peroration of Ofellus, wherein plain living and high thinking carry the day. The sober-minded farmer indoctrinating his sons in the rigors of life is a flesh-and-blood figure whose moral convictions have made him well and strong.

Just the opposite holds true for the madmen of the third poem in Horace's second book. No minds could be more diseased, no bodies more frequently abused, than those of the offending host whom the Stoic preacher flays alive from the pulpit. The congregation, furthermore, seems as large as the *sermo* is long: Horace shows how straight on *prosa oratio* can go, how prolix moral man can be when hipped on a subject. And as the parade goes by, we see more and more how everyone is out of step but the preacher. Much of the evidence Damasippus reviews for us has the same double edge: on a compulsive Stoic it looks suspiciously protestant; on the fools and knaves it sits just right. The germ of truth in the Stoic definition of madness grows to elephantine proportions, until, like some prehistoric monster, it becomes too heavy to survive. But of course all men *are* crazy except the wise man; folly is a weakness, vice a disease, crime a mental delinquency, stupidity perfectly absurd.

Therapeutic as they may or may not be, the preacher's views are expounded and pounded in until they redound in our ears by the time this *sermo* has run its course. A mere glance at the synonyms Horace found for *insanus* shows how ready his rhetoric is to serve the needs of the "discussion": *furiosus, excors, delirus, amens, amentia versatus, demens, cerritus, commotus, commotae mentis, mentem concussus, male tutae mentis, putidi cerebri.* The formidable length is divided up into a preface, introduction, main body, and ending, and so conquered. The introduction finds Horace confronted by the garrulous convert to Stoicism, Damasippus, who has become a considerable authority on the subject of busyness. Bankrupt and on the verge of suicide, Damasippus was rescued by Stertinius from his frustrations and now, back in business on a large scale, can afford to pass the word on to the poet who is afflicted with *nonposse laboritis.* Damasippus may have taken the truth Stertinius "rattled at him" (*quid Stertinius veri crepat*) a bit literally when he assumed that, since all men are in fact mad (*desipiant omnes*), the thing to do is profit from their whimsical behavior and set up in the antique business. There may be some slight trace of lunacy in the background of Damasippus' financial recovery, but he has been cured of his depression, and there's no zealot like a convert.

The preface having introduced to us a somewhat despondent Horace and the introduction having brought before us an overzealous Damasippus, the poem begins again with the "main body" of Stoic discourse à la Stertinius. Horace's device here is repeated elsewhere in the book—reliance upon hearsay evidence. Damasippus heard it from Stertinius, as in the fourth satire Catius hears it from the unidentified master, and in the seventh Davus picks up his philosophy from the janitor at Crispinus' lecture room. This route to truth via "unimpeachable authority" is precisely the sort of journey we often take to arrive at some of our clearest impressions, other people's opinions being the intellectual currency that circulates most rapidly and is most subject to inflation. But "I heard someone say" is also another sort of echo: it reminds us of Plato's gospel in the dialogues[2] and of Socrates' skilful fishing for truth in the streams of conversation. Here beginneth, at any rate, the gospel "according to" Stertinius, based on the text that all save the Stoic wise man are mad. Damasippus relates the sermon, divided into its four parts, Avarice, Ambition, Self-Indulgence (*a. Luxuria, b. Amor*), and Superstition. The matter is riotously unexceptionable (much like Chaucer's re-creation of the Pardoner's sermonizing in the turbulent prologue to *The Pardoner's Tale*) and amounts to uncompromising damnation on the part of the preacher. Stertinius goes on and on at such length and with such severity as to take on something of the Scotch Presbyterian character. This "eighth-wise man" threatens to turn into a latter-day Caledonian Bore.

Horace varies the matter in wondrous ways,[3] not the least of which are the adaptation into hexameters of a passage from Terence's *Eunuchus* (to caricature the *amator exclusus*), an

[2] Fraenkel, pp. 136–37, notes the similarity and traces Platonic origins for some of Horace's phrasings.

[3] What Fraenkel calls "glittering ornament" I would be rather inclined to consider easy and resourceful rhetoric.

imaginary interview between Stertinius and that madman Agamemnon, and snatches of vernacular dialogue, set within the monologue of Stertinius, as relayed through the original dialogue between Horace and Damasippus.

Ending with a reprise of the *de te / fabula narratur* theme, the third satire leaves Horace at the mercy of Damasippus, the world's foremost authority on foolishness. The frustrated satirist, at a loss for inspiration and subject matter despite his having deliberately withdrawn to the country to avoid the holiday distractions of big city life, is suffering from an inflated opinion of himself. Damasippus assures Horace that his trouble is simply an exaggerated view of his own importance: "building, writing, passionately loving." Ugh! Horace is like the mother frog in the story, puffing herself up in heroic imitation of the giant calf who crushed her little ones. "How big *was* it?" she asks anxiously, puffing up (*sufflans se*), "*this* big?" Inadvertently, the reader's mind turns away from Horace to the long-winded preacher and his pupil.

The fourth satire is an inspired plea for finer eating and more technical cooking. It is of course anti-Communist: *erst kommt die Moral, dann kommt das Fressen*. Catius' playback of his master's voice is again one of Horace's pieces of overheard information, and the main points in the lesson leave little to be desired. The short distance between this and the last satire of the book shows the nearness of *la haute cuisine* to *la nausée*, which is perhaps the point of both these virtuoso vocabular pieces. Engraved menus and expensive cookbooks might do the same work for the reader, but they would lack the personal touch. And how Epicurean it all is Horace seems to indicate in his deadpan closing quotation from the master, Lucretius. As for Catius' erudite concentration on the needs of the inner man, which has made him a kind of inner spaceman capable of soaring to unheard-of gastronomical heights, I suppose that, despite Horace's faithful recording of the phenomenon, the less said about it the better. Graduate students like Catius will go far, write more and more dissertations on Fine Food, and inherit the chairs of Intestinal Fortitude, or at least take degrees in Hotel Management, *summa cum fraude.*

The fifth dialogue summons Ulysses out of the vasty deep of the eleventh book of the *Odyssey,* carrying on where Homer had seen fit to leave off. Homer's Tiresias had told Ulysses originally how to get in touch with his mother's shade, but now Horace sees the man of many resources as standing in even greater need of his patrimony. The vicious practice of angling for legacies which Horace brings into view here must have been a sociological fact of some magnitude in his day; it grew to alarming proportions in Imperial Rome. And like many Roman customs, this art of forming profitable friendships could satisfy a literal urge, *worked.* But it could swiftly become a social evil and a ribald ritual, as Horace travesties the practice. You have some money? Count me in among your friends. Some editors compare Horace's drastic outline of the subject with De Quincey's *Murder as a Fine Art.* And such seems to be Horace's manner in the taut and cynical interview between Ulysses and the seer. Love thy rich neighbor, for thereby hang all the losses and profits.

There are many reasons for the overwhelming success of Horace's sixth satire. The town mouse and the country mouse play their roles with captivating ease in the dramatic scene Horace wrote for them to conclude and point the moral of the piece. The whole poem attains an effortless perfection as the poem builds and arranges its subjects. From prayerful beginning to melodramatic escape, the work sings and chants its delights and confusions, the treatment precise and consonant yet free and varied, the tone both casual and convincing, the tempos perfectly suited to the situations they mobilize and the scenes they change. Horace's concealed art of modulation, to be brought to uncanny perfection in the *Odes,* begins perhaps here for the first time to make itself felt and to secure its intricate aliveness of effect.

The sixth satire of Book II is like the satires of Book I in its autobiographical content and its soliloquizing; yet it partakes of both the direct and the double style when it begins in personal utterance and ends in dialogue. It is usually considered a "late" work, and I would conjecture that this was perhaps the last satire Horace saw fit to compose, that it stands for his satire of satires and brings into final focus the moral and the artistic preoccupations of his hexameter style. Having achieved this, he could proceed with the more restricted form of the *Epodes* and go on to polish the luminous lenses of the lyrics, to see finer and farther. At the end of the next period he could return with easy and familiar confidence to the hexameter style of the *Epistles.* The latter, surely, have more in common with the sixth satire of Book II than with any other satire. The imagery, diction, doctrine, and wit of the letters are deftly foreshadowed here, and although the satires as a group are far from lacking in good lines, particular images, memorable renderings, the *Epistles* contain a larger measure. The power of compressed formulation which Horace achieved in the lyric poems enters his work to a marked degree in the town mouse and country mouse, just as the delicate strength of image contained in the social confusions of these two amicable beasts defines the point of the poem. So far, Horace's satires have discovered their share of fine lines, as witness the noble passage in the second satire of the second book, beginning *cur eget indignus quisquam, te divite* . . . and rising to the subtle climax of *contentus parvo*. Or the candid limning of honest Lucilius, *quo fit ut omnis | votiva pateat veluti descripta tabella| vita senis*. The clever reprise of *comis et urbanus*, the modest assurance of *ubi quid datur oti | illudo chartis* and its counterpart in Book II, *quisquis erit vitae scribam color*— these phrases stay in our minds, as do such others as the notable passage on poetic genius in the fourth satire of Book I, the memorable sociological realism of the third satire of Book I, the two-line doctrine of the mean plus the *mutato nomine de te | fabula narratur* of the first satire of Book I, and the ideal shape of moral man as recorded in the seventh satire of Book II, *in se ipso totus, teres, atque rotundus*. There is ample evidence of good writing, of concern for arrangement and thematic relationships.

Horace has already acquired artistic prowess. But complete ease of style and perfection of form still lie ahead. For example, there suddenly appears in this sixth satire an arresting line, in which Horace is describing the moment when he is accosted by a "friend" who wants Maecenas to sign some papers and urges Horace to use his influence. The line goes, "If you say, 'Well, I'll try,' 'You can do it if you want to,' he hastens to add":

> dixeris experiar si vis potes addit et instat.

Now this line is perfect. It consists of eight words, six of which are verbs, the other two indispensable conjunctions. It has two rippling dactyls (denoting the quick brushoff), a "golden" caesura and a spondaic pause (denoting mutual uneasiness), then two more fast dactyls (denoting the friend's urgent anxiety), and finally the full stop *instat* (INSISTS). The line is a moving picture, and its rhythm the sound track, of the momentary invasion of Horace's privacy.

In the *Odes* Horace shows himself more and more capable of this compressed order of construction, and in the *Epistles* expert in reeling off limpid, self-contained hexameters (the most singularly famous one being *parturient montes nascetur ridiculus mus*, wherein the atomic weight of that vivid concluding monosyllable has to be seen and heard to be felt). His writing becomes more deftly "figurative." And yet the whole quality of Horace's verse at its consistent best is already here in the town mouse and country mouse satire, for this poem is genuinely prayerful, as melodic and weightless as the wind, and deeply eloquent.

Pastoral imagery and bustling metropolitan excitement vibrate together on subtle frequencies and matching amplitudes in the poem, and I would not be surprised if depth analysis of the aesthetic contours could assign inevitable attributes to each one of the 117 lines and poetic justice to every word. For example, the "natural" impatience, the urgent note on which *urbanus* persuades *rusticus* to light out for the city, his infectious enthusiasm for life, more life, the argument by the smallest of creatures on behalf of the biggest of things, his Epicurean insistence on delight. What's the good, he asks, of this slow and rather shaggy life in the woods (the words are quite deliberate, the rhythm cautious and slow)?

> quid te iuvat . . . amice,
> praerupti nemoris patientem vivere dorso?

But then he *hastens* to assure his friend of the countervailing joys of city life:

> vis tu homines urbemque feris praeponere silvis?
> carpe viam, mihi crede, comes. . . .

And then, with a steadying alternation of dactylic and spondaic rhythms, the grandest of notions is nimbly marshaled by the most sensitive of creatures, the sophisticated town mouse who has the source of all pleasure at the tip of his whiskers.

But I cannot pretend to explain the poetry to the reader. Horace, after all, invited us to it in the first place. If the town noises (to be heard even louder in *Epistles* ii. 2. 70 ff.) fail to drown out the murmur of the country; if *rusticus* escapes from the colorful private dining room unharmed by the noise and the dogs, and we are glad; if Horace the citizen and notorious friend of Maecenas has his farm to himself and can virtually measure, see, and hear his happiness, his art is also a success and of just the right size, like his "field": *modus agri, non ita magnus*. If he reminds us all too vividly of the busyness, the *aliena negotia centum* that stalk us all down and threaten to immobilize us in the midst of the big city whirl, of the connections that sometimes make us victims of envy by association, his sophistication is benign, not malignant. He has only turned with generous confidence to a subject matter absolutely germane to the satiric spirit, with its seemingly offhand ability to blend humor and antagonism for a moral purpose:

> ergo ubi me in montis et in arcem ex urbe removi,
> quid prius illustrem satiris musa pedestri?

He himself had come from the country to Rome. He had contracted the metropolitan madness and recovered from it. His slender art, like the "adequate bean" that is quite food enough for *mus rusticus,* was quite good enough to bring the poet back to his original senses. Some power had given him the gift to see himself in the eternal perspective of the countryside, where all creatures can sense the duration, the propriety, and the joy of all life. And so he had scampered back home to his soul.

The seventh poem of Book II plays with the problem of

freedom somewhat as the third toyed with wisdom. The Saturnalia (December 17 to 24) permits Davus to say what he wants without fear of reprisal, and the sprightly slave is ready to declare his independence of mind. Licentious as some of his examples may be, they are neither so obscene as matters mentioned in the second satire of Book I nor as crude as other random features of the same book; on the whole, Horace's second group of satires is a more elegant and better-balanced performance, and this poem is a scene from comic opera, not from a variety show.

Davus begins his aria with some familiar music (like the notes from *Figaro* that slip into the score of *Don Giovanni*), as if he had read the first book. Some people, he says, *are* perfectly consistent, unerring in their depravity; but most of the would-be upright waver, making a stab at good conduct, then backsliding. And I tell you, consistent misconduct is a lot less nerve-racking than this undulant moral fervor, *mio caro signore*. There follows a recitative passage between Horace and Davus, ending on the cadence *de te / fabula narratur*. Horace is just like the others, adhering to "The Concept of Interchangeability" either because he is hypocritical or because he is weak-willed. In the city he yearns for the country and in the country pines for the town. If he's not dining out, he wishes he were. But hold back your hand and your temper, *Signore*, while I tell what I learned from the janitor at the school where Crispinus instructs. Davus enumerates a brief little black booklist of love neuroses (as contrasted with the healthy peasant requital of passion) and then proceeds by a remarkable modulation to the theme of *libertà*. The slave of a slave, he continues, is called *vicarius* or *conservus*, but you, *maestrosissimo*, are enslaved to passions and worries I have no share in. You're being jerked about like a puppet, a "mere Adam in the motions," a piece of wood that moves, *mobile lignum: l'uomo è mobile lignum.* You call me your slave? Let me sing you my definition of freedom:

> quisnam igitur liber? sapiens sibi qui imperiosus,
> quem neque pauperies neque mors neque vincula terrent,
> responsare cupidinibus, contemnere honores
> fortis, et in se ipso totus, teres, atque rotundus,
> externi ne quid valeat per leve morari,
> in quem manca ruit fortuna.

The song soars as Davus delights in mentioning the unmentionable preoccupations that nibble away at Horace's freedom, his time, his tranquillity: love ("Take your neck out of that yoke"), a taste for good painting ("I like pictures too, but I don't know a thing about art"), a taste for good food (that brings on consumption of the purse). As he reaches the end, he modulates into the minor to evoke one of Horace's most famous figures, the Dark Companion Care who rides behind the rider. Even you, the master is assured by his man, know the anxiety of being yourself; even you try to drown the truth in wine or lull it to sleep. But worry keeps dogging the tracks of every free man.

> . . . teque ipsum vitas fugitivus et erro,
> iam vino quaerens, iam somno fallere curam;
> frustra; nam comes atra premit sequiturque fugacem.

At least Horace can threaten Davus with lese majesty, and does, although Davus mistakes Horace's anger for *furor poeticus.* The final presto passage brings us back to the major and lights up the stage. The actors can take their bows. But the crystalline music of a major psychological problem set in a minor key will sound in our ears for a good long time.

In the last poem of the book we are invited to a feast—not

INTRODUCTION TO BOOK TWO

this time to the recipes, blends, and concoctions but to the finished product. Is Horace parodying the Epicurean imagery of the picnic and the banquet? It is hard to say, for his satires comprise something of an intellectual smorgasbord themselves: Stoic and Epicurean offerings; samples of straight hedonism; heaping platters of Aristotelian ethics cut and served dialectically as judgments, not propositions merely; a dash of Empedocles and Pythagoras; the flavor of Plato and the spice of Socrates.

Of course the value of food is for Horace not quite commensurate with the cost of *la haute cuisine,* and in this *Cena Nasidieni* he enjoys tracing the lurid features of a Roman habit. The guests are ensconced on three triclinia surrounding the low altar of a serving table; their host, anxious to please and correspondingly unsettled, explains every fine point of the cookery *ad nauseam.* As the food and wine begin their antiphons, Fundanius reels off the guest list to Horace and then returns to his description of the action: fowl, sea food, a compleat fish course, with a sauce of the most unusual ingredients. Next comes the canopy course, as the décor flops down on the diners, reducing the host to tears and the guests to giggles. But, with the help of timely orations by Nomentanus and Balatro on the thousand natural shocks flesh is heir to, Nasidienus recovers his aplomb, as the guests make fun of him in whispers: *stridere secreta divisos aure susurros.* And he brings on the next course: cooked crane, forelegs of *lapin* (*arrachées*), singed breast of blackbird, pigeons en casserole—which would have tasted good, according to Fundanius, had not the host insisted on regaling the diners with a Lucretian discourse on the nature of things:

> suavis res si non causas narraret earum et
> naturas dominus. . . .

So, fed up and vengeful, the guests decide to dash off without taking a single taste more, and leave the host to his fete.

We may wonder why Horace has planted so much foodstuff in his second book: Ofellus said a mouthful on the subject in the second satire, Catius posed as a mystical initiate into the rites in the fourth, Davus described a fat master going to pot in the seventh; and the whole book ends with a banquet. Is this all a joke, a caricature of civilized man coddling his intestines far beyond the needs of his stomach? Is Horace again improving on precedent as he continues a tradition of Lucilian satire and serves up favorite dishes, which some ninety years later Petronius would prepare according to even more monstrous recipes in the *Cena Trimalchionis?* Much nearer to Horace in time than Lucilius or Petronius was the esteemed Marcus Terentius Varro (116–28 B.C.); among his some 620 volumes were 150 books of *Saturae Menippeae,* which in fact represented a kind of revival of Roman satire in its earliest form. And the earliest form of satire, the *satura* prototype of all later Roman humorous literature, was in fact originally a "savory dish," a mess of pottage, a mess, a potpourri, a medley, a stew. It was the literary equivalent, this *satura lanx,* of "the full platter of first fruits offered to Ceres and Bacchus . . . and the name was transferred from the rural basket or dish of various ingredients to a performance that was a blend of various materials."[4]

Satire *was* originally a vicarious meal. And the satire that Horace placed last in his series of eighteen performances parodies, while it perfects, the archetypal pattern of this distinctively Roman literary genre. True to tradition, conservatively and deliberately, Horace upheld the customs of his ancestors.

[4] J. Wight Duff, *A Literary History of Rome* (3d ed.; New York: Barnes & Noble, 1953), I, 81–82.

His satire, a new model based on their moral and stylistic ideals, displays a remarkable skill in engineering the hexameter; it is a superior construction, broader, smoother, longer-lasting. But it is still a Roman road leading straight from the dim hinterlands of Fescennine raillery and Menippean potpourri to the city and the world. Horace's two books of *saturae* are also medleys, meals with moral menus and a blackberry plenty of raisins. His successors, the "Neronian" Persius and Petronius, for example, would try in turn to profit from his work and cook up appetizing meals from his recipes. But each acknowledged the master's strength—Persius when he said of Horace *circum praecordia ludit*, Petronius when he alluded to Horace's *curiosa felicitas*. Juvenal, the last and perhaps chief chef of Roman satire, bustled busily about cultivating his own kitchen garden and proved to be, like Horace, a considerable master of these ceremonies. But nearly seventeen hundred years later Dryden found himself able to distinguish between the two great Roman satirists by saying that while Juvenal's cookery is more exquisite, there is more meat in Horace.

II · 1

TO WRITE OR NOT TO WRITE?
(A TALK WITH MY LAWYER)

Sunt quibus in satira videar nimis acer et ultra

Horace. To some, it appears, my satire is far too mean
And strains its aesthetic bounds, whereas others find
Whatever I write anemic, and claim that my lines
Can be turned out a thousand a day.
                                        Trebatius, my friend,
Advise me what to do.
   Trebatius.   Take a rest.
   Hor. And not write verses at all, you say?
   Treb.   That's what I say.
   Hor. Damn it! You're probably right! But I can't get to
     sleep.
   Treb. To one in default of sleep, I decree as follows:
Rub well with oil the party of the first part, then swim
(Transnatate) the Tiber thrice, then habeas your corpus
Well soaked with wine at night. Or, if so wild
A love of writing possesses you, have the courage
To write of invincible Caesar: recording his deeds
Will bring a good fee for the work.
   Hor.   Good father, the wish
Is there, but the skill is not. Not all can describe
The serried ranks bristling with pikes, and the Gauls
Going under, with splintered spears, a wounded Parthian

Slipping down from his horse to final defeat.

    Treb. You might just portray your hero as valiant and true,
As wise Lucilius did for his Scipio.

    Hor. I'll be equal to that when the occasion presents itself.
Unless the remarks of a Flaccus are properly timed,
They will not pass into the attentive ear of a Caesar.
Stroked the wrong way, the steed plays it safe and kicks
      back.

    Treb. How much more discreet this is than to lash out a
    line
That stings, consigning Pantolabus and Nomentanus,
The wastrels, to "Parasites Lost"; then everyone else
Fears he'll be next and, though still unmentioned, detests
    you.

    Hor. But what to do? Milonius starts to dance
As soon as the heat mounts up to his wine-bludgeoned brain
And as soon as he counts up twice as many lamps as there
    are.
Castor likes riding; his twin from the selfsame egg
Likes fighting; for every thousand people, you see
A thousand tastes. For myself, as best as I can,
I take delight in constructing verses that scan,
As Lucilius did, a nobler and better man
Than either of us. He confided his deepest thoughts
To his books, as if to his closest friends, and would not
Go running off elsewhere, whether things went right or wrong,
And the old poet's life is therefore as faithfully limned
As a votive tablet hung up for all to view.

    Like him, I'm a fighter. I come from frontier stock,
You know, for Venusia is part of . . . either Apulia
Or Lucania, it's hard to say which: Venusians plow
Right up to both borders. The history is, they were sent

To settle and guard the place when the Samnites were routed,
So that no enemy could rush through the gap at the Romans
If Apulians or fierce Lucanians rattled the sword.
But this stiletto, my stylus, will not assault
Any living soul, but defend me, like a sheathed sword.
Why should I try to draw it, as long as I'm safe
From malignant attackers? Jupiter, Father and King,
May my weapon, retired from use, be ruined by rust
And may no one injure me, who desire only peace!
But the man who provokes me will weep (HANDS OFF! I WARN
    YOU)
And his name will be widely rehearsed all over town.
The informer Cervius threatens to throw the book,
And the ballot box, too, in his rage, at his enemies;
That implacable witch Canidia menaces hers
With the poison Albucius used on his wife; Turius
Imposes a heavy fine if you go to court
While he's on the bench. So everyone would terrify
The ones he most fears by whatever natural means
He can wield. Come now, infer the way of the world
With me, from the following facts: wolves use their teeth,
Bulls their horns, to attack. Are they not so instructed
By instinct? Suppose you intrust to the spendthrift Scaeva
An aged mother who keeps living on and on:
His filial hands commit no capital crime—
But what's so amazing? The wolf won't fight with his hoof,
Nor an ox with his teeth. A honey-flavored cup
Of the very best hemlock will fix the old woman up.
To sum up my case: whether a calm old age awaits me
Or Death now circles above me on ebony wings,
Whether rich or poor, whether destined to live in Rome
Or ordered by chance into exile, I WILL STILL WRITE,

No matter what color or tone my life assumes.

    Treb. Dear boy, I'm afraid your life will be all too brief:
One of your prominent friends will strike you down
With the cold shoulder.

    Hor. What! When Lucilius, the first man who dared
Compose this kind of poem, stripped off the skin
Wherein everyone flaunts his good looks in his neighbor's
    eyes
While inwardly ugly, did Laelius take offense
At the play of wit, or did Scipio, named in honor
Of conquered Carthage? Did either make a show of grief
When Lucilius wounded Metellus and buried over Lupus
With lampoons in verse? Yet Lucilius laid hands on the
    leaders
And on the people themselves: he played no favorites,
But favored virtue alone, and virtue's friends.
In fact, when Scipio the wise, and Laelius the gentle
And wise, withdrew from the teeming spectacle of life,
They put aside pomp and amused themselves with Lucilius,
Having fun while the cabbage soup boiled on the stove.

    And, such as I am—inferior to Lucilius in rank,
Inferior in genius—even Envy will have to admit
That I too have lived with the great and, trying to sink
Her tooth into something soft, will grate on a rock.
Unless you, my learned friend, may wish to dissent?

    Treb. I can't make a dent in that. But still, be advised:
Look out for legal snags in our sacred laws.
Ignorance is no excuse. It is written: WHO WRITES
EVIL THINGS AGAINST SOME OTHER PERSON MUST HIMSELF
BY RIGHTS BE PREPARED TO BE SUED FOR REDRESS OF
    GRIEVANCE.

  Hor. That means who writes not wrongly but badly.
   Suppose
A man composes good verses, and Caesar approves,
As the judge? Suppose he has barked at one who deserves it,
The barker himself being quite a fine dog, free of faults?
   Treb. "CASE DISMISSED," in a hail of laughter. You will
    go free.

II · 2

PLAIN LIVING AND HIGH THINKING

Quae virtus et quanta, boni, sit vivere parvo

Gentlemen, hear the words of a sound old fellow,
The farmer Ofellus, a country neighbor of mine
Whose school of thought was his own indigenous wit.
From him learn the virtue and greatness of frugal living:
And the teaching, moreover, should not be acquired at a
    banquet
Where the eye dazzles, where the mind is especially inclined
To the wrong things, and turns down the better. Let's talk
    it over
Right here and now, before we sit down to our meal.
   "Why so?" I'll try to explain. Any judge who's been bribed
Is a poor judge of evidence. Suppose you've had a good
    workout—
Tracking down hares or riding a mettlesome steed,
Or—being averse to rough Roman military drill—
You've gone Greek to the extent of playing a fast game of
    ball,
Where the skill involved delightfully hides the hard work,
Or been busy with the discus: WATCH IT CARVE THE
    YIELDING AIR!
When the work has hammered you into shape—when you're
    thirsty
And hungry, but not finicky, you won't scorn plain food
Or refuse any wine that is not Mellow Muscatel.

104

The butler is out, and the ocean is also out
Of sorts: there are no fresh fish. Some bread, with salt,
Will quiet your growling stomach perfectly well.
   How or why, do you think, this result ensues?
The fact is, the ultimate pleasure exists in *you*,
Not in expensive aromas. Exercise is appetizing.
The man pale and bloated from self-indulgence can*not*
Enjoy his wrasse, his oysters, his Persian pheasant.
But once you've been offered a peacock, I'll never root out
Your urge to brush your palate with this, and not chicken.
You are taken in by appearace, the conspicuous expense
Of a rare bird who puts on a show with his colorful tail,
As if this had any real bearing on the case before you.
You'll eat the feathers you admire so? How's that bird look
When he's cooked? Yet, although the meat differs not a bit,
It's peacock for you, fooled by a superior exterior.
(All right, all right! Taste discrepancy if you like it!)
By the way, what tells you whether this pike was hauled in
At sea, or down by the Isola Tevere? You incomplete
Angler, you prize a three-pound mullet you'll have
To slice up to eat. Oh, I see. It's the *looks* you like.
Well, why not a nice long pike? Oh, they're long by nature,
The mullets normally light? Stomachs rarely hungry
Can scorn common food.
                        "Oh, for a great big fish
Stretched out on a great big dish! What a sight to see!"
Says a throat the equal of voracious Harpies'. O South Wind,
Blow, in your might, and spoil these gluttons' side dishes!
And yet the fresh flounder and boar are already rank
To the jaded taste of the gourmand, whose stomach is
      turned
By too much eating. Full up, he prefers some radishes

And some sharp pickles. Poor people's food is still not
    entirely
Absent from royal feasts: cheap eggs, black olives,
Have a place there even today. Not so very long ago,
Gallonius, the auctioneer, was roundly abused
For serving up sturgeon. And could there have been, in
    those days,
Fewer flounders afloat? They were safe in the sea, at least,
And storks were safe in their nests, until Rufus the praetor
First taught you to eat them. So, if someone now decrees
That sea gulls, roasted, are tasty, the Roman young set,
So eager to follow bad leads, will swallow this, too.
    Ofellus, of course, distinguishes simple living
From a sordid existence; there's no use avoiding one error
If you bump right into another. Avidienus,
Whose nickname "Dog" sticks to him, in view of the facts,
Eats olives five years old, with dogwood berries.
He hates to pour off his wine until it's turned,
And as for his oil—you couldn't abide the smell
As he pours it drop by drop from a two-gallon jar
On the salad when, clothed in white, he observes the feast—
A wedding, a birthday, some other occasion. Of course,
He is always lavishly free with his Olde Winegar.
What eating style will the wise man, therefore, adopt,
Gallonius the show-off's or the skinflint Avidienus'?
Here we're attacked by a wolf, and there by a dog,
As the proverb says. He will observe the proper amenities,
Not disgust us with dirt and disorder, but not be *too* elegant:
He will chart a sound course of conduct between the
    extremes.
He will not be Albucius, the compulsive perfectionist type,
Who bawls out his slaves in the act of assigning their jobs,

Nor so dense and careless as Naevius, whose guests get
    served
Greasy water to wash in: he errs in the other direction.
   Hear what blessings the simple life confers
And how great they are. First and foremost, good health.
You'll realize how harmful a many-course dinner is
If you think of old-fashioned food, which sat so well
On your stomach. Mixing boiled and roast meat, or shellfish
And fricaseed thrush, sours your liver and makes the phlegm
Act up in your stomach. You notice that guests rise pale
From the "bewilderment banquet" effect of a smorgasbord?
The body, weighed down and clogged up with last night's
    indulgence,
Drags the mind down with it—and a wisp of the spirit divine
Is imbedded in earth. By contrast, the temperate man
Puts his body in care of good food, then hands it over
To sleep that comes quick as a wink. He rises refreshed,
Alert to the next day's demands. Yet, mind you, he *has*
The capacity to have a good time, from time to time,
When an anniversary rolls round again, or when
His body's been under a strain and needs to be pampered,
Or when, as the years wear on, less vigorous age
Wants to be treated more nicely. But as for yourself,
If sickness comes or old age slows you down,
What margin of safety is left any longer to draw on
When, as a strong young man, you use it all up?
   Our fathers praised a boar that was somewhat rancid;
Not that they couldn't smell it, but rather, I think,
That they felt it more fitting to serve a meat that was high
To a tardy guest than for the greedy host
To devour it entire and whole. Had I but lived

In the age of such heroes!

                    To enjoy a good reputation,
Which chimes in human ears more charmingly than music,
Means something to you, no doubt. Big dishes, with big
    flounders
On them, bring big disgraces and ruinous costs.
Not to mention infuriated uncles, outraged neighbors,
Your mortified self, and your wholly impractical wish
To commit suicide when you haven't a cent to buy rope with!
    "It's all right to lace into Trausius like that," says he,
"But I have a big income, more wealth than three kings."
And therefore there's no better way for you to unload
The surplus? Why should a single deserving man
Be in need when you are so rich? Why do the gods' ancient
    temples
Fall into ruin? Why not dig into your pile
And measure some out for your own dear country, you
    wretch?
For you alone, things will always go well: how interesting!
Later on, your foes will get a big laugh out of you.
Of the following two, which one has the better chance
Of remaining self-assured in vicissitude:
The man who has accustomed his mind and magnificent body
To all the luxuries or the man who, content with little,
Fearing the future, provides in time of peace,
As a wise man should, the equipment required for war?
    To make you see this more clearly, do let me tell you
How, when I was a boy, Ofellus made use
Of his means on no larger scale than he now applies
When they're sharply reduced. You may see him there on
    his farm,
On his former farm (for now he's a hardy hired hand

On confiscated land) with his sheep, and his sons.
"I was never the one," as he tells it, "to eat anything
On a working day but some greens and a slice of smoked
    ham.
But if a guest appeared who hadn't been round to see me
For quite some time, or a neighbor paid me a visit
Some rainy day when I couldn't work—good fellow!—
We made out quite well with our meal of pullet and kid,
Not fish fresh from the city. We topped off the feast
With raisins, nuts, and split figs. Our sport after dinner
Was drinking as much as we felt we could take, until Ceres,
Invoked in our prayers—'May she rise on lofty stalks!'—
Smoothed out, with wine, the cares on our wrinkled brows.
Let Fortune rave and stir up new disturbances—
Can she detract from this? Have you or I
Lost our luster, my lads, since the new proprietor came?
Nature indeed has appointed not him, not me,
Nor anyone else as lord and master of the earth.
He drove us off; some force will in turn drive him out:
Inefficiency, ignorance of some subtle clause of law,
Or at least and at last, no doubt, an heir that outlives him.
The land now known as Umbrenus' was recently called
Ofellus'; it will never belong to anyone, really:
It is loaned to us for our use, now mine, now others'.
So live brave lives: stand up to the blows of fate!"

A STOIC SERMON

Sic raro scribis ut toto non quater anno

    Damasippus. You are writing so little these days that you
      don't call for parchment
Four times a year; you unweave the web of your lines;
You're angry at writing nothing worthy of mention,
While lavish of wine and sleep—what's going to happen?
You say that you even insisted on coming up here
To the farm on New Year's, and therefore stayed perfectly
      sober:
Well, say something worthy of what we've been led to expect.
Go ahead. Not a word? It's no good blaming your pens
Or pounding the innocent wall, which was hexed by the
      gods.
You looked quite pregnant with powerful stuff, which you
      threatened
To do something good with, once you got to the villa
And its heart-warming shelter, where you hadn't a thing on
      your mind.
What use was it packing your Plato in with Menander
And lugging Archilochus and Eupolis out to the country?
Did you mean to offset the ill feeling your satires aroused
By giving up your hard-earned success? You'll be despised
      now,
You oaf, as well as disliked. You must be on guard
To resist the unscrupulous siren who clangs like a streetcar

Named Sloth, or be perfectly willing to see laid aside
Whatever prestige you've acquired from nobler endeavors.
   Horace. For this good advice, Damasippus, may the gods
      and goddesses
Confer on you . . . the tonsorial rites all philosophers
Are heir to. But how does it happen you know me so well?
   Dam. My business on the Street went to pieces, and so,
      forced out
Of my own, I began looking after the business of others.
I got interested in uncovering antiques, the authentic
      bronze foot bath,
For instance, that sly old Sisyphus the King had washed
His Corinthian feet in. I'd note the crude strokes in the
      carving,
Or immalleabilities in casting, that made it antique:
As a connoisseur I'd price this piece, or some other,
At a round hundred thousand. And then, as for beautiful
      homes
And gardens, I was the one man who knew what to offer
To get them at bargain rates. So the street corner crowds
Called me "Mercury the Mettlesome Merchant."
   Hor.   I knew all that,
And I marvel at how you got over so bad a disease!
   Dam. What I can't get over is how an entirely new interest
Cured my old interest in interest. Isn't it interesting?
It's like the body's way of turning some pain in the neck
Or stitch in the side aside into stomach disorder,
Or the way a weak patient recovers and pummels the doctor.
   Hor. Well, as long as you don't try *that* cure out on me,
      you can have it
Your way.
   Dam.   Don't kid yourself, boy, You're out of your mind,

Like nearly everyone else, if truth can be grasped
From the speeches Stertinius raps out. I learned my lesson
From him, this miracle-cure prescription of dogma,
The very day he cheered me up and told me to grow
A philosopher's beard, and wend my way home again, happy,
From the bridge to the Isola Tevere. With my face
    concealed,
I was ready to jump—my business had failed so badly—
When he appeared on my right and uttered the following
Stoical Statements: HEAR THE WISE WORDS OF STERTINIUS:

Don't treat yourself in a way you don't really deserve;
You're obsessed by a false sense of shame when you fear
You are mad, in the midst of so many madmen. In the first
    place,
I will look further into just what it means to be "mad";
    then, if you
Alone are afflicted, I will not add a single word more
To prevent you from perishing bravely. Whoever is swept
Blindly through life, and by unbalanced folly is kept
In the dark as to truth, is by Stoics full witless yclept.
This formula holds for people and for powerful kings,
The wise philosopher alone excepted. Now learn
Why it is that all who have fastened the name on you
Are quite as crazy as you. Just as men in a forest,
Whom confusion forces to wander away from the right path,
Will veer off, one to the left, the other to the right,
Misled by the same mistake but misled in different
Directions, so you may consider yourself deluded
To the exact degree of the man who makes fun of you,
Who is dragging a tail behind himself all unawares.
    One class of fools invent the fears they're afraid of

And claim that a reef of rocks, or flames, or a river,
Blockade their path through an open plain. An alternative
Class, no wiser but certainly utterly different,
Walk right into a fire or a fast-flowing river,
Though a doting mother, a noble sister, a wife,
A father, and children, may each exclaim, "Look out!
There's a big ditch there, there's a big rock over this way!"
The fool just won't hear them, any more than Fufius did
The time he was playing the role of Iliona asleep:
Fufius slept, all right—he was dead drunk, in fact—
When Catienus, playing the part of Iliona's son,
Came on with "Mother! I call on thee!" No response,
So the whole house took up the chant: twelve hundred
     Catieni
"Appello-ed" the somnolent mother. All human madness
Is like this species of folly, as I will now prove.
    Damasippus is nuts to go around buying old statues.
Damasippus' creditor is quite *compos mentis:* oh, naturally!
Suppose I ask you to take this money, you WON'T
HAVE TO PAY IT BACK: are you out of your mind if you
    take it?
Or are you not more addlebrained to turn down a godsend
Mercury offers? Enter ten to be cashed by Nerius . . .
No, that's not enough: back it up with a hundred receipts
Advanced by Cicuta, the acute moneylender, who's famous
For freezing your assets; put on a thousand more chains
Of financial bondage. The fiendish debtor, this Proteus,
Will still wriggle loose from his bonds. When you drag him
    to court,
That's not *you* laughing, it's old Proteus grinning with glee,
As at will he's a boar, a bird, a stone, or a tree.

If it's crazy to mismanage property, and the contrary,
    wise—
Then, believe me, Perellius' brain is more decomposed
When he makes out a letter of credit you can never repay.

A TYPICAL STOICAL SERMON ON SANITY

(*Introduction*)

Now I bid you arrange your togas and listen to me,
  (1) Whoever is pale with passionate love for money,
  (2) Whoever is chill in the gruesome grip of ambition,
  (3) Whoever is running a fever for luxury living,
  (4) Whoever is all inflamed with religious fears
Or some other mental disease. Draw near to me,
And I'll prove that you all are mad, from the first to the
    last.

(FIRST, *Avarice*)

To the avaricious, by far the largest dose
Is due of the drug hellebore that cures insanity:
Or, perhaps, the wisest thing would be to reserve
Anticyra's whole crop for their use. Staberius' heirs
Were forced to engrave the sum of his wealth on his
    tombstone,
Or furnish a hundred gladiatorial pairs
For the mob's amusement, as a penalty, and a funeral feast
To match extravagant Arrius', and consume all the grain
North Africa grows. THIS IS THE WAY I WANT IT,
Staberius wrote, DON'T UNCLE ME, YOU LITTLE SQUIRTS!
I imagine Staberius had the presence of mind
To foresee what his heirs would think. "But what *was* the
    use
Of his wanting his heirs to carve the sum on the stone?"

As long as he lived he considered poverty evil,
The grossest of evils, and avoided nothing more zealously,
So that if by chance he had died one penny the poorer,
So much the more worthless he would have considered
      himself.
Everything else is the slave of gorgeous wealth:
Virtue, renown, moral dignity, all things divine
And human. When someone has heaped up a good big pile,
He will be famous, brave, and just. "And wise, as well?"
Right you are! And king, and anything else he desires.
Staberius thought that his wealth would bring him prestige,
As though it resulted from merit.
                    "What likeness obtains
Between the man we've discussed and the Greek Aristippus,
Who instructed his slaves to heave out a mass of gold
In the middle of Libya—it made him travel too slow?
Which is the more insane?" You can't solve one problem
By raising another, so that illustration won't do.
If a man buys up harps and puts them all in a warehouse
But doesn't like music and is no devotee of the arts;
Or, not being a shoemaker, corners the market on lasts
And shoe knives; or, dead set against the seafaring life,
Does the same with sail canvas, he deserves to be called
      deranged
And goofy. But what's the difference between these pile-its
And a man who hoards silver and gold without knowing how
To use what he's stashed away, and is afraid to touch it,
As though it was sacred?
                If a man stretched out with his cudgel
Beside his huge pile of grain, intending to keep
A continuous watch on it, and yet never dared, though
      hungry

And in possession, to touch a grain, but preferred
To dine like a miser on dandelion salad; or if,
Surrounded by a thousand casks of vintage Falernian
Or Chian stored in the cellar . . . make it three hundred
    thousands . . .
He drank rank vinegar; or if, on the verge of eighty,
He still slept on straw while expensive covers and quilts
Lay moldering away in the chest as excellent food
For moths and worms, amazingly few would think
Him mad. After all, the vast majority of men
Keep tossing and turning in their beds with the same disease.
   Do you guard your hoard, you godforsaken old goat,
So a son or a freedman heir may drink it away?
So as not to be short? How tiny a tab will your daily
Consumption tick off, if you begin to dress your salad
With a better-grade oil, and dress your uncombed hair,
Now scurfy with dandruff? If anything is really enough
For you, why perjure, pilfer, and plunder? You, all there?!!!
If you started to pelt the people with stones, and the slaves
You paid hard cash for, the kids would call you insane.
   When you strangle your wife and poison your mother,
    in the bosom
Of the family, there's nothing wrong with your head. After
    all,
You're not doing this at Argos, where mad Orestes
Murdered a parent with steel. Or perhaps you hold
That Orestes did not go mad until after the fact,
That he was not unhinged by the fiendish Furies before
The sharp steel edge of his sword grew warm with the gore
From his mother's throat? For the moment madness set in
Orestes did nothing, in sooth, to merit reproof,
Didn't dare go so far as to carve up Electra or Pylades,
But merely cursed them both out, calling Electra a Fury

And Pylades whatever name the shiny black bile,
Surging up in the hero's stomach, commanded him to.
    Opimius, impoverished in spite of the gold and silver
He kept stored away, drank only the local red wine
Of Veii on festive occasions, and on working days
Used to drink sour wine right out of the earthenware ladle.
One day he fell into a coma so deep that his heir
Started dancing in triumph and joy around the strongboxes
And the keys to them. His quick-witted loyal doctor
Revived him by means of this ruse: he ordered that a table
Be set up, and bags of money poured out on top of it,
And that lots of people be invited in to start counting.
This way, the doctor soon had his man sitting upright,
As he pointed out to Opimius, "If you don't watch your
        money,
Your greedy heir will lug it all off." "While I'm
Still alive?" "Wake up, if you want to live. Come on!"
"What are your orders?" "In your weakened condition, your
        veins
Won't hold up unless you support your collapsing stomach
With food, and take *much* better care of yourself." "*How*
        much?"
"You *won't?* Come on, drink down this nice rice gruel."
"I'm sick! How much did it cost?" "Oh, hardly anything."
"But, how much?" "Oh, only eight cents." "Well, what's the
        difference
Whether I die of disease or am robbed and plundered to
        death?"
    "Who, then, is sane?" The man who is not a fool.
"And the covetous man?" A fool and a madman. "Ah,
        therefore,
If a man is no miser, this means he is not insane?"
Not at all. "How's that, my Stoic?" Well, let me explain.

(SECOND, *Ambition*)

Let's assume Craterus furnishes this diagnosis:
My patient is not dyspeptic. Does that mean he's well
And ought to get up? Oh, no: his lungs or kidneys
Are gravely affected. Here's a man in a similar case
Who is no miser, no perjurer. Let him offer a pig
To the kindly gods. But he is ambitious, and reckless:
Let him sail off to Helleboreland. For what is the difference
Between never using your savings and pouring them all
Down some deep dark drain?
                       Servius Oppidius is said
To have divided his two estates at Canusium between
His two sons—he was quite well off, by old-fashioned
    standards—
And on his deathbed he called them to him and said:
"Ever since I saw you, Aulus, carrying marbles
And chestnuts around loosely in a fold of your toga
And giving them away on an impulse, or gambling a bit,
And you, Tiberius, counting yours over and over
And hiding them cautiously off in a hole somewhere,
I've been worried that two different kinds of madness might
    seize you:
That you, Aulus, might follow in Nomentanus' footsteps,
And you, Tiberius, the ways of the Shylock named Hemlock.
Therefore, I beseech you both, by our household gods,
The one of you not to reduce, nor the other increase,
What your father considers ENOUGH and what nature allows.
Moreover, to see that ambition does not captivate you,
I will bind you both with this oath: whichever of you
Becomes aedile or praetor thereby becomes accursed
And loses his rights. Will you throw your money away
On handouts of beans and lupine and vetch for the mob,

So that you can expansively promenade all round the Circus
Or stand there in bronze—and be stripped of your land,
Stripped of the money your father left to a madman,
In order, of course, to get a big hand, like Agrippa?
You foxy fox, can you copy this lordly lion?"

(*Imaginary interview. Scene: the camp before Troy*)

    Stertinius. Agamemnon, you refuse us the privilege of
        burying Ajax.
Why do you do so?
    Agamemnon.   Because I'm king around here.
    Ster. As a commoner, I, of course, seek no further redress.
    Agam. And I govern perfectly justly. If I seem unfair,
I will hear the complaint and grant the critic immunity.
    Ster. Oh, greatest of kings! May the gods place Troy in
        your hands
And steer your fleet safely home. Am I now permitted
To ask a few questions and in turn advance a few answers?
    Agam. Put your case.
    Ster.   Why should Ajax, a hero second
        only to Achilles,
Rot unburied, a man who so famously saved the Greek cause
So often? Is it so that Priam and Priam's people
May heartily rejoice in the body's being left unburied
Which made so many young men in the Trojan ranks
Miss out on their chance of being buried at home?
    Agam. But Ajax went crazy, he slaughtered a thousand
        sheep,
Yelling out, all the while, that he was killing off the famous
        Ulysses,
Menelaus, and me.
    Ster.   Were you well preserved in your mind,

Unscrupulous rogue, when you brought your child to the
        altar
At Aulis, instead of a heifer, and sprinkled her head
With salted meal? Ajax, for all his insanity,
Slew sheep with his sword, which amounted to what?
To withholding his hand from wife and child. Oh, he cursed
Menelaus and you, but he didn't attack even Teucer,
Not to mention Ulysses.
    Agam.   But at Aulis my ships were
        shore-bound
By hostile winds, and to pry them loose I piously,
Thoughtfully planned to appease the gods with bloodshed.
    Ster. Your own bloodshed, you swellhead.
    Agam.   My own blood,
        I grant,
But my head was quite unaffected, I sincerely assure you.

(*Interview fades away*)

The man whose impressions fail to square with the truth
And are further confused by a tumult of guilty emotions
I consider somewhat disturbed: it makes no difference
Whether folly or anger leads him away from the path.
When Ajax slays innocent lambs, he's out of his mind.
When you perpetrate a crime on purpose to win
Empty titles and fame, is your mind on an even keel?
Is your heart free of faults when it seethes and billows with
        pride?
    Suppose a man loved to carry a shiny white lamb
In a litter, and furnished it clothes and maids and gold,
And planned to marry it off to a gallant husband:
The praetor would write an injunction declaring
        incompetence

In the eyes of the law, and he would be handed over
To his sane relatives. Now, really, is someone who kills off
His own daughter in the place of a speechless lamb
Sound in his mind? Say not so. The height of insanity
Is misguided folly; the criminal is simply a raving
Lunatic; the man who is seized by a glittering vision
Of fame can already hear the thunder rolled round
By Bellona, who revels in blood.

(THIRD, [a] *Self-indulgence*)

                        Now come, let's attack
Nomentanus together, and luxury right along with him.
Reason will prove that spendthrifts are fools and mad.
As soon as he came into the millions his father had left him,
He decreed grandiosely that fish sellers, fruit sellers, fowlers,
Perfumers, the riffraff of Tuscus Street, the cooks
And the scroungers, bringing in tow the whole meat-and-fish
      market,
Should appear at his house the next morning. And what
      happened then?
They showed up, in droves. And a pimp was the spokesman
      for all:
"Whatever I have, whatever we, all of us, have
At home, believe me, old fellow, is yours, all yours,
Whether you want it today or tomorrow."
                        Now hear the response
Of our fair-haired boy:
                     "You there, you sleep in your boots
In the snow of Lucanian hills, so that I may banquet
On boar. You there, you sweep the tempestuous deep
For the fish I fancy. I'm lazy and really should not
Have so much money. Take some! You there, take a million;

121

You there, take a million more; and you over there,
Yes, you: the obliging husband whose ever-running wife
Must be ready to go at midnight with whoever calls her—
You take three times as much!"

                                    The fabulously rich
And prodigal son of Aesop the actor once took
A pearl from Metella's ear and drenched it in vinegar,
Intending to swallow a cool million at one fool gulp.
Wouldn't it make as much sense if he threw her jewel in the
        sewer
Or into a fast-flowing river?

                                    That fine pair of brothers,
The sons of Quintus Arrius, identical twins
As regards their perverted pleasures, their simply
        nogoodhood
And all-round stupidity, paid out enormous sums
To breakfast on *rossignol* en casserole.
How are they to be listed? In chalk, as befits the sane,
Or in charcoal?

(THIRD, *[b] Love conks them all*)

    To delight in building toy houses or hitching up mice
To a cute little cart or playing "you're it!" or riding
Horsie on a willowy cane would be sure signs of madness
In a grownup. If reason can prove that being in love
Is even more childish than this, that it's really no different
Whether you play at building in the sand, as you used to at
        three,
Or whimper and fuss if your mistress won't muss up your
        hair.
I ask you, why not just STOP IT? Polemon did.
The moment he heard Xenocrates' voice expounding

The beauty of self-restraint, and on an empty stomach,
Polemon guiltily slipped off the wreath he was wearing,
Sobered completely up, and lived a good life
From then on. Won't you, too, take off the signs of your
    sickness,
The wristlets, anklets, the soft little wrappings and pads?
  If you offer some fruit to your boy when he's having a
    tantrum,
He'll refuse it. "Come on, darling, have some!" He turns you
    down cold.
If you don't give it to him, he wants it. How different, really,
From this is the excluded lover who debates with himself
Whether to go or not to the place that he meant to return to,
Though quite uninvited, and hangs around the hateful doors?
    Lover. To go now, or not to go now, when she herself calls
      me?
Or, thinking more deeply upon't, why not end my troubles?
She herself shut me out, she herself calls me back: shall I go?
No! Even if she begs me.

(*Enter his slave, much smarter*)

    Slave. Oh master, a matter that doesn't submit
        To methodical handling or rational wit
        Will not be conquered by reason or rules.
        In love, the feelings are wicked tools.
        First it's war, then it's peace, then both together:
        La donna è perpetuum mobile, just like the weather.
        The situation is fluid, subject to chance:
        The scenes shift, *and* their inhabitants,
        And it's done in the dark. To eliminate sadness
        By a rational scheme to promote your gladness
        Would only be as right as devising a method for
            madness.

When you take the seeds of delicious apples of Picenum,
Squeeze them between the thumb and forefinger, and shout
For joy if you hit the ceiling, because then "she loves me,"
Are you really all there, *chez vous?* If, when you are old,
You lisp out some sweet baby talk on your slippery lips,
How are you wiser than a child building castles in the sand?
Pythagoras said, "You must not egg an angry man on,"
But I say, stir up the fire with a sword, add blood
To your portion of folly. A few days ago, for example,
When Marius made mincemeat of Helen and then threw
    himself
Out the window, wasn't he as touched in the head as a loaf
Of bread full of caraway seeds? Or will you absolve
Him of mental guilt and convict the same man of crime,
Applying, as we usually do, a different name
To things that, like folly and crime, are really the same?

(FOURTH, *Superstition*)

There was an old freedman who used to go running around
To the shrines at every street corner first thing in the
    morning,
Having fasted and washed his hands. He prayed: "Just me—
It's not such a big request [he added], just me—
I ask you to grab back away from the brink of death.
For the gods it's easy!" The man was physically sound
In ears and eyes, but his mind? No master could vouch
For that if he sold him, unless he wished to be sued.
This whole crowd of blind superstitious believers
Chrysippus would place in the fertile tribe of Menenius.
"Jupiter, who givest and takest away great griefs,"
Prays the mother of a child confined to his bed for five
    months,

"If the chilling quartan leaves my boy, I promise
  That he will stand naked in the Tiber on the day thou settest
  For fasting." (In those days Jovesday was Jewsday, not
      Thorsday.)
Should the doctor, or just good luck, rescue the patient
From his crisis, the mother will kill him by stationing him
On the cold river bank, thus reintroducing the fever.
And what malady hit her mind? Sheer superstition.

  This is the armor that Eighth Wise Man, Stertinius,
Equipped me, Damasippus his friend, with—so that none
      thereafter
Might insult me and not be insulted in turn. From now on,
Whoever says I'm mad will hear the same charge flung at him
And will learn to look over his shoulder to see what hangs
      down
From his back he wasn't aware of.
  Hor.   Good Stoic, I hope
You now sell your goods at a profit, after your losses.
But now tell me what particular form you think
My madness takes, since there are so many forms it can take.
To myself, I seem perfectly sane.
  Dam.   What's that! Does Agave
Seem mad to herself when, in a demented state,
She brings in the severed head of her ill-fated son?
  Hor. I yield to the truth, I confess that I'm foolish, admit
That I'm mad. But, please: expound this much to me—
What mental failing, would you say, is making me ill?
  Dam. Well, listen. First of all you're building, which
      simply means that you
Are trying to act like the big shots when, after all, you
Only measure two feet over-all—the very same you

                                                    125

Who laugh at the tiny gladiator Turbo, who stalks
And storms in his armor a world too wide for his frame.
Are you so much less laughable than he? Is it proper for you
To do what Maecenas does when you're so unlike him
And hardly a match for him?

                    While mother frog was away,
Her children were crushed under foot by a calf; only one
Escaped to tell mother how monstrous a beast had demolished
His brothers. "How monstrous? This big?" she asks, puffing
    up.
"Half again as big." "Big as this, then?" she wanted to know,
And kept puffing and puffing. "Even if you burst," her son
    said,
"You still won't be as large as IT was!"

                        That's not a bad picture
Of you, Horace. Next, add in your poetry, that is,
Pour oil on the fire. If anyone who writes verse
Is acting sensibly, then of course you act sensibly.
And third . . . well, I won't go into your furious temper . . .
    Hor. STOP IT!
    Dam.   Your living beyond your means . . .
    Hor.   HOLD IT!
Just mind your own business, Damasippus.
    Dam.   The thousands of girls,
The boys by the thousands, you're forever passionately
    chasing . . .
    Hor. Oh, you superior madman, spare your inferiors!

GOURMET À LA MODE

Unde et quo, Catius? Non est mihi tempus, aventi

> *Horace.* Where are you coming from, and where are you
> going, Catius?
> *Catius.* I haven't a minute, I'm so anxious to write up my
> notes

On a lecture I've heard full of precepts bound to surpass
Pythagoras, erudite Plato, and the man accused
By Anytus.

> *Hor.*   Oh, my fault, I must admit, for disturbing

Your train of thought at such a poor time. I beg you,
Do pardon me. If something has slipped your mind,
It'll come right back to you. Whether because of your
> training

Or because of some native power, your memory is amazing.

> *Cat.* I was just trying to think how to keep the whole thing
> in mind:

It was clever stuff, worked out in a clever style.

> *Hor.* Do tell me the fellow's name. A Roman, or a stranger?
> *Cat.* Let me tell you the points he established—I've got
> them by heart:

I don't think the name of the teacher ought to get out.

A RECIPE FOR GOURMET À LA MODE

> Be sure to serve oval eggs: their flavor is better,

Their whites are whiter, than round eggs; they're firm in
> consistency,

And contain male yolks. Cabbages grown in dry fields
Are sweeter than those raised on farms near the city: there's
    nothing
More tasteless than the food produced in an overwatered
    garden.
    If a friend suddenly lands on you some fine evening
For supper, to insure that your chicken will not be too tough,
You'll be smart to plunge it alive in diluted Falernian:
This will make it tender.
                        Mushrooms from open fields
Are by far the best; no others should ever be trusted.
    A man will get through the summer in very good health
If he finishes off his luncheon with the black mulberries
He's picked from the tree before the sun gets too scorching.
    Aufidius mixed his honey with strong Falernian;
But this was unwise, for when the veins are empty,
It is not a good practice to intrust any but the mildest
Of things to them. You'd do better to wash out your stomach
With a weaker mixture. If your bowels are sluggish, some
    limpet
Or common shellfish will drive out the trouble, or sorrel
From the low-growing bush, but not without white Coan
    wine.
    New moons fill out the flesh of slippery shellfish,
But not every sea produces the choicest variety:
The Lucrine mussel is better than the Baian cockle;
Oysters come from Circeo; sea urchins thrive
At Cape Miseno, while the well-heeled town of Taranto
Prides herself on her fine fat scallops.
                             And no one
Can claim to have mastered the art of good dining until
He has acquired a detailed knowledge of the subtle theory

Of flavors, become, as it were, a Brilliant Savorant.
It's not quite enough, for example, to sweep up the fish
From the most expensive fish stalls if you don't know which
Go better with sauce and which, when served up broiled,
Will make your jaded guest sit up and take notice.
    The host who wants to avoid serving tasteless meat
Will hold out for the Umbrian boar that, fattened on acorns
From the holm oak, makes the platter bend under his weight;
The Laurentian boar, who lives on marsh grass and reeds,
Tastes poor. Roes raised in vineyards are not always edible.
Your true epicure will be found to favor the forelegs
Of the prolific hare. As for fish and fowl, I'm the first
Whose palate has made unquestionably clear what age
And what quality they should be. Some gourmets are gifted
Only in finding new sweets. But, heroes, I swear
It is not heroic enough to lavish your care
On one point—as if, for instance, someone took pains
To see that his wines were perfect but was quite indifferent
To the type of oil poured over his fish.
                                                    Set out
Your Massic wine on a fine clear day, and its roughness
Will be well toned down by the good night air, and its scent,
Which is hard on the nerves, will evaporate. But if you filter
The same through linen, it spoils and loses its taste.
The cunning contriver mixes Sorrentine wine
With the lees of Falernian and draws off the sediment neatly
With pigeons' eggs, for the yolk sinks right to the bottom,
Dragging the dregs down with it.
                                            The blasé drinker
Will perk up again if you offer him prawns and snails.
Fried prawns, *fried African* snails; but lettuce swims around
In the acid stomach, after wine. The belly's craving

To perk up and drink some more is much better met
By ham and sausages, better still by piping hot food
From a short-order joint.

         It's worth while to do some research
In the field of the compound sauce: the simple part made up
Of sweet olive oil, to be mixed with thick wine and the brine
Of the strong-smelling sort in the cask your Byzantine fish
Are preserved in. You pour this over chopped herbs and boil
    it,
Then sprinkle with Corycian saffron, set it aside
To stand, and, finally, add the juice distilled
From the fruit of Venafrian olives.

         The apples of Tibur
Look better than those of Picenum, but are not as juicy.
Venuculan grapes are good to preserve, but the Alban
Had better be dried in smoke. You will find it was I
Who invented the trick of serving these Alban raisins
With apples. Another of my firsts: caviar in wine lees.
Another: black salt and white pepper, sifted on their own
Special dishes.

         It's an unforgivable sin
To lay out three thousand at the fish market, only to squeeze
Those vagabond fish close together in a dish that's too
    narrow.
It's revolting when your slave hands around the drinking cup
In hands grease-stained by the snacks he's been licking up
On the sly, or when some offensive crud still sticks
On the bowl you prize as antique. Ordinary brooms,
Plain napkins, some sawdust, don't cost much, do they?
If you fail to provide them, however, you're grievously at
    fault.
To think of your sweeping mosaic floors with a broom

Made of dirty palm leaves, or spreading your Tyrian drapes
Over dirty couch covers! Forgetting that the less these things
    cost
And the less thought they require, the more justified the
    blame
For neglecting them. Surely, you're more to be blamed for
    this
Than for failing to provide a menu that equals the rich.
    Hor. O learned Catius, in the name of the gods and of
    friendship,
I beg you, remember to take me to hear the next lecture,
Wherever it is. For although you report it verbatim
To me, from your fabulous memory, to hear it firsthand
Would afford me even more pleasure. There's the man
    himself, too:
His appearance, the way he handles himself! You forget,
Having seen him, how lucky you are, and discount it.

    But I am on fire with no slight desire
    To dwell near this sacred well and the king
    Whose saws are laws; I aspire
    To drink deep, not sip from, this so Superior Spring.

HOW TO RECOUP YOUR LOSSES

Hoc quoque, Teresia, praeter narrata petenti

Ulysses. Tell me one thing more, Tiresias, in addition to all
You've told me about: what tricks and what means should I
 use
To recoup my losses? Why laugh?
 Tiresias.   Isn't it enough
For the man of many wiles to be borne back safe to Ithaca
And see his house and his home and his household gods?
 Uly. Oh, you, who have never lied to a soul, don't you see
Me returning home nude as a number, resourceless,
As you foretold? And at home, my cellar and herd
Raided and stripped by the suitors? Upper-class birth
And good character are worth even less than seaweed
If there's no real money to draw on.
 Tir.   To put the case plainly,
Since you admit you dread being poor, hear now what ways
You can use to get rich.
       If a thrush or some other dainty
Is given to you, let it wing its way right away
To some place where money is evident, and the owner quite
  old.
Let the rich fellow taste your first fruits ahead of the
  lares—
He is, after all, even more to be worshiped than they—
The tangy apples and whatever glories your farm,

With its well-tended crop, supplies. He may be a perjurer,
Of unrespectable birth, a runaway slave,
A fratricide; nevertheless, if he asks you to go
For a walk, make sure that you don't refuse.
    Uly.   What! Me
Take the left side of some Sporca Miseria! That's not how I
Conducted myself at Troy, where I always competed
With my betters.
    Tir.   Then you'll continue to be a poor man.
    Uly. No . . . I will order my valiant soul to endure
This affront. In former times I've experienced worse.
So come on, my prophet, inform me immediately how
I can scrape up some wealth and pile up a heap of cash.
    Tir. I've said it, of course. But now I'll say it again.
You'll craftily fish all the waters for old men's wills—
Don't give up hope, even though one rascal or another
Escapes the hook after nibbling off all the bait.
Don't stop angling, even though you're baffled. At some
    point,
When a big lawsuit, or a small one, is in full progress
In the Forum, make a point of becoming defense attorney
For the one of the two contestants who is rich and childless,
The disreputable hard-hearted type, who hales into court
A superior man; turn your back on the good citizen
With the better reputation and the better case, if at home
He has a son or a fruitful wife. Suppose you start out
With "Quintus, old fellow" or "Publius" (sensitive ears
Prick up at the sound of first names) ". . . your excellence
    itself
Has made me your friend. I know the dubieties of law:
I can plead your case. They can pluck out my eyes before I
Let you be made a fool of, or suffer the loss

133

Of a single nutshell. I'll make it my business to see
That you not lose the case or get laughed at." Bid him go
     home
And take care of his own precious hide. Become his attorney:
Stick to it and brazen it out, whatever the weather—
Whether

> "The blazing Bitch Star shatters the obstinate mien
>   Of unspeakable statues, or the wintry sheen
>   Of snow drools over the Alps its white spleen,"

As that modern poet Furius so exquisitely puts it,
When his lungs are inflated by a dinner of good, fat tripe.
Someone will surely nudge his neighbor with his elbow
And say, "Look how patient he is, how perfect a friend,
How persistent!" Then more tuna will swim up obligingly
To stock your fish ponds.
                         Then again, if a sickly son
Has been born as the one to be reared in a wealthy
     household,
Worm your way into the father's good graces, in the hope
Of being named second heir—you mustn't make it obvious
That you specialize mainly in bachelors—and also in the
     hope
That if some chance spirits the child off to the hereafter
You may come into the property. This kind of gambit
Seldom fails.
              If someone gives you his will to read,
Refuse, and push the tablets away, with a sidelong
Glance at the second line on page one. Run your eyes
Swiftly across it to see if you are the sole heir,
Or share with many co-heirs. Some night-court judge,
Newly tricked out in the professional robes of a scribe,

Will often be able to outwit the ravenous crow,
The way Coranus made a fool of the legacy hunter,
Nasica.
 Uly. Are you out of your mind, or purposely muttering
These dim prophecies to make fun of me?
 Tir.   What I say,
O son of Laertes, will either come true or will not,
For great Apollo has gifted me with loss-and-profit-see.
 Uly. But what's the point of that story? Please point it out.
 Tir. When, in the fulness of time, a fine young hero,
A menace to the Parthians, a descendant of lofty Aeneas,
Shall be mighty on land and sea, to the dauntless Coranus
Shall be wed the stately daughter of Nasica (who dreads
Paying back the money he owes Coranus). The son-in-law
Will proceed as follows: he will hand the father-in-law
The tablets whereon his will is inscribed and ask him
To read. Nasica will refuse them repeatedly, at last
Giving in and reading the words to himself. He will find
That nothing is left to him and to his but to hell with them.
 Now here's another tip I can give you: if a shrewd dame
Or freedman happen to have wound their way round the
   heart
Of some goofy old duffer, you become an ally of *theirs*.
Build them up, and when you're not there, they'll sing your
   praises.
This usually works. But what prevails first and foremost
Is to storm the fortress itself. Will the poor fool insist on
Writing bad verses? Praise them! Will he go in for women?
Don't let him even have to ask you: hand over your wife,
Give Penelope to lover number one. BE OBLIGING!
 Uly. Do you think that she could be led astray, that marvel
Of modesty and self-control whom the suitors could not

Deflect from the righteous path?
  Tir.   That group of young Greeks
Came not bearing gifts, you know, but to get them. Their
    appetites
Were trained not so much on Venus as they were on the
    menus.
Penelope was, accordingly, virtuous. But once she has tasted
The gain to be made from an oldster, in partnership with
    you,
She'll be no more kept from it than a dog can be frightened
    away
From a piece of skin that has pieces of fat still on it.
    Let me tell you something that happened when I was
    an old man.
A wicked old witch at Thebes was carried to the pyre
As follows, by the terms of her will: her heir had to carry,
On his own bare shoulders, the body well coated with oil—
Just to see if she couldn't slip out of his clutches at last.
I suppose he bore down too hard when the crone was alive.
    Make your approach carefully: don't be too eager,
Don't be too meager of your interest. If you talk a lot,
The irritable, close-mouthed type will resent it; but then,
You mustn't clam up entirely. Be like wily Davus
In comedy, and just stand there, your head bowed,
    registering
Servile respect. Make advances with flattering words;
When the breeze springs up, remind him to be so wise
As to keep his precious head covered; shoulder your way
In the crowd and extricate him; when he feels like talking,
Cup your ear. Is his appetite for flattery endless? Lay it on
Thick, blow up the bladder with fulsome remarks
Until he's been forced to lift his hands skyward and say

"Wow! That's enough for now!"
                          When at last he's relieved you
Of your anxious concern and your long-drawn-out servitude,
And you hear, wide awake, these words read out from the
    will:
ULYSSES IS HEIR TO A FOURTH PART OF MY ESTATE,
Start saying, every now and then, this kind of thing:
"Ah! Is my old friend Dama no longer with us?
Oh, where shall I ever find one so faithful and true?"
And if you can shed a few tears over him, it will hide
The delight your expression betrays. If it's left up to you
To arrange, give orders that the tomb be built in style.
Let the neighbors all find the funeral very impressive.
If one of the co-heirs happens to be older than you,
And happens to have a hacking cough, just assure him
That if he should want to pick up some land or a house
That has fallen to you, you're only too glad to sell out
To him, right off, for a nominal sum.
                        But Proserpina
Orders me home. Farewell, and long life, my friend!

II · 6

THE TOWN MOUSE AND THE COUNTRY MOUSE

Hoc erat in votis: modus agri non ita magnus

This was what I had prayed for: a small piece of land
With a garden, a fresh-flowing spring of water at hand
Near the house, and, above and behind, a small forest stand.
But the gods have done much better for me, and more—
It's perfect. I ask nothing else, except to implore,
O Son of Maia, that you make these blessings my own
For the rest of my life. If my property has not grown
By my making a series of deals, neither will it shrink
By my mismanagement. If I'm not one of those who think:
"If only that corner were mine, that lies adjacent
To my strip, cutting in in a manner that's really indecent!"
Or, "If only some luck came my way, like the find which,
Leading the plowman to buried treasure, made him rich
Enough to buy the land he formerly plowed for hire,
Thanks to Hercules!" If what I have is all I desire
And makes me content, then to this one last wish I aspire:
Make my herd grow fat, and everything else I lay claim to,
Except my brains. And, Mercury, still be the same to
Horace as you have been, his great good guardian. To
    complete
My removal from city streets to mountain retreat,
What else should I do but celebrate it now satirically,
Dwelling, far from town (and far from lyrically),
In my pedestrian style, on how far from that bit of hell

Known as big city life is life in my citadel.
Social-climbing can't get me down here, or the lead-weight
        blows
Of siroccos, or for once and for all plague-laden falls
Lay me out, and enrich the layout in funeral halls.
    Instead, I begin this morning by addressing you, Monarch
Of Morning, or more openly, Janus, if you prefer it:
In allegiance to whom men begin all the work of their days—
For so heaven wills it. Be the principal source of my praise.
    At Rome the mornings are different: you rush me right off
To court to vouch for a friend. "Hey there! Get going!
Or someone else will answer this call before you!"
And I *have* to, whether the north wind is raking the land
Or winter drags snow-laden days through diminishing curves.
    After saying in court, good and loud, things that may
        some day
Incriminate me, I fight my way back through the crowd
In the streets, tripping over some slowpoke's toes. "What's
        up,
You blockhead? What gives?" some stupid assails me. "Oh,
        Horace,
It's you, is it, racing back home to Maecenas, so full of
The fact that you knock over everything blocking your
        path!"
Well . . . the name of Maecenas *is* honey to me, I admit it.
    But as soon as I reach the depressing Esquiline Quarter,
A hundred conflicting concerns pour down on my head
And stream around me. "Roscius wants you to meet him
        tomorrow
Before seven in the morning, at Libo's Wall." "Oh, Quintus,
The clerks request you to remember to return to the Forum
Today for a big new matter of mutual interest."
"Do have Maecenas affix his seal to these papers."

If I say, "Well, I'll try," he insists, "You can *do* it if you
    want to."
   It is now seven years—actually, nearer the eighth—
Since Maecenas began to admit me into his company
Of friends, insofar as a friend is just good company
On a trip, someone to talk to about such subjects as:
"What time is it?" . . . "Oh, about the fight: is the Thracian
    Bantam
A match for the Sheik?" . . . "These frosty mornings can
    nip you
If you don't wrap up." And small-change talk like this,
Which it's perfectly safe to deposit in leaky ears.
And the whole time, daily and hourly, our intimate Horace
Was *envied*. He watched the games from the stands with M.
He played some ball on the Campus, *and* with M.
"Fortune's Favorite Son," they thought in unison.
   A hair-raising rumor rolls through the streets from the
    Rostra,
And whoever bumps into me seeks my advice. "Dear
    fellow,
You ought to know, you live so much nearer the gods,
What's up in the Balkans?" "Nothing, as far as I know."
"Oh, you're still making fun of us!" But may the gods undo
    me
If I've heard a word. "What about the veterans' allotments
Of land Caesar promised? Will they be on the three-cornered
    isle,
Or Italian soil?" When I swear I know nothing about it,
They marvel at me for being the sole human being
Who knows how to keep an important unfathomable secret.
   Amid such lightweight concerns the light of my day
Sputters out, leaving me limp, only able to pray:

Oh, countryside mine, when will I see you again,
Read my favorite classical authors, and then
Get some sleep and get back to my lazy routine of life,
Of pleasure mercifully free from worry and strife?

When shall we dine on beans, Pythagoras' cousins,
And eat, cooked in bacon, country greens in their dozens?
Those nights and feasts of the gods! When friends and I sup
In *my lar*'s presence, while the saucy slaves lick up
What's left untouched on the plates. Each guest drains his
    cup,
Big or small, as it suits him: no Prohibition
To govern his choice except his free disposition
To toss off heroic amounts and keep a clear head,
Or gradually mellow with moderate potions instead.
And then we start talking, not about other men's lives
And property and assets but of things on which wisdom
    thrives.
Not whether Lepos is really a good dancer or not
But whether happiness comes from the money you've got
Or, rather, derives from virtue. What makes men friends?
Self-interest, or rectitude? This subject lends
Interest to us: the good life, and its ends.
    From time to time, my good old neighbor, Cervius,
Rattles off an old wives' tale, to make a point:
If someone praises Arellius' wealth, without knowing
What worries it brings, Cervius starts off like this:
    "Once upon a time, a country mouse
Welcomed a town mouse in his poor little hole of a house
In the sticks, both host and guest being quite old friends.
The country mouse roughed it, of course; he kept a close eye
On his larder, but not so myopic he couldn't enlarge

141

His view, with a view to a friend's entertainment. What
    else?
He was not the mouse to begrudge a friend the choice
    chick-peas
Set aside in a special place, or the long grains of oats;
But, eager to conquer the fastidious disdain of a guest
Who tended to turn up his tooth after sampling each dainty,
He brought in by mouth and served, to vary the meal,
A dried grape seed and some half-nibbled pieces of bacon.
The master of the house, stretched out on his couch of chaff
(New chaff), ate spelt and darnel, leaving the best
For his guest to digest. Finally, the town mouse spoke up:

'What pleasure can it be for you, my friend,
    Roughing it out here on the edge of a precipitous
        forest?
    Surely you put *people* and *the city* ahead of this
        wildwood?
    Take my advice, and my road, with me as your guide.
    All earthly creatures, after all, have drawn as their lot
    A mortal life: there is no escape from death
    For large or small. Therefore, while you still can,
    Enjoy a happy career, my good man, live well;
    Live mindful of how short life really is.'

                                        When these words
Dawned on the yokel, he bounced off gaily from home,
And both set out together, according to plan,
Hoping to sneak through the walls of the city by night.
And night was poised, midway across the heavens,
When both set foot in a rich man's house, where crimson
Coverings blazed against ivory couches, and leftovers
From last night's feast were stacked up high in the baskets.

Well, the host then made his rural guest stretch out
On the crimson covers and began dashing madly about,
With his clothes tucked up like a waiter's, serving up dish
After dish and taking a taste, as a proper slave does,
Of each course before serving it. The other mouse meanwhile
Leaned back at ease, delighted with the change in affairs
And with all this good living, and was playing to perfection
    the part
Of the satisfied guest, when a sudden loud rattling of doors
Shook them both right off of their couches. Frightened,
    they scampered
Across the whole length of the room, and, even more
    frightening,
The big house began to ring, at the very same time,
With the barking of colossal hounds. Says the country
    mouse:

    'I have no use for this kind of life. And good-by!
    My woodland and hole, where I'm safe from traps like
      these,
    Will be quite good enough, my slim pickings quite
      food enough.' "

MY SLAVE IS FREE TO SPEAK
UP FOR HIMSELF

Iamdudum ausculto et cupiens tibi dicere servus

 Davus. I've been listening for quite some time now,
  wanting to have
A word with you. Being a slave, though, I haven't the nerve.
 Horace. That you, Davus?
 Dav.   Yes, it's Davus, slave as I am.
Loyal to my man, a pretty good fellow: *pretty* good,
I say. I don't want you thinking I'm too good to live.
 Hor. Well, come on, then. Make use of the freedom
  traditionally yours
At the December holiday season. Speak up, sound off!
 Dav. Some people *like* misbehaving: they're persistent
  and consistent.
But the majority waver, trying at times to be good,
At other times yielding to evil. The notorious Priscus
Used to wear three rings at a time, and then again, none.
He lived unevenly, changing his robes every hour.
He issued forth from a mansion, only to dive
Into the sort of low joint your better-class freedman
Wouldn't want to be caught dead in. A libertine at Rome,
At Athens a sage, he was born, and he lived, out of season.
 When Volanerius, the playboy, was racked by the gout
In the joints of his peccant fingers (so richly deserved),
He hired a man, by the day, to pick up the dice

For him and put them in the box. By being consistent
In his gambling vice, he lived a happier life
Than the chap who tightens the reins and then lets them
    flap.
   Hor. Will it take you all day to get to the bottom of this
    junk,
You skunk?
    Dav.   But I'm saying, *you're* at the bottom.
    Hor.   How so, you stinker?
    Dav. You praise the good old days, ancient fortunes, and
    manners,
And yet, if some god were all for taking you back,
You'd hang back, either because you don't really think
That what you are praising to the skies is all that superior
Or because you defend what is right with weak defenses
And, vainly wanting to pull your foot from the mud,
Stick in it all the same. At Rome, you yearn
For the country, but, once in the sticks, you praise to high
    heaven
The far-off city, you nitwit. If it happens that no one
Asks you to dinner, you eulogize your comfortable meal
Of vegetables, acting as if you'd only go out
If you were dragged out in chains. You hug yourself,
Saying how glad you are not to be forced to go out
On a spree. But Maecenas *suggests*, at the very last minute,
That you be his guest: "Bring some oil for my lamp,
    somebody!
Get a move on! Is everyone deaf around here?" In a dither
And a lather, you charge out. Meanwhile, your scrounging
    guests,
Mulvius & Co., make their departure from your place
With a few descriptive remarks that won't bear repeating—

145

For example, Mulvius admits, "Of course, I'm fickle,
Led around by my stomach, and prone to follow my nose
To the source of a juicy aroma, weak-minded, lazy,
And, you may want to add, a gluttonous souse.
But you, every bit as bad and perhaps a bit worse,
Have the gall to wade into me, as if you were better,
And cloak your infamy in euphemism?"

                                         What if you're found out
To be a bigger fool than me, the hundred-dollar slave?
Stop trying to browbeat me! Hold back your hand,
And your temper, while I tell you what Crispinus' porter
Taught me.

                Another man's wife makes you her slave.
A loose woman makes Davus hers. Of us two sinners,
Who deserves the cross more? When my passionate nature
Drives me straight into her arms, she's lovely by lamplight,
Beautifully bare, all mine to plunge into at will,
Or, turning about, she mounts and drives me to death.
And after it's over, she sends me away neither shamefaced
Nor worried that someone richer or better to look at
Will water the very same plant. But when you go out for it,
You really come in for it, don't you? Turning yourself into
The same dirty Dama you pretend to be when you take off
Your equestrian ring and your Roman robes, and change
Your respectable self, hiding your perfumed head
Under your cape?

                    Scared to death, you're let in the house,
And your fear takes turns with your hope in rattling your
      bones.
What's the difference between being carted off to be scourged
And slain, in the toils of the law (as a gladiator is),
And being locked up in a miserable trunk, where the maid,

Well aware of her mistress' misconduct, has stored you
    away,
With your knees scrunched up against your head? Hasn't
    the husband
Full power over them both, and even more over the seducer?
For the wife hasn't changed her attire or her location,
And is not the uppermost sinner. You walk open-eyed
Right under the fork, handing over to a furious master
Your money, your life, your person, your good reputation.
    Let's assume that you got away: you learned your lesson,
I trust, and will be afraid from now on, and be careful?
Oh, no! You start planning how to get in trouble again,
To perish again, enslave yourself over and óver.
But what wild beast is so dumb as to come back again
To the chains he has once broken loose from?
                              "But I'm no adulterer,"
You say. And I'm not a thief when I wisely pass up
Your good silver plate. But our wandering nature will leap
When the reins are removed, when the danger is taken away.
    Are you my master, you, slave to so many
Other people, so powerful a host of other things, whom no
Manumission could ever set free from craven anxiety,
Though the ritual were conducted again and again? And
    besides,
Here's something to think about: whether a slave who's the
    slave
Of a slave is a plain fellow slave or a "subslave," as you
    masters
Call him, what am I your? You, who command me,
Cravenly serve someone else and are led here and there
Like a puppet, the strings held by others.
                             Who, then, is free?

The wise man alone, who has full command of himself,
Whom poverty, death, or chains cannot terrify,
Who is strong enough to defy his passions and scorn
Prestige, who is wholly contained in himself, well rounded,
Smooth as a sphere on which nothing external can fasten,
On which fortune can do no harm except to herself.

    Now which of those traits can you recognize as one of yours?
Your woman asks you for five thousand dollars, needles you,
Shuts the door in your face and pours out cold water,
Then calls you back. Pull your neck from that yoke!
Say, "I'm free, I'm free!" Come on, say it. You can't! A
    master
Dominates your mind, and it's no mild master who lashes
You on in spite of yourself, who goads you and guides you.

    Or when you stand popeyed in front of a painting by Pausias,
You madman, are you less at fault than I am who marvel
At the posters of athletes straining their muscles in combat,
Striking out, thrusting, and parrying, in red chalk and
    charcoal,
As if they were really alive and handling these weapons?
But Davus is a no-good, a dawdler, and you? Oh, MONSIEUR
Is an EXPERT, a fine CONNOISSEUR of antiques, I ASSURE
    you.

    I'm just a fool to be tempted by piping-hot pancakes.
Does your strength of character and mind make much
    resistance
To sumptuous meals? Why is it worse for me
To supply the demands of my stomach? My back will pay
    for it,
To be sure. But do you get off any lighter, hankering
After delicate, costly food? Your endless indulgence
Turns sour in your stomach, your baffled feet won't support

Your pampered body. Is the slave at fault, who exchanges
A stolen scraper for a bunch of grapes, in the dark?
Is there nothing slavish in a man who sells his estate
To satisfy his need for rich food?
                                        Now, add on these items:
(1) You can't stand your own company as long as an hour;
(2) You can't dispose of your leisure in a decent fashion;
(3) You're a fugitive from your own ego, a vagabond soul,
Trying to outflank your cares by attacking the bottle
Or making sorties into sleep. And none if it works:
The Dark Companion rides close along by your side,
Keeps up with and keeps on pursuing the runaway slave.
   Hor. "Where's a stone?"
   Dav.   "What use do you have for it?"
   Hor.   "Hand me my arrows!"
   Dav. The man is either raving or satisfying his craving
For creative writing.
   Hor.   If you don't clear out, instanter,
I'll pack you off to the farm to be my ninth planter.

II · 8

NASIDIENUS HAS SOME FRIENDS
IN FOR DINNER

Ut Nasidieni iuvit te cena beati

   Horace. How did you like the dinner you went to yesterday
At the home of that rich man Nasidienus? When I tried
To get you to come to my place, they told me you'd been
      there
At dinner since noon.
     Fundanius.   I've never enjoyed myself more.
   Hor. Tell me, won't you please, what was the first peace
     offering
Made to your growling stomach?
     Fun.   First course: wild boar
Snared when the south wind was light, as the father of the
     feast
Kept informing us. Savory turnips, lettuces, radishes,
Things that whip up your drooping taste buds, surrounded
     it—
Caraway, pickle, and wine lees. When these plates went off,
One slave with a silk serviette and his apron tucked up
Wiped off the maplewood table quite clean; another swept up
The scraps lying round on the floor, odds and ends, and
     crumbs,
Whatever might trouble the guests. Dark-skinned Hydaspes
Marched in with the Caecuban wine, like a maid of Athens
Bearing the emblems of Ceres in solemn processional,

150

And Alcon came in with the Chian (no salt water needed
To bring out the tang of the vintage). Our host then
    announced:
"Maecenas, if Alban is more to your taste, or Falernian,
We have both."
    Hor.   Oh, those poor rich people! Who else was
    there,
Fundanius? I'm dying to know whom you had all that fun
with.
    Fun. I was at the head, Viscus of Thurii next,
And next below was Varius, as I recall it.
Then Vibidius, and Servilius Balatro, the "shades" of
    Maecenas
(They weren't invited; they just came along in his train).
Nomentanus' place was above our host's, and below him
Sat Porcius, who made us all laugh, gulping down
    cheesecakes
Whole, in one bite. Nomentanus was present, apparently
To point his finger at everything, so we wouldn't miss
Anything. The rest of us, far less canny than he,
Ate fowl, oysters, and fish that tasted far different
From any familiar food, as was soon made clear
When Nomentanus passed me a dish I'd never tasted:
Flounder livers, and livers of plaice. He next pointed out
That the honey apples were red because they were picked in
    the light
Of a waning moon. To learn what the difference is,
You'd better appeal to him.
                    Then Vibidius said to Balatro:
"Unless we drink him bankrupt, we'll die unavenged,"
And called for much bigger cups. Our host's face went pale:
There's nothing he fears like hard drinkers, either because

Wine loosens their tongues or because it deadens their
    palates.
Vibidius and Balatro upended whole decanters
Into their goblets: the rest followed suit, except Porcius
And fastidious (of course) Nomentanus: sitting by their
    host,
They made no great dents in the bottle.
                              Next course: a lamprey,
Flat on a platter, with shrimp swimming round it. The matter
Was gravely explained by the master: "It was caught before
    spawning;
The flesh would have been less delectable later. The sauce?
Its ingredients are: (1) oil from Venafrum (first pressing);
    (2) roe
From the juice of mackerel *espagnol;* (3) five-year-old wine
(Domestic), poured in when it's boiling—the best wine to use
After boiling is Chian; (4) white pepper; (5) and be sure to
    add vinegar
Fermented from vintages of Lesbos. One of my 'firsts'
Has been to show that the boiling-in of a sauce like this
Should be done with *eruca sativa,* and *inula campana;*
Curtillus would use sea urchins still dripping salt water,
On the grounds that the sea itself is the best of all pickle
    jars."
  At this point the canopy pulled loose and flopped on
    the fish plate,
Dragging with it more black dust than the north wind stirs up
On the fields of Campania. We crouched, in fear of what else,
    even bigger,
Might fall, then realizing there was no further danger,
Recovered. Our host hung his head and shed bitter tears,

As if his son had met an untimely fate. Lord knows
How it all would have ended if Nomentanus had not
Made his friend buck up with these words: "Oh, Fortune,
    what god
Is more cruel to us than you are! You always have fun
Making fun of mankind!" With some difficulty,
Varius smothered a laugh in his napkin. Balatro,
Who turns up his nose at the world, said, "It's the condition
Of living! Rewards are never equal to the efforts to attain
    them!
You, for instance, are racked, torn limb from limb by
    anxieties
Of every imaginable sort: Will the toast be burnt?
Will the sauce be served up ill-seasoned? Will the slaves be
    dressed
All right, all of them, neatly turned out to serve,
Just so that I may be lavishly looked after? It's a fete
Worse than death! Think of the risks, the canopy slipping,
The way it just did; or a dumb slave loses his footing,
And a dish goes crash! But the host plays a role like the
    general's:
When things go wrong, his genius comes most into play;
When the going is smooth, you'd never know he had any."
    Nasidienus replied, "May the gods gratify
Every wish you express! You're a nice man, and such a good
    guest!"
And called for his slippers. You can imagine the sort of
    whispers
That percolated through the guests slouched on the couches.
    Hor. I'd rather have seen all this byplay than gone to a
    good play!

But tell me, what happened next to provide you with laughs?
  Fun. While Vibidius, with Balatro as straight man, was
    asking the slaves
If the flagon was smashed, since the cups he called for
    weren't brought,
And kept the company in stitches with his feeble jokes,
You marched back into the room, good Nasidienus,
With a brand new look on your face, like one who intended
To repair the damage by skill. The servants followed after,
Bearing in the joints of cooked crane dusted with salt
And meal, on a big breadboard, and a white goose's liver
(A goose fattened up on figs) and the severed front legs
Of wild hare (much tastier this way than joined to the
    body).
We next saw blackbirds, their breasts crisply done to a turn,
And pigeons minus their rumps—tasty, these rare birds,
Had our host not mouthed so much gastronomical learning.
  We scampered away! Our sweet revenge consisted
Of tasting nothing, as if everything had been breathed on
By Canidia, whose breath is sharper than a serpent's tooth.

EPISTLES

INTRODUCTION
TO BOOK ONE

After he had published the two books of *Satires* and the
Epodes, Horace set to work on what was to be his master-
piece, the three books of *Odes,* which occupied him from the
years 30 to 23 B.C. And as he ruefully admits in the nineteenth
letter of the first book of *Epistles,* the lyrics, or *carmina,* did
not take the Roman public by storm. Although they were undoubtedly admired and appreciated by friends and critics capable of judging and comparing, the collections of lyric poems
moved very slowly at first toward their ultimate fame. Horace
therefore turned back to the earlier style of the hexameter and
during the years 23 to 20 B.C. wrote the poems we now know
as the first book of *Epistles.*

In form the *Epistles* continue where the style of the *sermones* leaves off: they can condense that style or expand it,
and seem to be gradually altering it to something less exclusively generic. The letters have immediate definition as documents written for and addressed to particular persons and are
in one sense entirely specific. But in another sense, they are
less limited and bounded than the individual satires. Except
when very brief and held to the demands of the situation, they
are discursive literary reflections, "essays." It has been said
that what makes a letter an epistle is the predominance of general content over topical interest and that these poems were
not so much letters, written on the stated occasion to the person in question, as compositions born of *l'esprit d'escalier* and
aimed generally at a cultivated audience.[1] It has been said

[1] E. P. Morris, "The Form of the Epistle in Horace," in *Yale Classical
Studies,* II (1931), 79–114.

that the poems are very distinctly letters, and the best sort of letters, which reveal an interest in the person addressed, being about him as well as from Horace—and that they always proceed from the particular to the general, whereas the *Satires* tend to particularize the general.[2] It has been said (of Horace's style in the *Satires*) that "il part toujours du particulier, il tend toujours au général et il y atteint."[3]

All three interpretations apply to the letters, I think, and point to important qualities in them. Horace's letters are often general and philosophical. They are always cultivated and clever. They are often particular, definite, personal. They are always literary compositions. When Horace turned from the exacting confinements of lyric verse to the hexameter again, he discovered new opportunities for exploring and expanding the medium and in this artistic process realized its potential capacity as that most protean of literary forms, the familiar essay. Like any first-rate artist, he can lift the familiar out of the realm of the commonplace—as in the *Epistles*, he puts the essay on a par with poetry—but here, as throughout his work, he moves with natural ease and unprecedented grace among traditional forms, converting the old to a substantially new and remarkably individual use.

And so there came into being the collection of twenty epistles, the most harmonious of Horace's books. Philosophical problems had been discussed in letters before, and letters in verse had occasionally been written before, but nothing comparable to Horace's *Epistles* had ever existed in Greek or Roman literature.[4]

[2] Fraenkel, pp. 308–10.

[3] A. Cartault, *Étude sur les satires d'Horace* (Paris, 1899), p. 359.

[4] Fraenkel, p. 309.

The first book arranges itself somewhat along the pattern of the *Satires,* varying in tone from serious affirmation to whimsical or devastating criticism, varying in audience from world-renowned friends to personal acquaintances, varying in subject from philosophical themes to anecdotal satire, modulating its moods, looking at landscapes and city scenes, scrutinizing personality and behavior, attentive to ethical problems, conscious of literary problems. The second book is of another order entirely—the essay rises to heights and achieves a length unrivaled elsewhere in Horace (except for the "Stoic Sermon" of *Satires* ii. 3). The three "great" epistles comprising the second book show us that Horace is not only wielder of the word but defender of the word as well. Each one, a temperate but lively and broad approach to the whole domain and tradition of ancient literature from a different avenue, reinforces Horace's defense of his literary faith. The first book is Horace's correspondence *ad familiares,* the second his *summa literaria,* adroitly balanced against his whole creative career.

I will not delay the reader with detailed analysis of each letter in Book I but will try instead to suggest a few ways of looking at this new style, and offer a few comments on the significance of this whole group of poems. What Horace says in the first letter holds true throughout: his mood, his aesthetic interests, his artistic pace—these are all now quite different from the concentration that upheld the production of the first three books of *Odes.* He has become more ruminative and wants to familiarize himself again with his ideas, to consort with thought in its pedestrian form, not to soar and shine in quest of the translucent images of the lyric. A man who is moral and civil and an artist who is quite unusually amicable, Horace naturally gravitates toward literary subjects in many

of the letters of the first book; in the second book he is clearly
the artist, thinking reasonably and therefore morally, and his
mind likes to dwell on the thing it knows best. If the *Satires*
were a curiously consistent brand of moral literature, the *Epistles* often end by pointing a literary moral.[5]

In the first book Horace has framed the picture of his correspondence nicely, beginning with an apology to Maecenas
and ending with an appeal to his judgment and good sense,
the first epistle avowing his intention to philosophize, not
"write," and the nineteenth being a philosophical attitude toward his own reception as a lyric poet, and resting its defense
on the fact of his poetic achievement. In the first letter he refuses to "write" again; in the nineteenth he refuses to be
drawn into literary feuding—and both times gets the last
word. The twentieth letter, a "signature," also has this lastword tone, an envoy and at the same time a deft reminder of
the artist's mature prowess. The second modulates from literature to moral philosophy, then back to literature the teacher;
the seventeenth and eighteenth swing calmly at anchor in
moral waters. The intervening letters vary in tone and in
stress, as the persons and occasions they befit differ one from
another—standing now for ethical time exposures, now for
candid camera shots of action and scenery, now for surprisingly well-ordered and charmingly personal notes dashed off
on impulse.

As elsewhere in his work, Horace plunges into his epistolary

[5] At the geometric center of the epistle to Augustus (ii. 1) Horace offers a
noble, convincing, and delightful defense of the poet's aesthetic morality, in
the lines beginning: *Hic error tamen et levis haec insania quantas / virtutes
habeat, sic collige* ("And yet this craze, this mild madness, has its merits.
How great these are, now consider"), and ending *carmine di superi placantur,
carmine Manes* ("Song wins grace with the gods above, song wins it with the
gods below") (ll. 116–38).

subjects, follows them quickly along, pauses to land hard on a concept that attracts him. So the first letter states his refusal to "write" any more: his mind and his age have changed. He is an old athlete, an old soldier, an old horse. He wants to be left to browse, having put aside such childish things as verse, and wants as a man only to come to grips with life:

nunc itaque et versus et cetera ludicra pono;
quid verum atque decens curo et rogo et omnis in hoc sum.

Throughout the two books of letters Horace is *omnis in hoc*, holding to the decency of man and the dignity of literature. He is more and more the subjective philosopher, choosing among schools and creeds the elements suitable to his own attitudes and judgments, not addicted to any one brand of philosophy: *nullius addictus iurare in verba magistri*. Beginning with the first letter, the reader will notice how powerful in its compression a line of Horace has become. There is a lapidary strength of phrasing, an agility of diction, and an aptness of imagery in the *Epistles* that far surpass the poetry of the *Satires*. Here, for instance, to exemplify the purifying power of a book of philosophy on the mind, he unleashes a line of adjectives characterizing the confused and cluttered mind: *invidus, iracundus, iners, vinosus, amator*. And then he quietly proceeds to assure us that no one is so wild that philosophy cannot tame him. At the end of the first letter he drives home the "good" words, as if in riposte to those reeled off above (at line 38), the attributes conferred on the mind by philosophy: *liber, honoratus, pulcher, rex denique regum*. Again, in the second letter, to characterize the injustices visited upon the mass of men by their war leaders (a radical enough view of the *Iliad!*), Horace engraves the fact on our minds in a single line: *quidquid delirant reges plectuntur Achivi*. And he follows this with a series of vicious nouns: *seditione, dolis, scelere atque libidine ira.*[6]

All the latent "poetry" of the *Satires,* beautifully adumbrated in the town mouse and country mouse piece, developed and mastered in the *Odes,* surges through these *Epistles.* Horace's modulations are supreme, his ear absolute, as he glides "casually from one topic to the next."[7] He arrives at excellent sound effects, is in complete command of his rhetorical resources from minute alliterations[8] to jaunty syllepses;[9] and propriety plus muscular co-ordination rules his diction.[10] For

[6] Horace seems to favor this one-line word-series effect in the *Epistles,* as in the three instances mentioned and as in the itemizing of qualities (ii. 2. 203) : *viribus, ingenio, specie, virtute, loco, re;* and again in the description of Achilles in the *Ars poetica* (1. 120) : *impiger, iracundus, inexorabilis acer.*

The lapidary lines are numerous and varied in the *Epistles,* many of them best known to us from the most frequently read poem, the *Ars poetica.* But elsewhere we also have (e.g., i. 14. 43) *optat ephippia bos, piger optat arare caballus* (a fine animal example of the concept of interchangeability!) ; the one-line definition of the mean, already referred to (i. 18. 9) : *virtus est medium vitiorum et utrimque reductum;* and in the same poem a one-line syllepsis (37) : *cum pulchris tunicis sumet nova consilia et spes;* a fine "irrevocable" unit: *et semel emissum volat irrevocabile verbum* (71) ; and the quiet Epicurean ideal, the words of which perhaps influenced Gray's "Elegy": *an secretum iter et fallentis semita vitae* (103) ; or a neighbor's house on fire, dangerously close to our own: *nam tua res agitur paries cum proximus ardet* (i. 18. 84). In the the first two epistles of the second book we have such lines as *scribimus indocti doctique poemata passim* (ii. 1. 117) ; *singula de nobis anni praedantur euntes* (ii. 2. 55) ; *vehemens et liquidus puroque simillimus amni* (ii. 2. 120).

[7] Fraenkel, p. 341. Also his phrase "the many gentle transitions," p. 324.

[8] E.g., *librum cum lumine,* i. 2. 35.

[9] E.g., the line unit, *caelum non animum mutant qui trans mare currunt* (i. 11. 27), and the graphic *forte roget cur / non ut porticibus sic iudiciis fruar isdem* (i. 1. 71).

[10] Strong phrasing often results from a sparing but forceful use of anaphora, as at i. 7. 25–27, i. 14. 32–34, i. 18. 21–24. Sometimes it just results! As in *naturam expelles furca, tamen usque recurret* (i. 10. 24, also a line unit) ; *strenua nos exercet inertia* (i. 11. 28) ; *concordia discors* (i. 12. 19) ; *decipit exemplar vitiis imitabile* (i. 19. 17). Not to mention *Graecia capta ferum victorem cepit et artis/intulit agresti Latio* (ii. 1. 156–57) and *genus irritabile vatum* (ii. 2. 102), or the consistently memorable phrasing of the *Ars poetica.*

instance, he can if he wants give us a whole story in two lines, the fable of the country yokel who came to a stream, only to find it too wet and too deep to cross. So he decided to wait until it flowed by:

> rusticus expectat dum defluat amnis: at ille
> labitur et labetur in omne volubilis aevum.

The first line *is* the country fellow, in gingerly doubt; the second *is* the stream, slipping and splashing past his feet, as interminably twisting as time. When he gives credit to his friend and fellow poet Tibullus for his capacity to enjoy life—*di tibi ... dederunt artemque fruendi*—it is almost as if Horace himself were alluding to the subtle enjoyment he senses in the continuity of his own art.

In this book, just as he can trace a story in a few strokes, so can he spin one out at luxuriant length, as in the narrative of Mena and Philippus in the seventh epistle. That forceful episode, moreover, is in some ways a summing-up of the doctrine of the previous letter, the famous *nil admirari* indictment of enthusiasm, of excited worship of *regina Pecunia* and obsequious political ambition. The Horace who was so widely respected and imitated in English literature of the eighteenth century comes into view in this sequence, with its restrained hedonism and commonsensical attitude toward hopes and fears. And the landscape poetry reflected in the tenth and fourteenth epistles, and picked up again at the beginning of the sixteenth, again reflects the Horace English writers of the Augustan Age loved most for his ordered and serene sense of tangible reality and his exquisite, grown-up simplicity.

As Cartault said of the *Satires*, "Il se confesse avec bonhomie, et il se défend avec vigueur"[11]—but I would say that

[11] *Étude*, p. 353.

Horace does this everywhere, in the lyric poems as well as in his hexameters. He confesses to a weakness for a life subtly flavored by art, by landscape and clear air, by urbanity and friendship. He defends his view, his philosophy of life, by means of a sophisticated doctrine, mirrored in numerable sprightly examples of happiness—a happiness won by the moderation of desire, by the management and appreciation of one's actual resources (*ars fruendi*), by giving rein to intellectual curiosity:

> inter cuncta leges et percontabere doctos,
> qua ratione queas traducere leniter aevum;
> num te semper inops agitet vexetque cupido,
> num pavor et rerum mediocriter utilium spes;
> virtutem doctrina paret, naturane donet;
> quid minuat curas, quid te tibi reddat amicum;
> quid pure tranquillet, honos an dulce lucellum,
> an secretum iter et fallentis semita vitae.

Man is firmly enough endowed against fate by the gift of life itself. And the artist is doubly fortified, by the fact of his sensibility and the evidence of his work, to furnish the necessary mind and bring his judgment into play:

> me quotiens reficit gelidus Digentia rivus,
> quem Mandela bibit, rugosus frigore pagus,
> quid sentire putas? quid credis, amice, precari?
> sit mihi quod nunc est, etiam minus, et mihi vivam
> quod superest aevi, si quid superesse volunt di;
> sit bona librorum et provisae frugis in annum
> copia, neu fluitem dubiae spe pendulus horae.
> sed satis est orare Iovem qui ponit et aufert,
> det vitam, det opes: aequum mi animum ipse parabo.[12]

[12] *Epistles* i. 18. 96 ff.

TO MAECENAS (20 B.C.)

Philosophy has clipped my wings

Prima dicte mihi, summa dicende Camena

The first line the muses moved me to write, Maecenas,
Was addressed to you, and the last line I write will be, too.
But how can you ask me to pick up my pen again?
I've performed already; I've fought in the ranks of the poets.
And now, if I re-enlist, who'll listen to me?
Why not award me the wooden sword and my discharge?
My age and my mind have changed. The athlete Veianus
Hangs up his gloves on Hercules' doors and retires,
To bury himself in the country and never again
Pray for "thumbs up" from the crowd when time and again,
Helpless and vanquished, he stands at the outermost edge
Of the ring. And a voice dins into my rinsed-out ears: *in Pope, voice*
    "Be wise in time. Turn the old horse out to pasture,   *is reason*
Or he'll stumble at last and end up with caved-in flanks
And win for his efforts plenty of laughs, but no thanks."
    So I lay down my poems and other toys of my youth
To devote myself to one main subject: the truth. *Philosophy*
What is right and honest? This I would like to know.
I am laying up stores, setting them all in a row,
Of the only thing that will keep on helping me grow.
    And who is the head of my house? With whose ideas
Am I most at home? I'm not obliged to swear
By the words of any one trainer. Wherever the storm

Drives me in, I take shelter. At times, I'm the Practical Man,
The heroic, Stoical Man, who takes Part in Life,
And Care of Truth, and Charge of inflexible Virtue.
At times, I slip off unseen to the opposite side,
To fit the world to myself, not me to it.

   As the night drags on and on for men whose mistresses
Fail to show up; as the day lasts forever for men
Who work for wages; as the year, for boys whose mothers
Keep a strict watch over them, lags like a lazy lout;
So the time flows slow and surly for me, whenever
It makes me abandon my hopes and intentions to do
The work that benefits poor and rich alike,
That neglected will ruin the young and the old alike.
It remains for me to comfort and direct myself
With common-sense stuff like this: your eyes aren't as keen
As Lynceus', but this doesn't mean that if they're inflamed
You shouldn't put drops in them. Glycon's muscular limbs
Will never be yours, but still, you ought to take steps
To insure that the gout doesn't tie your body in knots.
Your strides may be modest: they'll still take you farther
     along.

   Is your soul on fire with greed and painful desire?
The words of the wise are magic charms you can use
To soothe the pain and practically rout the disease.
Or is your tumor ambition? Miracle cures
In the booklet will renovate you: just read them through
Three times, in the right frame of mind. The envious man,
The sorehead, the lazy lout, the drinker, the lover:
No one is such a beast as not to be tamed
By lending a patient ear to moral advice.

   Virtue means keeping from vice, and wisdom begins
When you stop being stupid. Notice what serious work
You make yourself do, mental endeavor, encounters

With physical danger, to fend off such serious evils
As a low bank account or not being elected to office.
To escape being poor you light out, on business, to India,
Thrusting your way overseas, past rocks, through fire.
Won't you listen to, learn from, and trust someone wiser than
    you,
And not fuss about things it's absurd to crave and admire?

    What athlete, making his living by touring the sticks
In free-for-alls, would turn down an Olympic crown,
If given the chance to wear it and stay at the top,
Nor even be made to sweat to defend his title?

    Silver is worth less than gold, but gold is worth less
Than virtue. "Citizens, Citizens! Money comes first!
Go after it! Then you can go on out and be good!"
This doctrine is bawled from the top to the basement of Wall
    Street.
This is the lesson old men say over and over,
As well as the young, "shouldering their satchels and slates."
You're a sensible, well-spoken lad, trustworthy, good:
But you're short six or seven of the four hundred thousand
    you need
To get in the horsy set; so you'll keep on being
Plebeian. When boys play King of the Hill, "You will,"
They chant, "be king if you cling to the height: you'll be
    right."
And this bronze wall should be ours: to let no shame
Steal across our faces, no guilt steal into our hearts.

    Tell me, quite frankly, which is the better rule,
The Roscian Law (that publicizes your rank
On the principle of how much money you've got in the bank),
Or the rule kids sing at school: "You will be king
If you do the right thing, every inch a king, every foot
A ruler"? Is the rhyme absurd that connects the word

KING with the THING named ruler, when the best thing for
        both
Is living along right lines? When boys sing this song
They're manly enough; after all, some lads named Curius
And Camillus used to recite it. Now, whose advice
Is better, his who tells you, "Make money, make money,
If possible in the right way, if not, in *some* way,
Any way you can manage, make money," to rank with those
Who sit up front at the shows (by Roscian Law
They're assigned the first fourteen rows), privileged to weep
Copious tears at Pupius' plays? Good advice?
What of his who stands by you and helps you to stand
By yourself, to stand straight and free and say NO to fortune?
    But the Voice of the Roman People may ask me why I
Refuse to join in her views as I join in the crowd
Strolling along her arcades, ask me why I
Don't follow or disregard what she esteems
Or doesn't; I give the answer the wily fox
Returned to the ailing lion: "Because those footprints
Scare the life out of me. They all lead *toward* your den."
Your Voice of the Roman People is a many-tenored thing.
Follow Whom, for instance, or do just exactly What?
Some men derive their income from government contracts;
Some hunt down rich widows, with fruit and glazed candy;
Some cast their nets for old men to put in their fishponds;
Some people's capital keeps on growing, kept going
By interest (fostered by time, just like a tree).
    Absorbed as they are in different things, absorbed
In different pursuits, even so, can men really stick
To any one thing for as much as an hour at a time?
"There's not a spot in the world as brilliant as Baiae."
If a rich man has spoken, the ocean AND its lagoon
Will FEEL his love POSSESSING them all too soon.

But his vicious whims are his most auspicious omens:
"What ho, my lads! Tomorrow we're off to Teano!
So pack up your tools: we'll build us a house 'way inland."
Or he's just put the bridal bed on display in the hall
And promptly finds nothing as worthy of praise or as fine
As the bachelor's state. Or if he stays unmarried,
He swears there's nothing to rival connubial bliss.
What sort of a knot can I use on old Proteus? His outlook
Keeps changing! And suppose our man is poor: oh, laugh
If you must, but he's never too poor to change, changing
    garrets,
Changing beds, changing baths, changing barbers. If he hires
    a boat
To go for a ride, he gets just as sick, does he not,
As a rich landowner out for a sail in his yacht?
If you meet me soon after I've been to my cross-eyed barber,
You laugh at my hair. You laugh at my shirt, worn smooth,
When it shows underneath the rough new nap of my tunic,
And chuckle whenever my toga's askew. But I ASK YOU:
What if my judgment is off, at odds with itself,
And spurns what it just now wanted, and asks once more
For what it just now turned down? If it ebbs and flows
Like the tide, is all out of true in its whole scheme of life,
Wrecking, then building, making the square one round?
You find my malady normal, and nothing to laugh at.
You don't think I need a guardian assigned by the court,
Or a doctor, though you are in charge of all my affairs,
You whom I always depend on and always look up to,
Who get into a towering rage if my nails are cut wrong.
In conclusion: the wise man is only surpassed by Jove.
He is well off, respected, handsome, the free king above
All kings. And above all, being RIGHT in the head,
He's always quite well . . . if a cold doesn't keep him in bed.

TO LOLLIUS MAXIMUS (22 B.C.)

Homer teaches us all how to live, but we must do it ourselves

---

Troiani belli scriptorem, Maxime Lolli

Maximus Lollius, while you study the art of rhetoric
At Rome, at Praeneste I'm reading the poems of Homer.
He's neither a schoolbook, you know, nor just a poet:
He can state more clearly and state more surely than
    schoolmen
The idea of the beautiful and the base, of the useful and
    useless.
Hear why I think this is so, if I'm not intruding.
   The story of Greece and Barbaria smashing together
In a long, slow war brought on by Paris' amours
Has in it the foolish passions of kings and their people.
Antenor proposes to excise the cause of the war:
And Paris? No, *he* can't be forced into living in peace
And contentment. Nestor bustles about: he'll settle
The quarrel between Agamemnon and savage Achilles.
Love warms Achilles, but both are inflamed by the anger
They share. Whatever folly their kings commit
The Achaeans must pay for. Inside the walls of Troy,
And outside, the sins of the soul flourish like weeds:
Crime and wrath and guile; treachery, lechery.
   On the other hand, Homer gives us a useful example
Of virtue and wisdom at work in the noble Ulysses:

"The tamer of Troy, whose piercing glance traveled into the
    hearts
Of men, as he entered into their cities. Borne to the ends
Of the world to discover the homeward path overseas for his
    friends,
He tossed on his troubles, UNSINKABLE, a true man of parts."
    You know about Circe's drink, and the siren voices:
Had Ulysses let himself go and drunk what he wanted,
He'd have lost his true shape and from then on lived like a
    nitwit
At the mercy of a sleazy mistress, lived like a hog
Settling cozily down in the mud, lived like a dog.
In comparison with him, the rest of us look rather weak:
As they put it in Greek, we simply don't COUNT. WE
    CONSUME.
We're Penelope's suitors, cloudbrains; we're like the young
    men
At Alcinous' court who spend more time than they should
On appearance, who pride themselves on sleeping till noon
And lulling their cares by strumming on languid guitars.
    Robbers get up at night to cut a man's throat:
Won't you get up in the morning to save your own neck?
If you won't run when you are well, you'll run, or else,
When dropsy attacks you: that's the prescribed therapy.
If you don't call for a book and a light before daybreak
And bend your mind to the study of interesting things,
You'll twist and turn all night with passion and spite.
Why hurry so to take out that mote from your eye,
But put off until next year the time to take steps
To arrest your soul erosion? Well begun
Is half done. Dare to be wise. Get under way!

He who puts off the hour to begin living rightly
Is like the yokel who stands at the stream with a sigh:
"I can't get across. I'll wait here till it runs dry."
Meanwhile, it flows, forever flows on and rolls by.
    We seek after money, a wife well off and well able
To bear our children. The plow domesticates wild woods.
Let the man who has acquired Enough not ask for MORE.
A house and acreage, a pile of bronze and gold coins,
Have never been able to lower the sick master's fever
Or drive out his worries. The proprietor must be well
If he plans to enjoy the good things he's gathered together.
His house and estate are as much of a pleasure to him
Who wants something more (or is deathly afraid he won't
       get it)
As dazzling canvases are to a man with sore eyes,
Or nice warm robes to a man who suffers from gout,
Or the music of mournful guitars to infected ears.
If the vase isn't clean, whatever you put in turns sour.
    Push pleasures aside: when you buy them with pain,
      you're worse off.
The miser is always in need; draw a boundary line
Around your desires. The envious man loses weight
When he sees someone else getting fat. The tyrants of Sicily
Never discovered a worse form of torment than ENVY.
The man who cannot control his temper will regret
What his grievance made him do when he hurried ahead
To slake his unsatisfied rage. RULE YOUR DESIRES:
If they don't obey, they'll command. BRIDLE THEM. CHAIN
    THEM!
    While the colt's neck still can be turned and he's able
      to learn,

The groom can train him to go where the rider decides.
As soon as your puppy has started barking ferociously
At the stuffed deer in the front yard, he's begun his training
As a future hunting companion.
                              Therefore, drink in my words
While you're still a boy with an innocent heart. TRUST
YOURSELF TO YOUR BETTERS. A jar will retain the scent
Of what is first poured in it when new, a very long time.
    But if you should hang behind, or dash out in front,
    And think I'll wait or try to catch up: I WON'T!

I · 3

TO JULIUS FLORUS, CAMPAIGNING
WITH TIBERIUS (20 B.C.)
How are you out there with all those officers?
What are you doing with your spare time?

Iuli Flore, quibus terrarum militet oris

Julius Florus, on what far fringe of the earth
Is Tiberius campaigning at present? I'm anxious to learn.
Are you up to your knees in the snow of Thrace? By the
    Hebrus?
Stuck at the straits of the Hellespont racing between
Leander's tower and the neighboring tower of Hero?
Off in the fertile plains and hills of the East?
   What kind of work are your erudite group getting done?
This too I wonder about. Who has the job
Of recording the deeds of Augustus, unfolding to time
His triumphs in war and peace? What of that name
Shortly to rise to the lips of all Romans, our Titius,
Who fearlessly quaffs from Pindaric streams and refuses,
With fastidious taste, to recur to more commonplace sources?
Is he well? Does he still think of me? Work on his lyrics,
Fashioning Theban lines to a Latin lyre,
With the help of the muses? Or is he stark raving tragic,
Giving us, and his art, a much more considerable jar?
What is Celsus at work on? Although he's been told,
He needs to be told again to find his own stuff
And keep his hands off the books in the Palatine Library,

Which Apollo hospitably harbors; the rest of the flock
Will fly up some day to strip from our bird the fine feathers
He stole to dress up in, and make him their laughing stock.
And what beds of thyme are *you* busy hovering over?
What are you up to? Your talent cannot be dismissed;
Your "field" has not been left untended, to bristle
With unsightly weeds. Whether you sharpen your tongue
For pleading cases at court, or prepare to act
As a legal consultant in matters of civil dispute,
Or build your enchanting models of verse, you will win
The first prize and wear the crown of victorious ivy.
If you'd only stop worrying, take that cold compress, Care,
Off your head, you'd mount where heavenly wisdom would
        lead you.
We all of us, great or small, should proceed with this task,
Make it our whole endeavor, if we wish to live
To endear ourselves to our country and to ourselves.
    When you write back, do let me know, if you will,
Whether you and Munatius are getting along better now.
Were the stitches awkwardly taken, so that the cut
Didn't close right and keeps coming open again?
Does your turbulent blood and inexperience with life
Continue to drive you wild and keep both your backs up?
    On whatever fringe of the earth you now live, I assure you,
Who are both too good to abandon your brotherly bonds,
I've a fatted calf at my place, against your return.

I · 4

TO ALBIUS TIBULLUS (24 B.C.)
Don't be depressed, my friend. I'm not!

Albi, nostrorum sermonum candide iudex

Tibullus, honest judge of these satires of mine,
What may I say you are doing at Pedum these days?
Writing some verse that will outshine those nice little things
By Cassius of Parma? Stealing off into the woods
By yourself, for a healthful walk, and thinking about
What a good and wise man ought to reflect upon?
You were never just body, deprived of a soul. The gods
Gave you beauty; the gods endowed you with money enough,
And the art of enjoying your life. What more could a nurse
Want for a cherished child, with a mind to think
And a tongue to express, one granted a generous share
Of favor, of fame, of health, of civilized living
And the money required to maintain it?
                                    Between your hopes
And cares, between your rages and fears, believe
That each day's dawn is the last to shine upon you:
The unhoped-for hours will be welcome.
                                    And when you feel
Like having a laugh, call on me. I'm fat, I'm fine!
One of Epicurus' sleek, well-cared-for swine.

I · 5

TO TORQUATUS (22 B.C.)
Come to dinner tonight, the twenty-second

Si potes Archiacis conviva recumbere lectis

Torquatus, you're expected at my house this evening at
    sunset,
That is, if you think you can stretch out your legs
    comfortably
On the old-fashioned couches that Archias designed for me,
And can put up with a modest meal served on plain plates.
The wine we'll drink is Second Consulate Taurian,
Poured off at Villa Petrinum, near Sinuessa,
Below the salt flats of Minturnae. Or have you a better
Vintage to offer? If so, send it round by your boy.
If not, you'll have to take your orders from me.
My hearth has been gleaming for days now, just for your
    sake,
My furniture cleaned up and set to rights. Drop everything,
Those airy ambitions, that drive to make still more money,
Your defense of Moschus on that poisoning charge.
      Tomorrow
Is Caesar's birthday—we're all *excused,* to sleep late,
To stretch the summer night with copious talk.
  What is my fortune for, if I can't make use of it?
Someone who, out of regard for his heir, is stingy,
And much too hard on himself, sits next to a madman.
So I will begin the rites, the scattering of flowers,

177

The drinking, and let you think me unhinged, if you want.
What wonders drink can perform! It unseals the heart,
Tells hopes to turn into facts, makes cowards fight,
Takes weight off worried minds, teaches new arts.
Whom has the flowing bowl not rendered eloquent?
Not made free from the grinding need of money?

   I take it upon myself to vouch for the following—
And do so gladly: that no tattered linen of mine,
No dirty napkin, will make you turn up your nose
In disgust; that pitchers and plates reflect your image
Like mirrors; that no one is present who will gossip outside
About what is said among faithful friends—so that equals
May be intimate with equals.

                    I'll invite Septicius
And Butra to meet you, and add Sabinus to the list,
Unless a prior engagement or a slyer girl
Detains him. There are places enough for a few of your
    "shades":
But when goats get too close together, the air's a bit thick.

   You've only to write back how many you want us to be,
Then drop everything: the client you're supposed to see,
Your business. Sneak out the back. Come to me!

I · 6

TO NUMICIUS (NO DATE)
Nil admirari

Nil admirari prope res est una, Numici

If you want to make yourself happy and stay that way,
Numicius, perhaps the only successful rule
To follow is: marvel at nothing; never be spellbound.
There are those who can gaze on our sun, our stars, our
    seasons
Revolving in fixed progression, and not feel a drop
Of fear. And what point of view do you think we should take
Toward things like the treasures of earth and sea that
    enrich
Far-distant Arabs and Indians with pearls worth a fortune,
Or things like the Roman awards of acclaim and
    appointments
By admiring voters? What should our attitude be?
    Fearing to lose these things is like craving to win them:
Either man "marvels," either man gets upset
When some unforeseen event puts them both in a tizzy.
What does it matter whether he grieves or gloats,
Whether he craves or trembles, if his eyes are glued,
His body and mind locked and frozen in feeling,
Whenever he sees something better, or worse, than he hoped
    for?
Even the wise man must be thought quite insane,
The just man quite unfair, if he goes beyond

The proper bounds in pursuit of virtue itself.

   So, go and feast your eyes on a fine silver service,
On antique marble groups, on *objets d'art,*
On bronzes; marvel at gems and Tyrian cloths
In their myriad colors. Revel in the fact that thousands
Of eyes are fixed on you when you speak. Be busy—
Off to the Forum early, not back home until late,
So that Mutus doesn't haul in a bigger harvest
From his wife's estates (shameful thing, for a man
Of lower birth than you) and thereby win
The chance to be the one who's marveled at
By you, when it's you who should be marveled at
By him.

            Whatever now lies beneath the soil
Time will bring up to the light. What now lives and shines
It will bury and cover up deep. When the Appian Way
And Agrippa's Arcade have seen your familiar figure,
You'll still have the journey down to make, where Numa
And Ancus have gone before you.

                        If your chest or back
Is assailed by twinges of pain, find some relief
From the ailment. You wish to lead a good life (who
    doesn't?)?
If Virtue alone can grant this wish, have the courage
To busy yourself about her and stop fooling around!
You consider *Virtue* entirely a matter of terms?
Or the Sacred Grove just so much wood for the stove?

   Look out! A competitor will make his way back to port
Ahead of you, or you'll lose the money you've sunk
In ventures in Cibyra or some Bithynian coup.
See to it that you round off your earnings with a cool
    thousand talents:

You'll add on a thousand more, and a thousand more,
And, just to square off the pile, one more, making four.
Pecunia Regina gives a wife with dowry, and friends,
Good standing, good looks, and a family tree. The goddesses
Venus and her sister Persuasion beautify the man
Who's well heeled. Of course, you mustn't get into the
    plight
Of the King of Cappadocia, long on slaves, short on cash.
Remember what they said of Lucullus: when asked for
    cloaks,
A hundred of them, for a spectacular stage production,
He answered, "Where would I get a hundred cloaks?
But I'll look around and send over all that I have."
A few days later he wrote. "I seem to have
Five thousand of these darned cloaks lying around the
    house;
Have them all, or as many as you need." It's a pretty poor
    house
If there's not quite a lot of stuff for thieves to make off
    with,
Which the master hasn't even kept track of! So, I would say,
If money alone makes you happy and keeps you that way,
Work at it first and last, without further delay.
    But if influencing people and keeping in the public eye
Constitutes bliss, let's buy us a slave to stand by
And tell us their names, give us a dig in the ribs,
And hustle us across the street to shake their hands:
"*He* has pull with the Fabians. *This man*'s a wheel with the
    Velines
This fellow can make you a consul or judge, or break you,
If he feels in the mood." When you reach out your hand
    for their vote,

Say "brother" or "father"—*adopt* your constituent,
    adapting
Your words to his age.
                    Now, if he who dines well, lives well,
Well then—come on, it's dawn—let's go where our throat
Leads the way. Let's go hunting or fishing the way old
    Gargilius did.
First thing in the morning, he ordered his slaves to march off
And tramp through the Forum, lugging their nets and
    spears
Through the midst of the crowd so that every last person
    could see
The boar he bought at a store, on one of the mules
In the train.
            Gorged and stuffed with food, let us bathe,
Unmindful of whether it is proper or not, and deserving
To rank among second-class citizens like Ulysses' crew,
Those rogues to whom forbidden pleasure meant more
Than sailing back to their native shore.
                     Was it proved
By Mimnermus that not to have lived is not to have loved
And not to have laughed? Then live in love and laughter:
May you live forever, and be happy forever after.
    Now, if you have better advice than this to proffer,
    Impart it, old boy. If not, just take what I offer.

I · 7

TO MAECENAS (NO DATE)
I won't be coming to town this winter. Sorry!

Quinque dies tibi pollicitus me rure futurum

I said I would stay in the country no more than a week,
But, false to my word, I've made myself scarce all August.
Even so, if you want me to live safe and sound, Maecenas,
You will pardon me as much when I fear falling ill
As you do when I am in fact sick. This is the season
When the first figs and heavy heat elevate undertakers
And their black-robed attendants to positions of great
     importance,
The time when every father and mummy blanches
With fear for the children, when nerve-racking social
     functions
And minor details of business-going-on-as-usual
Bring on fevers, and bring out wills to be read.
But when winter whitens the Alban fields with snow,
Your bard will go down to the seaboard to care for himself,
And huddle up and read. He'll come back to you, dear
     friend
(By your leave), when the winds blow warm and the first
     swallow flies.
   You have made me rich, but not as the Calabrian host
Urges the guest to sample his pears. "Oh, try some!"
"I've had enough, thanks." "Well, take some home with you,
     then."

"Oh, I couldn't!" "But your kids will like you for bringing
      them presents."
"I'm as much obliged for the offer as if I were leaving
With my toga full." "As you wish. Whatever you leave
Will make a good meal for my pigs to relish today."
    The foolish prodigal gives what he no longer wants;
The good, wise man stands ready to aid the deserving
But knows the difference between real coins and the beans
They jingle on the stage. And I would prove myself worthy
In a manner befitting your manifold goodness to me.
But if you want me to stay by your side, give back the
      strength
Of my lungs, give back my raven tresses, nestling
On a narrowly visible forehead, give back the times
We sat chatting gaily or gracefully laughing and drinking
Or deploring the flight of Cinara (under whose reign
I was not as I am).
                A lean and hungry fox
Happened to squeeze his way through a chink in the box
Where the grain was kept, and ate as much as he could.
With his stomach full he tried to get out: no good!
A weasel who was hanging around then said to him, "Hey!
You went in there thin: you'll have to get out the same
      way!"
If I were called on to plead my defense on these terms,
I'd give up the case. "In fair round belly WITH
Good capon lin'd," I don't praise the poor man's sleep.
Nor would I trade my freedom and time to myself
For all of Arabia's wealth. You have often praised
Me as modest, have been addressed quite frankly by me
As "Boss" or "Sire" (nor do I spare these words
When you aren't around): so test me now and see

If I can't return your gifts, and do it with glee.
    That wasn't a bad reply Telemachus gave,
The son of patient Ulysses, when offered the horses;
"Ithaca's no place for horses. It's not flat enough
And there's not much pasture. Son of Atreus, your gift
Is much better suited to you, I leave it to you."
Small things suit small people: to royal Rome
I now prefer tranquil Tivoli or tame Tarentum.
    That well-known defense lawyer, vigorous, bold Philippus,
Was walking back home from work one day around two.
Somewhat along now in years, he complained of how far
The Carinae still was from the Forum. Then he saw, so they
        say,
A clean-shaven man sitting alone at ease in the shade
Of a barber's booth, and quietly cleaning his nails
With his own pocketknife. "Demetrius, just see who that is
Over there. Go find out where he's from, who's his father
        or patron,
What he's worth." The lad was quick to get the idea.
He went, he returned, he explained: It's Vulteius Mena,
The auctioneer, a fine fellow, if not a very rich one,
Known to work hard when he ought to and stop when he
        should,
To take in money and spend it, completely content
With a few humble friends and a home of his own, with
        his time
Free after business to go to the games in the Campus.
"I'd like to hear from him what you say about him:
Invite him to dinner." Mena can hardly believe it
And marvels silently inwardly. Finally, *"Non, merci!"*
"He turns me down?" He turns you down, the rascal,
Either afraid or insulting. The next day, Philippus

Comes across his Vulteius selling cheap remnants
To the prolies in work shirts, and offers his greetings first.
Vulteius excuses himself, on the grounds of business
And work, for not having paid a morning call
On Philippus, for not having seen him in time to speak first.
"You can earn your pardon by coming to dinner today."
"As you wish." "After three, then. Now get back to work.
     Make more money."
When Vulteius came to dinner, he chattered along
On every conceivable and inconceivable subject,
Until at last he was allowed to go home to bed.
   When the man I've been describing was regularly seen
Running, like a fish to the hidden hook, to his patron,
A morning caller, a regular guest at dinner,
He was invited to go with his host to a country estate
During Latin Holidays. A brace of smart French ponies
Drew the coach; Vulteius couldn't stop praising the scene,
The Sabine soil, and its climate. Philippus looked on
And laughed, and anxious to amuse and distract himself,
No matter how, what with offering seven thousand outright
And a loan of seven thousand more, persuaded Vulteius
To buy a small farm. And he bought it.
                 To end the suspense:
Our city slicker becomes a yokel, and his fine talk
Rattles on, but now it's about his furrows and vinestalks.
He prunes his elm trees, just about kills himself
Fixing *this* and trying out *that*, and ages rapidly
From his love of possession. When his sheep are taken by
    stealth,
His goats by disease, and his crop deceives his hopes,
And his ox lies dead from too much plowing, Vulteius,
Frantic in the face of his losses, saddles up his jade

187

At midnight and furiously gallops to the home of Philippus.
As soon as Philippus sees him unshaven and dirty,
He says, "Vulteius, it looks to me as if you
Have been under a strain and working yourself too hard."
"If you call me my true name, *padrone*," Vulteius replies,
"*Accidenti!* It's Sporca Miseria! I beg and beseech you,
By your Genius and household gods, by your strong right
        hand,
Give me back my former life!"
                                    As soon as one's seen
How the life he left behind surpasses the one
He gained by giving it up, he ought to go home
In time to become again what he ought to have been.
The best rule by which to measure ourselves is: OUR OWN.

TO CELSUS ALBINOVANUS,
CAMPAIGNING WITH
TIBERIUS (20 B.C.)
I'm depressed. Hope you aren't

Celso gaudere et bene rem gerere Albinovano

Muse, take a letter to Tiberius' friend and scribe
Celsus Albinovanus. At my request,
Greetings and all good wishes. If he wants to know
How *I* am, say that in spite of my good intentions
I'm neither quite right nor quite happy. Not that the
    hailstones
Have ruined my vines, or the heat gotten into my olives,
Or that my herds are wasting away in some far-off pasture:
But simply because my mind is a lot more weak
Than my whole physique. And I won't get over my pique.
I won't listen to, much less learn from, those who would
    cure me;
I find fault with my trusted physicians and badger my
    friends
For hurrying to keep at bay my fatal depression.
What's bad for me I pursue, and then run away
From the thing I am sure might do me some good. Like
    the wind,
I keep changing—at Tivoli longing for Rome, and at Rome
Pining for Tivoli.

            When you've told him all this about me,

Celso gaudere et bene rem gerere Albinovano

Ask how he is, how it goes with himself and his pelf,
How he stands with the prince and his staff. And if he says
    "Fine!"
Be sure to remember, O Muse, to register joy,
And then to drop this advice in his ears: good Celsus,
We'll stand by you, in proportion as you stand up to your
    fortune.

I · 9

Recommending to you my friend Septimius

Septimius, Claudi, nimirum intellegit unus

Tiberius, it seems that only Septimius knows
How I stand with you. He asks, nay insists, that I try
To introduce him to you as a person who shows
Abilities equal to those of the family
And mind of a Nero, who attract good things to your side.
When he thinks that I rate a place as your intimate friend,
He sees far better than I where my powers reside.
Of course, I made excuses and tried to defend
Myself from encroaching on you: ah, but that won't do,
I reflected, it looks too much like self-deprecation,
Self-interest. Therefore, I have the effrontery to
Comply with his wish, to avoid the worse reputation
Of a snob. And if this response to a friend's request,
Immodestly offered, merits your praise, inscribe
The man in your tribe: you'll find him one of the best.

TO ARISTIUS FUSCUS (21 B.C.)

You can have the city. I'll take the country

Urbis amatorem Fuscum salvere iubemus

Fuscus, you love to live in the city: I DON'T.
But good afternoon, anyway. I hope you are well.
It's the only difference between us, this city vs. country—
For in all else we're practically twins or brothers-in-mind.
Like two old familiar doves, we nod our heads mutually,
Bobbing up to say "yes" and down to say "no" and
  "no, too."
 But while you keep to the nest, I praise the brooks
Flowing through the sweet countryside, its stones overgrown
With moss, its delightful groves. Need I say more?
I begin to live, I reign, as soon as I've left
The very same things you people praise to the skies—
Like the runaway slave of a priest, I don't want any wafers:
I need plain bread now, much more than honeyed cakes.
 If it's only proper to "live in accordance with nature"
And we must put our house somewhere, do you know
  anywhere
Better than the country, naturally so well situated?
Where winters are warmer, and welcome winds can soothe
The Dog Star's fury or the Lion's impatient thrust,
When goaded to rage by the first hot rays of the sun,
Where fewer frustrating worries ravel our sleep,

Where the grass smells finer and shines more than African
  mosaics.
  Is the water purer that pounds its way through the pipes
In the city than that which scampers and murmurs along
Our sloping streams? After all, you grow trees in town
Among the many-colored columns that set off your fine
  inner courts,
And you praise the home with a view of fields in the distance.

> DRIVE NATURE OUT WITH A PITCHFORK. SHE'LL BE
>   BACK AGAIN.
> SHE'LL OUTWIT AND BREAK THROUGH ABSURD
>   CONTEMPT! SHE WILL WIN!

  The man who cannot distinguish the false from the true
Sustains as heavy a loss and blow to his heart
As the "expert" who thinks he can tell the two dyes apart
When he can't tell Sidonian blue from the similar hue
We get from the moss of Aquinum and use for our cloth.
  One whom a favorable turn of events OVERjoys
A change for the worse undermines. *Nil admirari*—
You'll simply be sorry! And incapable of giving it up.
Shun BIGNESS. Your humble estate may offer the chance
To outpace kings and the friends of kings, as you dance
Your way along life.
                        The stag, in time past, could drive
The horse from the feeding ground, and beat him in fighting,
Until the perpetual loser came crying to man
To ask for his help, and accepted the bit. Then the horse
Fought the stag once again to a bitter conclusion, and won.
He walked off and left his foe, but now couldn't shake
The bit from his mouth or the rider down from his back.
So one who, fearing poverty, loses the liberty

That is worth even more than a gold mine will carry a
    master,
And cravenly slave for another, simply because
He can't subsist on a little. If what you have
Won't do, well . . . it's like the wrong size shoe:
If it's too big for your foot, you trip and fall all over yourself;
If it's too small, it pinches.
    You will live the right sort of life, Aristius Fuscus,
If you're happy with what you have, and lay into me
When I seem to be gathering in much more than enough
And seem unable to stop. Money stored up
Is every man's master, or slave. A well-woven rope
Ought to follow and not lead the way.
                        That's all for today.
I dictate these lines near the shrine of Our Lady of Vacuity:
I'm fine, although she's far gone, by now, in her ruinty;
I'm completely content—except that I don't have you
    with me!

I · 11

TO BULLATIUS (NO DATE)
How was your trip?

Quid tibi visa Chios, Bullati, nataque Lesbos

How was your trip, Bullatius? How were the islands?
What did you think of Chios, of world famous Lesbos,
Of stylish Samos? What about the royal home
Of Croesus, Sardis? And Smyrna, and Colophon?
Were they more, or less, than their reputation implies?
Do they all look poor when compared with our Campus and
    Tiber?
Did you lose your heart to one of Attalus' cities?
Or perhaps you're sick of oceans and highways, and find
Even Lebedus charming? You know Lebedus: a burg
Even more in the middle of nowhere than our Gabii
Or Fidenae. But still, I wouldn't really mind living there,
Forgetting my friends, forgotten by them, and watching
The enchafèd flood from my vantage point on the shore.

    But the traveler heading for Rome from Capua, splattered
With rain and mud, wouldn't spend his life in an inn.
Nor would someone chilled to the bone praise stoves and
    baths
As supplying the things that alone make life worth the living.
If a rough south wind has knocked you about at sea,
You don't automatically sell your ship when you land
Across the Aegaean.
                Fair Mytilene and Rhodes

Quid tibi visa Chios, Bullati, notaque Lesbos

Do about as much good for a man with a good reputation
As a heavy cloak in the summer, or light linen shorts
When snow's on the way, or a winter plunge in the Tiber,
Or a stove in the middle of August.
                                    As long as you can,
While Fortune continues to smile, let Samos be praised,
And Chios, and Rhodes—at a distance, while you stay in
    Rome.
Whatever excellent hour a god has bestowed
Upon you, take it gratefully, graciously take it in hand—
Do not postpone your pleasure from year to year.
Thus, you'll be able to say, "I've *lived* today,"
Wherever you are.
                    If it's true that reason and sense
Alone can dispel your worries, and not some spot
Looking out on a wide stretch of sea, then people who race
Overseas change, NOT their minds but their place.
Our world is full of people with nothing to do
And no time to do it! We cruise around in our cars
Or our yachts, pursuing our happiness. But what you pursue
Is right here, in Frogville, or Swamptown, or Rattlekazoo,
If you can just piece together the mind that accompanies
    you.

I · 12

TO ICCIUS, IN SICILY (20 B.C.)

Hope you are doing well in your work for the Department of
External Revenue. But do look up Pompeius Grosphus.
Here's the latest news from Rome

Fructibus Agrippae Siculis quos colligis, Icci

With the revenue coming your way in Sicily, Iccius,
As Agrippa's agent, you have only to handle it right:
Jove himself couldn't shower you better with gold.
So stop complaining! The man is certainly not poor
Who has everything that he needs. A king's own ransom
Can't add a bit more, if your stomach and lungs
And feet are all right. Suppose it's a frugal life
You lead—not that there isn't a lot within reach,
But that you're used to nettles and grass—you'll go on that
     way
When the Fortunate River gilds you from head to foot:
Either because mere money can't change your nature
Or because you consider all else subordinate to virtue.
   We wonder that Democritus' herds ate up his fields
And meadows, while his fast-moving mind wandered off by
     itself,
Without his body. Yet you, surrounded by wealth,
Seem immune to the filthy disease, and think nothing of it,
And still keep turning your mind to loftier objects:

What keeps the ocean's volume ever constant,
What regulates the seasons of the year,
Whether stars roll on by pattern or by chance,
What animates the phases of the moon,
What "the harmony of discord" really means
And where it tends, and whether the real truth lies
Where Stertinius claims or Empedocles denies.

But whether it's fish or only scallions and onions
You slaughter (if it's fish you may get yourself in hot water
With Empedocles, who claimed to have been one himself),
Take good care of Pompeius Grosphus for me,
And if he needs anything, please don't wait till he asks for it.
I'm sure that he won't bombard you with unfair requests.
The asking price for friends is far from exorbitant
When you consider how few good men are around today.
And now for the news from Rome: Cantabrians Prostrated
By Agrippa's Valor in Spain. Armenians Yield
To Tiberius' Strength in the East. Vindicated,
Crassus' Banners Back on the Roman Field
As Parthian King Bows Knee to Western Caesar.
Prosperity Flows As Italy Is Found To Please Her.

TO VINIUS ASINA (23 B.C.)

Please give these odes to Augustus, and watch what you're doing!

Ut proficiscentem docui te saepe diuque

Vinius, as I repeated to you when you started,
You will hand these volumes of odes, still sealed, to Augustus,
If he's well and happy and . . . oh, yes, if he asks you for
    them.
Follow my orders so as not to ruin my chances
By being too keen and ardent an agent of mine.
If three slim tomes gall your flanks, just throw them away:
Don't slam the saddlebags down at Augustus' feet
Like an obstinate ass, or your family name, Asina,
Will be joked about all over town and ring in your ears.
    Take your stouthearted way over hill and dale,
Past streams and mudholes. And when you've won through
    at last
And reached the goal, please carry your book bundle
    properly.
Don't sling the package under your arm like a farmer
Picking up a lamb, or like Pyrria stumbling onstage
Tipsy, hiding the ball of wool she purloined,
Or like a poor man invited to dine at the home
Of his district political leader, who crooks in his elbow

His sandals and woolen cap.
                              And don't stop and tell
Everybody you meet you're all in a sweat, bringing poems
Which are bound to attract the eyes and ears of Caesar.
Now that you've heard out my urgent instructions, DON'T
      STOP!
Be off. Fare well. Don't stumble. DON'T DROP IT!

I · 14

TO THE FOREMAN ON MY
FARM (NO DATE)
You can have the city; I'll take the country

Vilice silvarum et mihi me reddentis agelli

Let's have a contest, steward, to see which one
Can defend the farm: the man by whom it is run,
Or the man by whom it is owned. For me, it's home,
This wooded sight that brings me back to myself,
Shelters five families, and sends five worthies to vote
And to market at Varia. It's obvious you don't dote
On the place as I do. But let's see which hired hand
Weeds better: you when clearing the thorns from the land,
Or I when clearing my mind. Let us now debate
And see which is better: Horace or his estate.
Detained in town as I am by Lamia's sorrow
And affectionate need for me—he's beside himself
With inconsolable grief for his brother's death—
My mind and heart bear me off to the very place
Where you are, and avow they will break through into the
    open.
I say that living in the country makes a man happy.
You say the city. Small wonder, that one discontent
With his own lot prefers another's. Each is absurd
To pretend the place is at fault: *it's* innocent;
The mind is to blame. It has to live with itself,
Wherever it is. When you were an unskilled laborer

For hire by the hour in town, your secret sighs
Went out to the country, but as foreman now on my farm,
You pine for the city, longing for the baths and the games.
But you know how consistent I am, how I hate to leave
Whenever some depressing business drags me to Rome.
We ADMIRE, but not the same things, and that's just the
      difference
Between your fickle delights and my steady pleasures.
The man who shares my views finds utterly charming
The mesas and badlands you detest, while he hates
What you find entrancing. Some hole-in-the-wall of a brothel,
Some greasy short-order joint, inflames your desire
For the city, I see, and the fact that the hole-in-the-ground
Where you're buried at present will as soon grow pepper
      and spice
As it will good grapes, that there's no good tavern nearby
Where you can get wine, no flute girl doling out music
For you to clomp and to stomp to. Nothing to enjoy,
You still have much to endure: working those fields
Long left untouched by the hoe, tending that ox
After work when his yoke comes off and you fill him up
With the fodder you've cut and dried. The brook makes work
After rain, when you throw up earthworks to try to teach
The damned thing to steer away from your sunny meadow
      grass.
Come, hear what discord undermines our concord:
A man whom expensive clothes and well-groomed hair
Once suited, a man you knew as one quite able
To please, and without bringing gifts, an unquenchable
      wench
Like Cinara, a man who'd drink his good clear Falernian
In the middle of the day, now takes his chief delight

In a simple meal and a snooze on the bank of a stream.
The shame lies not in the fact that you've played the game
But in not being able to stop. Out where you live,
No one fixes his basilisk eye on me when I bask
In comfort or, whispering hypocritical thanks,
Sinks his fangs in my back when it's turned and poisons
  the pleasure
I enjoy at my leisure: that's the metropolitan way.
Out there, my neighbors just laugh to see how I toil,
Moving rocks around and digging a bit in the soil.
You'd rather be here in town with the slaves on the dole
Munching their food—you're for them, body and soul.
My shrewd servant here in town discovers more good
In the access you have to a flock, a garden, and wood.
The ox wishes he were caparisoned like a fine horse;
The horse wants to plow—it's a nice slow existence, of
  course.
I fail to see why each of us shouldn't enforce
The things he does best—and do it without remorse.

I · 15

TO NUMONIUS VALA (22 B.C.)

I'm planning to come south for the winter. What's it like down there?

Quae sit hiems Veliae, quod caelum, Vala, Salerni

Vala, what is it like in winter at Velia
And Salerno? How's the climate, what sort of people
Live there, and how are the roads? Antonius Musa
Has made the hot springs of Baiae superfluous to me,
And me unpopular there, by prescribing cold baths
In the middle of winter. That town laments to see
Its myrtle groves abandoned, its sulphur baths
In disrepute, famous for their power to drive off
Chronic rheumatic attacks. That town resents
Its valetudinarians' daring to plunge
The heads and stomachs under cold-water showers
At Clusium, traipsing off to Gabii
Or some such cold winter spot. I have to change
My watering place, and change my horse's mind,
Driving him past the places he usually stops at.
When he starts to turn off to the right, I'll have to say
"Where in the world are you going? The road I'm now taking
Doesn't go to Cumae or Baiae." Angry, the rider
Saws on the left-hand rein; the horse's ear
Doesn't hear: he feels the words in his bridled mouth.
    Now, which of the two has a better supply of food?
Salerno or Velia? Is the rain water stored in tanks,

Or can they drink from springs that never go dry? The wine
Of the region I won't go into. Of course, when I'm home
I'm not so fussy, but when I go to the coast
I insist on a pedigreed wine, smooth to the tongue,
Banishing care, making my veins and my heart
Surge with luxurious hope, making me witty—
A dashing young figure in the eyes of a Lucanian lass.
  Which place, incidentally, has more hares,
And which more boars, and which of the two sea fronts
Conceals more fish and sea urchins—so that I'll come home
Fat as a Phaeacian?—I wish you'd write about this.
I'll believe what you say, for you're no Stranger to Elea.
  Maenius valiantly ran right through the inheritance
His father and mother had left him, and then showed up
In the city as a "Parasites Lost" who prowled all over
In search of his meals, having no immovable manger
To feast at. If he'd had no dinner as yet that day,
He'd bring his nasty gossiping tongue to bear
On friend or foe, saying piquant things, not true:
Whatever he made from this he just took and threw
In his greedy belly, thereby knocking the bottom
Out of the market—a veritable plague, or cyclone,
Or bottomless pit. If he happened to get no response
From those who indulged or feared his wicked remarks,
He restricted his diet to a few fat platters of tripe
Or cheap lamb stew—downing enough of a meal
To satisfy three hungry bears. And at times like this
He'd announce that prodigal sons really ought to be branded
With a hot plate on the belly—so he would tell you,
This fine, reformed, now so frugal and fair-minded fellow!
Of course, if he then had a windfall, he'd promptly convert
The substance to smoke and ashes, and solemnly aver,

"*Ma foi!* No wonder people *consume* the good things!
 Nothing's better than thrush or tastier than fat sow's
  paunch."
  As a matter of fact, I'm just like that, you know.
 When the means are lacking, I praise a retired way of life:
"Small things for small people," oh, I'm quite strong-minded
 When it comes to cheap living. But when something a cut
  above this
 Happens to come my way, something quite a bit *tastier*,
 Then I insist that you alone are the wise fellows,
 Whose firmly based wealth shines out from your dazzling
  white villas.

I · 16

TO QUINCTIUS (25 B.C.)
Virtue is wisdom

Ne perconteris fundus meus, optime Quincti

Quinctius, in case you might be writing to ask
How my farm supports its master—whether grain or olives,
Cattle or vine-clad elms, are what make me rich—
I'll ramble on a bit about the natural shape and roll
Of my Sabine Farm.
      There's a nearly unbroken skyline
Of mountains, cut into by a single thick-shaded valley
Whose right side the morning sun looks upon, whose left
He warms and mellows as his chariot drives away.
You'd like the feel of the place and its looks, my friend,
If you saw the friendly face of my fruit-bearing shrubs
Rosy with wild cherries, crimson and gold with plums,
My oak and ilex groves, where the cattle can browse
On the berries and acorns while the master enjoys the
  shade;
You'd say a greener Taranto had drawn nearer Rome.
I've a fine spring, worthy of bearing the name of a river,
Pure and cool as the Hebrus winding through Thrace,
Whose flowing waters bring relief to ailing heads
And relief to wavering stomachs. This dear hideaway,
This beautiful spot (you're convinced by now?), keeps your
  Horace
Sound in health in the direst hours of September.
 You, of course, live aright if you see that you are

What people say that you are. All of us at Rome
Have been boasting loud and long of how happy you are.
I can only hope that you won't trust anyone else
To know more about you than you, and that you don't think
A man can be happy in possession of anything else
Than intelligence and virtue. Even if people insist
You're in excellent shape, perfectly sound, you won't hide
The fever you secretly feel, just to put up a front
At dinner, until your grease-stained fingers start trembling.
THEIR WOUNDS ONLY FOOLS CONCEAL: THE WISE LET THEM
    HEAL.
   Suppose a poet were to hail the wars you fought
On land and sea, and beguile your willing ears
With words like these: "Jupiter alone, who guide
The fate of This City and This Citizen, please hide
The answer to this (and don't force *us* to decide):
Whether the people's interests safely and solely reside
In him, or his in them—when both coincide."
You'd know the words were addressed to Augustus, not you.
But if you hear yourself called infallibly wise,
Do you take the words as applying to you? "Well, of course,
I don't mind being called a sound and sensible man,
Any more than you do." One who confers today
A title like this, tomorrow may take it away,
As political office, conferred on the wrong incumbent,
Is whisked right out of his hands. "Hand over the keys,"
They say, "they're ours." I hand them over again
And mournfully walk back out through the door I came in.
What if the same guys shout, "There he goes, the thief . . .
The lecherous, treacherous . . . and besides, he strangled
    his father!"?
Will I smart or blush under such notorious falsehoods?
For whom does lying slander terrorize

Or undeserved approval gratify
Except a man who's full of faults in the first place
And needs a doctor in the second place?
                                    And who is the good man?
"He who abides by the Senate's decrees, who adheres
To the statutes and laws, whose private judicial opinion
Can be brought into play to settle many big disputes,
Whose standing bail means that the property is safe,
Whose taking the stand as a witness, that the case will be
    won."
Yet this same man, as his household and neighbors all know,
Is rotten inside, foul where the skin doesn't show.
    "I've never stolen; I've never tried to escape."
If a slave told me this, I'd reply, "You have your reward:
You're not being whipped to bits." "I haven't murdered
Anyone, either." "Then you won't feed the crows from a
    cross."
"And so, you see, I'm a good and reliable person."
But our Sabine friend rather shakes his head at this.
The careful wolf is afraid of the pit, and the hawk
Of suspected snares, the gurnard of the hidden hook.
Through love of virtue the good have come to hate crime;
Fear of punishment keeps you from going astray.
If you thought you could pull it off without being seen,
You'd steal the money from the poor box to buy kerosene
To burn down the orphans' home, which would be quite
    mean.
When from my thousand bushels you steal one bean,
My loss is not sharp; your guilt is terribly keen.
    When your "good" man prays in public to placate the gods
With a pig or an ox, and the public entirely approve
As he peals out "Apollo!" in clarion tones, or intones
"Oh, Janus, Our Father!" he keeps on moving his lips

In private prayers: "Laverna, Protectress of Thieves,
Cover my tracks, make me seem to be upright and just,
Wrap my sins in night and my lies in the dust."
    I fail to see how a miser can be more free,
Or better than a slave, if he stoops to scoop up the coin
Some boys have glued to the street. The man who craves
Is also the man who fears, and the man who lives
In fear will NEVER, in my view of things, be free.
He throws down his arms, he deserts the field of virtue
Who busily ruins himself to add to his money.
When you've got a captive like this, don't kill him: SELL HIM.
He'll make a good slave; let him work outdoors, if he's
        tough,
As a shepherd or plowman; let him spend the winter at sea
As a merchant sailor and keep down the price of grain
By increasing our imports from Egypt; let him be a porter,
Carrying wheat and foodstuffs.
                        The truly good man,
The truly wise man, will dare speak lines of this sort:

> *Dionysus.* Pentheus, ruler of Thebes, what will you
>   force me
> To undergo and endure?
>   *Pentheus.*   I'll take away your goods.
>   *Dio.* My cattle, money, furniture, silver? Take them!
>   *Pen.* I'll throw you in handcuffs and chains and into
>   clutches
> Of a cruel jailer.
>   *Dio.*   God Himself will release me
> As soon as I want.

                    I believe this meant, "I will die."
Death is the finishing line on the racecourse of life.

TO SCAEVA (NO DATE)
How to win friends and influence patrons

Quamvis, Scaeva, satis per te tibi consulis, et scis

DEAR LEFTY:
    You seem to know how to look after yourself,
And seem to know how to handle the higher-ups, too.
But take a tip from your insignificant friend,
Who could use a few lessons himself but wants to show you
The way, blind though he is. What I have to say
May be something you can make use of: if it is, please do.
 Unhurried pleasure and sleeping right on until sunrise
Delight you? And dust, and screeching wheels, and taverns
Annoy you? I will order you off to secluded Ferentino.
Happiness does not befall the wealthy alone,
And he has not lived badly who has lived unknown,
From birth to death.
      If you wanted to be nice to your friends
And not be so hard on yourself, you'd aim a bit higher—
Heading for a sumptuous meal on an empty stomach.
 Remember Diogenes' remark to wise Aristippus
When the latter passed by his door on the way to dinner?
"If Aristippus knew how to subsist on cabbage soup
And make the most of it, he wouldn't kowtow to kings."
Aristippus turned this around, of course, and replied,
"If Diogenes knew how to get the most out of kings,
He wouldn't have to stoop to soup." Which made more sense?

Tell me which one's expression and action you like best—
Or better, since you're younger, let me tell you why I
Find the sense of Aristippus the stronger. He slipped past the
    Cynic,
Who snapped at him as he went by, with the following words:
"I play for profit, at least; you play to the mob.
I earn my keep, in order to be fed by a king,
To have a horse to ride; you say you don't need a thing
Or a single person, yet you beg for food and alms,
And are lower than the man who supports you. My royal road
Is a much higher, less inferior way—and it's straight!"
    Aristippus made the best of it, no matter what
Color or form life assumed. He aimed rather high
But generally proved quite equal to what came along.
And the opposite type, whom sturdy indifference clothes
In a single garment which he wears folded over and under:
How would he carry off a radical change in his life,
I wonder? The former doesn't wait for a crimson cloak,
But throws something over his shoulders and wades through
    the crowds
And decently plays either part, as man or philosopher.
The latter recoils from a fine Milesian wool cape,
More than he would from a dog or a snake, and will freeze
If you don't give him back the tattered gown that says he
Is a doctor of philosophy. Give it back! Set him free
To live his neurotic life to a compulsive degree.
    To do big things, to display the enemies you've taken
To your fellow citizens, is touching the throne of Jove,
Scaling the heights; to have been the friend of the foremost
Is no mean honor itself. But of course every man
Can't wind up eventually at Corinth. The man who feared
He wouldn't be able to win never entered the race.

Voila! But what of the man who comes through, who arrives?
Has he performed like a man? Here lies our question.
The man who just sits there shudders at the effort involved
And decides it's too much for his little body and soul.
The other one undertakes it and brings it off.
Now, either virtue is an empty name, or the man
Who tries for it rightly pursues a praiseworthy end.
　　Those who don't mention their needs in the patron's
　　　　presence
Will get more than the person who begs. It makes some
　　　　difference
Whether you meekly, sensibly take what's given or grab it:
The point, after all, was to *get it.* "My sister has no dowry;
My mother's on relief; I can't find a buyer for my farm;
Yet it doesn't bring me in a cent." Someone taking this line
Is really setting up the beggar's cry, "Give me food!"
And another will soon chime in, "Me, too!" The handout
Will be split several ways, the loaf sliced thinner and thinner.
If the crow could light on a piece of food without cawing,
He'd have more to eat and less of his fellow crows' jawing.
　　If you bundled off to busy Brindisi as someone's
　　　　companion,
Or perhaps instead went to sweet Sorrento on pleasure,
And complained of the jagged roads and the cold, wet rain,
Or kept moaning over the fact that your traveling case
Had been broken into and rifled, you'd find that these tricks
Were just what a spoiled mistress tries who complains and
　　　　complains
Of how someone stole her gemmed anklets or golden chain:
Soon no one will trust what she says even when she has cause
For grieving over some real loss. A man who's been fooled
Won't trouble himself to bend down and lift up a beggar

Quamvis, Scaeva, satis per te tibi consulis, et scis

With a broken leg, at the crossroads, though the tears stream
    down
His cheeks and he swears by Crisis and Osiris: "No joke!
Believe me, you bad-hearted men! My legs is broke!
Lift up the lame!" They all stand around and croak:
"Find some stranger; they're easy to fool."

                                    That's the chorus
We raise against us—too bad it's not for us.

                                        Yours,
                                            HORACE

I · 18

TO LOLLIUS MAXIMUS (20 B.C.)

How to influence patrons: be yourself!

Si bene te novi, metues, liberrime Lolli

If I know you aright, my frankest of friends, good Lollius,
Once you've declared your attachment to one in high station,
You'll go to any lengths to avoid the impression of being
Your patron's servile dependent. The attachment as friend
Is as different from the scandalous scrounger's, who *uses* his
    patron,
As a matron is different from a mistress in clothing and
    conduct.
So you won't be the obsequious toady. The opposite vice,
Perhaps even worse, is to play the part of the sourpuss
(The rough-hewn type of buffoon, with your hair
    close-cropped
And your teeth discolored), which is offbeat and hard to take,
Though it's meant to suggest liberty and self-neglect,
And Virtue Pure and Simple. But Virtue withdraws
From both extremes and lies at the mid-point between them.
The yes-man, more prone than is right to lay himself out
At the rich man's feet and crack smart jokes as he sits
Beside the host at his couch, is so cowed by the nod
Of the rich man's head that he says all over again
What *he* just said, picking up the words as they fall
From the rich man's lips. You'd think he was a boy at school
Gradgrinding the lesson back to a vicious teacher,

Or an actor who plays the second part in a play
(And always has to learn by heart the first actor's role).
The buffoon gets into a brawl when discussing the texture
Of goat hair! Is it *wool* or hair, that's the question.
Armed to the teeth, he belabors the silliest notions:
"Oh yeah? They don't put no trust at all in my words,
Right off? Oh, no? I'm not gonna be let to bark?
What're they afraid of? Somebody gonna get bitten?
The gift of a second life won't hardly repay
Me for being treated this way!" And what's at stake?
Whether Long John fights better than Beaver; or which road
    to take
To Brindisi, the Appian or Minucian Way, for heck's sake!
  A rich man is sure to shun and despise some friend
Whom Venus has ruined or reckless gambling stripped bare,
Or whom Vanity dresses and manicures way beyond his
    means;
Racked by insatiable hunger and thirst after riches,
Ashamed and in fact in a panic at the thought of poverty,
This man is hated by his well-to-do erstwhile friend,
Who is probably ten times more schooled in scandal than he
    is.
Or if he doesn't hate the poor sinner, he tries to berate him
And straighten him out and, just like a goodhearted mother,
Wants him wiser and nicer than he is, and tells him the truth,
Or something pretty close to it. "Look here, my income—
But don't try to match it—can stand a bit of tomfoolery.
But your means are small. A client with sense in his head
Wears a narrow, conventional toga. So cease competing
With me." Eutrapelus said that if he intended
To wreck someone, he'd give him a good suit of clothes:

The happy man, as he slipped on his handsome new tunic,
Would slip on some new ideas and plans as well:
He'd start sleeping late, putting aside business affairs
For a date with his girl, increasing his debts, and so
End up in the driver's seat of some vegetable cart
Or in a gladiatorial show.

       But back to your patron:
Don't pry into secrets, but if he confides in you,
Keep it to yourself even though you're tempted to tell it,
When drunk or angry. Don't praise your own pursuits
Or ridicule others'. Nor, when he wants to go hunting,
Will you be just in the mood, at that moment, for writing.
This is what pulled asunder the bonds of brotherhood
That linked Antiope's twins, Amphion and Zethus,
Till to keep the peace, Amphion silenced his lyre.
Amphion, you see, *gave in* to his brother; you, too,
Should obey the mild commands of your powerful patron.
When he's off to the fields with his nets and mules and his
  dogs,
Rise up and desert your grim, unsociable muse.
You'll earn your meal with your host: "exercise is
  appetizing."
After all, it's an Old Roman Custom for heroes to hunt:
Improves your circulation and your reputation when you beat
The hound in running, the boar in a contest of strength.
You're good at handling your weapons: hear all those cheers
Rocking the Campus from the spectator's ring when you fight
In the games! As a boy, you fought in the Spanish campaign
Under a man who, at this very moment, reclaims our
  standards
From the Parthian temples and consigns to Italian arms

What has so far lain outside their sphere and the reach of
    their power.
  And don't withdraw or absent yourself from this sport
Without any valid excuse. When you're in the country
At your father's estate, although you make it a point
Never to strike a false note, you go in for play:
The army divides up its boats, and the Battle of Actium
Takes place once again on your pond. Your slaves are
    Egyptians,
Hostile *and* servile; your brother can make his mark
As Antony; the pond is the wild Adriatic Sea.
One of you will surely be crowned by winged Victory.
Anyone (a patron, for instance) who thinks that your
    interests
Coincide with his will squeeze both thumbs in approval.
And proudly commend the virtues of your avocations.
  Let me give you some more advice—not that you need it.
Be careful of what you say and *to* whom and *of* whom.
Steer clear of inquisitive snoopers: they're usually gossips.
Open ears will not keep safe what's deposited in them,
And a word once launched on its way cannot be revoked.
Don't fall for a boy or girl residing inside
The marble precincts of your honorable patron: the master
Might make you happy by making the charming thing yours
As a modest gift, just a token; or he *might* drive you wild
By refusing to come across. Be careful of whom
You recommend to your patron: look him over and over,
Lest he fall far short of your hopes and put you to shame.
We misjudge people, at times, and present the wrong person.
And if you're taken in, don't come to his rescue:
Let him stew in his juice. When someone you know really
    well

Gets in trouble, you can stand guard over your trustworthy
    friend
And protect him. When Theon the Venomous sinks his tooth
In someone you know, aren't you entitled to think
That the slanderous danger will quite soon fasten on you?
When your neighbor's house catches fire, your place is
    threatened,
And flames that are disregarded usually burn brighter.
    Those who haven't yet tried it think it's quite fun
To cultivate the friendship of patrons; one who has done so
Is afraid. But as long as your vessel is still out at sea,
Take care that the wind doesn't shift and carry you back.
The sober sort despise the gay, and the gay
Despise the sober; active types can't stand
The sedentary type; the relaxed—or languid?—man
Dislikes the busy beaver; people who drink
Don't take very much to your pushing the cup away,
Even when you insist you're afraid of fever at night.
And chase those clouds from your brow! Shyness too often
Takes on the aspect of guile, silence of jaundice.
    In the midst of all this, read and examine the wise:
Let philosophers instruct you in living out your days in peace.
Ask *them* whether greed and need will hex you or vex you,
Or fear and hope about things that don't matter much;
Whether learning imparts, or nature imports, virtue to us;
What lessens your cares, and keeps you in good with yourself;
Where tranquillity lies, in fame or in money
(Just a tidy little sum) or along sequestered ways
Where alone you can keep the noiseless tenor of your days.
    What do you think *I* think over every time
I dip my hands in the limpid, icy Licenza
Which waters the town of Cantalupo, wrinkled with cold?

What, my friend, do *I* pray for? For what I now have,
Or even less; that I live out the rest of my days
In my own sweet way, if the gods mean me to survive
A while longer; for a good supply of books and food,
Enough for the year. Beyond that, SIMPLY NOT TO WAVER
On the hope that sways back and forth each hourly quaver.
I ask Jove for what he gives and takes from mankind:
Life, and its means. I'll furnish the well-balanced mind!

TO MAECENAS (20 B.C.)

My lyric poetry is not derivative, *it's* contributive

Prisco si credis, Maecenas docte, Cratino

Learned Maecenas, no lyric poems live long
Or please many people (if you trust the words of Cratinus)
Which are written by drinkers of water. Ever since Bacchus
Recruited unhinged poets in the ranks of his satyrs
And fauns, the delightful muses have regularly reeked
Of wine in the morning. By lavishing praises on wine,
Homer shows that he was a drinker. Good father Ennius
Never dashed off to fight in the front lines of epics
Until he'd downed one or two. "To the sober I assign
A career in business or public affairs; from the grim
I withhold the right to write poems." But once I DECREED
That wine was for drinking, other poets picked up the beat,
And began to compete in drinking all night and in stinking
All day of the stuff. You can't *put on* the virtue
And conduct of Cato by donning his gown and his frown,
And padding around barefoot, acting like a hardhearted
    Stoic.
When Iarbitas copied Timagenes, his tongue tripped him up:
He tried too hard to be suave, to be thought of as witty.
A model whose faults you can all too easily acquire
Is sure to mislead you. If by chance I started looking pale
The "poets" would switch, as a man, to straight vinegar.
Oh, you me-imitators, you servile flock,

Prisco si credis, Maecenas docte, Cratino

How often your fussing makes you my laughing stock,
Or the butt of my anger!
                              I was the first to plant
My feet on an untrodden path; I went forward freely,
Not tracing another man's steps. Who trusts in himself
Will rule the swarm as its king. I first displayed
The iambic lines of Paros to a Latin land,
Following the meter and tone of savage Archilochus,
Not the subjects or words he unleashed against old Lycambes.
But don't award me a wreath made of smaller leaves
For fearing to change the meter and style of his lines:
Masculine Sappho smoothed out Archilochus' muse
By her use of meter; and so did Alcaeus, who differed
In his choice of subject and arrangement of lines,
And in not hunting down a father-in-law to be smeared
With poisonous pen, and in not devising a noose
Of notorious verse for his bride. Alcaeus transformed
His model, and I, the lyric poet of Latium,
Have brought in turn Alcaeus to people's attention,
Which no one had done before. And I take some pleasure
In making the unknown known, in being looked over
By the eyes, and held in the hands, of civilized readers.
    If you'd like to know why an ungrateful reader will praise
And love my odes, as long as he reads them in private,
But once he's in public disparage them quite unfairly,
It's because I don't try to buy the popular vote.
I won't trim my sails to that wind, and invite them to
        dinner—
Not I! I won't give away my old clothes as a bribe.
I won't go to poetry readings, to hear "famous writers,"
Or recite my verse, as a form of professional revenge,
Or hang around the tribes of critics and play for their votes,

221

Dignify their pedantic pulpits with my personal presence:
And that's why they cry and complain. Oh, well, when I say,
"But I'd be embarrassed to hear my poems read out
Before such masses of people—my things don't rate that,
And I wouldn't want to make so much of mere trifles,"
My inquisitor answers, "You're just having fun with us,
And keeping it all for His Ears. You look pretty good
To yourself, and exclusively feel that only your lips
Drip such harmonious honey." I'm a little afraid
To turn up my nose and, when he starts fighting, get raked
By his sharp fingernails. "I don't like the place you've picked
For the fight," I complain, and ask for his armistice terms.
This game gives rise to violent quarrels and anger;
Anger breeds fierce hostility, and deadly war.

TO MY FIRST BOOK
OF EPISTLES (20 B.C.)
I guess it's up to you to make your own way in the world

Vertumnum Ianumque, liber, spectare videris

Well, Book, how well I see
You want to look like a book
And be *liber*, be free of me!
You see the city in sight, the world at your feet,
Like a girl who comes out at night and offers a treat.
You're all polished up, dark hair shaved off: you're clean!
Maybe children, after all, should be not heard but obscene.
My fine boy, my slave, I didn't bring you up this way,
But kept you at home under lock and key, till today.
Slip down now, into the world
Where you're burning to be: no returning
To me. And the first time you're hurled
Into pain by discovering what it means to be hurt,
To be rolled up and tossed aside to lie in the dirt
By a lover who's had enough, you'll hear yourself say,
"Poor me! What game *was* this I wanted to play?"
If my power of prediction is not neutralized by your sin,
Rome will adore you so long as you're young and thin;
But when at last you begin
To feel hacked from lying on your back,
Pawed and soiled by the skin
Of the sordid fingers that held you, and silently feel

The lice in your hair, of your own volition you'll steal
Off in exile to Utica, or be sent on your way in a chain
To an unpronounceable village somewhere in Spain.
I'll laugh, who could have advised you sensibly, IF
You'd listened—like the man who pushed his mule off the
    cliff:
When he slipped, the man pulled from above,
But the mule pulled the other way, the fool,
So his master just gave him a shove.
No one wants to keep on an unwilling slave,
So please go ahead and have the experience you crave.
You'll grow old, of course, and probably have as your fate
Teaching young boys how to SPELL their words on a slate.
Word-stumbling old age will find you living in the suburbs,
Where a slave or a book can be used, at least, to learn verbs.

ENVOI

As you sit there thinking and blinking in some southern sun
With a crowd gathered round to listen, talk about ME.
Tell them how I was poor, just a freedman's son,
But spread my wings too wide for that nest and flew free:
What you take away from my birth, you'll add to my worth!
Tell how I made my mark, in peace and war,
With the foremost men of my time. Prematurely gray,
A short man, who liked to sit in the sun, I got sore
Pretty quickly at times, but also calmed down right away.
And if someone asks you how long I stayed on the earth,
Well . . . as of now, it's forty-four years. You'll remember
That Lollius became Lepidus' colleague just this December.

INTRODUCTION
TO BOOK TWO

During his last productive period Horace wrote both lyrics and hexameters. For the festival of 17 B.C. he composed the solemn *Carmen saeculare*, and by 13 B.C. he had completed a fourth book of *Odes*. Of the three letters, the "Epistle to Florus" was written first (around 20 B.C.), the "Epistle to Augustus" last (by 13 B.C.), and the *Art of Poetry* sometime in between, we cannot say definitely when. Suetonius' *Life of Horace* tells us that Augustus "pressured" Horace into writing the letter which now stands at the first of Book II:

> Post sermones vero quosdam lectos nullam sui mentionem habitam ita sit questus: "irasci me tibi scito, quod non in plerisque eiusmodi scriptis mecum potissimum loquaris. an vereris ne apud posteros infame tibi sit quod videaris familiaris nobis esse?" expressitque eclogam ad se, cuius initium est "cum tot sustineas . . . tua tempora, Caesar."[1]

In all three letters the main interest for the modern reader undoubtedly comes from the subject matter, for each "chapter" of this last book contains a share of Horace's *biographia literaria* and his principles of literary criticism. In his late forties and early fifties he seems ready to take stock of his lifework, to review the canons and practices of literary art from the standpoint of the experienced craftsman. That he should

[1] "[Augustus appreciated his writings so highly that], after reading some of his *Sermones* and finding no mention therein of himself, he sent him this complaint: 'Know that I am angry with you, because in your several writings of this type you do not address me—me above all. Is it your fear that posterity may deem it to your discredit, that you seem to be intimate with me?' And so he wrung from the poet the selection addressed to him, beginning *cum tot sustineas*" (trans. Fairclough).

do so with a sure and steady hand is no surprise; that he still has a sense of humor as well as a sense of purpose is to be expected. But what is sometimes overlooked is that this final book completes the cycle of Horace's hexameter seasons. It is a plentiful harvest, the fruit of good taste and sensibility which Horace has gathered in the autumn of his life in the garden he once planted and has been caring for all along. It stands naturally alongside the previous three books of hexameter verse, like each of them separate and new in substance, of an equivalent length,[2] *totus, teres, atque rotundus.*

If Horace was "forced into" writing the "Epistle to Augustus," he simply made a virtue of the necessary words. With skilful independence of thought and ironic self-deprecation, he refuses to burden Caesar with fulsome remarks and then with an amazing conviction proceeds to assess the ancient literary tradition, to comment on the purpose and spirit of the writer, to side with modern art against the revivalists. And at the end, with consummate tact and genuine grace, he hands the problem over to Augustus again, as a matter still pertaining to his command, while confessing that it is not so unpleasant to be asked by the emperor to write something new.[3]

Acknowledging the supremacy of his friend in power, Horace chooses to begin by making Augustus an exemplary instance of the new dispensation in Roman affairs. He believes that Augustus has restored order and insured continuity to Roman life, and at the same time grasps a useful argument on behalf of the present state of Roman literary taste. The leader's innovations have strengthened Rome, and Rome admires her novel deity; why, then, is the Roman temperament still so

[2] *Serm.* I: 1,030 lines; II: 1,083; *Epist.* I: 1,006; II: 961.

[3] Cf. 226–28. In the whole passage, 219–28, there is gracious acknowledgment as well as racy irony. From here to the end, there is realism and self-respect.

hidebound in matters of art, arch-conservative, antiquarian? Why must a poet be dead before he is admired, and every old book be sacred? The public, Horace suggests, is sometimes a better judge than the critics; fallible as its opinions may be, it sees better than the Société des Choses Anciennes when it discerns flaws, crudities, and quaintness in old works.[4] The truth is, of course, that neither antiquity nor novelty can be an adequate criterion, but we should welcome the new effort, if for no other reason than that the "classics" themselves were all new once.

This observation leads into a review of the Greek and Roman literary tradition which occupies the next 123 lines of the poem. Informal, an insight into rather than detailed coverage of literary history, Horace's sketch has the ring of experience and study. He has worked with these subjects and knows them at first hand, although he seems to handle them lightly. To begin, he touches on the sociology of art momentarily, saying that the Greeks were playful, inventive, childlike, and that art was what they did with their leisure. Aesthetic pleasure, like all pleasure, furthermore, *is* changeable and varied. But Romans, in former times, were conscientious, conservative, commercial, and cautious, not artistic. Now, curiously enough, they're ALL WRITERS, man and boy, scribble, scribble, scribble. Me too, he adds—if I say I *don't* get up in the morning before daybreak and call for my writing materials, I lie worse than a Parthian. I am addicted to this modern Roman habit. Obviously, it's a dangerous state of affairs and probably means some unevenness in quality: *scribimus indocti doctique poemata passim.*

But suddenly Horace turns from this rather scandalous

[4] And, Horace adds, I remember studying the classics at school: *quae plagosum mihi parvo / Orbilium dictare* (70–71).

227

comparison and denigration to undertake the defense of poetry
and point a resounding literary moral, in lines 120–38. The
poet, he argues, instructs the new age in old truths, brings
solace to the sick and comfort to the needy; he educates and
improves the young and lives a frugal, non-aggressive life of
quiet concentration. He is *utilis urbi*—and what more could
Rome ask of one of her citizens?

He turns back now to his sketch of literary history, noting
the characteristically Roman severity and ribaldry combined,
evident in the very beginnings of their dramatic literature, the
Fescennine verses. No sooner was the rude and abusive primitive art improved to some extent, however, than Roman cul-
ture was swamped by Greece, in Horace's intellectual chronol-
ogy: *Graecia capta ferum victorem cepit et artis / intulit
agresti Latio.* The victim of Roman military might, "Greece"
nevertheless civilized her wild and primitive conqueror. Horace's phrase is so perfectly turned that one is tempted to take
it as the literal truth of the whole matter of the Roman "imitative" genius, although by the time Horace had engraved this
stunning epitaph on the tomb of Roman art, he and his friend
Vergil had together succeeded in giving it an ironically new
meaning. They had in fact reconquered "Greece" and completely Romanized the tradition by virtue of the transforming
original powers of their native genius.

In any case, Horace goes on, traces of the primitive past
lived on in Roman literature until they disappeared when Roman writers turned to the models of Greek tragedy, looking
for something useful in Sophocles, Thespis, and Aeschylus.
Furthermore, when the Roman tried his hand at serious drama,
Horace observes, he did it well, being by nature a forceful
and dignified creature, at home with the tragic temperament:
nam spirat tragicum satis. . . . Horace only regrets that the

first Roman tragedians were not as painstaking in their work as they were gifted in this direction.

He now begins to poke fun at Roman comedy, that of Plautus in particular, reasoning that because it lies more on the common level than tragedy it requires more, not less, skill and is the more burdensome art form of the two. The comic muse is a tough and tricky adversary. Horace himself refuses to face her, to risk a subject where success and failure stand perilously close together. Farewell, he says, to the ludicrous urge, when it can make you or break you so quickly, fatten you or flatten you: *valeat res ludicra si me / palma negata macrum, donata reducit opimum.* And now in full cry, he parodies the modern theater, playwright and playgoer alike. Ruled by sensationalism and monstrosities, majoring in noise and Tarentine Technicolor, the Roman theater in the present has nothing in it but scope, Cinemascope and Horrorscope. But the fact is, Horace is prompt to admit at the conclusion of his sociological tirade, the drama is the form of forms: there is no power to equal the dramatist's for moving the mind and mirroring the magical vision of art.

Horace's survey has been kaleidoscopic and swift, to say the least, and at the end he turns back with an audible sigh of relief to what he knows best, to the book a reader holds in his hands. On this subject he can pronounce authoritatively. About "literature," as distinct from "drama," not only can he give advice, he can inspire conduct. Demoting himself to the ranks of imperfect poets—*ut vineta egomet caedam mea*—he warns, scolds, analyzes. He wittily reminds the emperor that a good subject deserves a good poet:

> sed tamen est operae pretium cognoscere, qualis
> aedituos habeat belli spectata domique
> Virtus, indigno non committenda poetae.

And from here on to the end he is somehow delightfully serious. Alexander the Great was a good judge of painting and sculpture, but a bad judge of poetry. Augustus is a good judge of poetry, as witness his predilection for Varius and Vergil:

> At neque dedecorant tua se iudicia atque
> munera, quae multa dantis cum laude tulerunt
> dilecti tibi Vergilius Variusque poetae.

I myself, he continues, would sing of your might, majesty, dominion, and power, except that I can't. I must abide by my *sermones . . . repentis per humum.* I wish I could! *si quantum cuperem possem quoque.* But your majesty would not be enhanced by a feeble song, and my modesty forbids my embracing more than I can hold:

> sed neque parvum
> carmen maiestas recipit tua, nec meus audet
> rem temptare pudor quam vires ferre recusent.

Moreover, I mustn't detain you with wordy attentions: it's rather nauseous. I hope no one ever tries to praise me in some gauche composition. People ought to be more careful about what they put down on paper!

The "Epistle to Florus" combines the satiric with the epistolary style. It is Horatian satire: anecdotes, examples, *de te fabulae narratae,* figure freely. It walks the chalk line of ethical self-sufficiency without tottering. It is funny, heartfelt, autobiographical.

But in many ways this poem epitomizes the charm and force of all the *Epistles.* It draws a swift and sure portrait of the artist, touching on temperament, ideals, and Bohemia. It stresses the importance of the critical faculty and defends aesthetic experience as strongly as it defends conduct.

The Julius Florus to whom Horace is writing here, as earlier in the third letter of Book I, is a young subaltern on the staff of the young Tiberius (now in his early twenties), currently campaigning in the Near East. Horace is clearly interested in Florus, and we might expect the older man to take a paternal or avuncular line with his junior. But Horace is not patronizing or condescending; he is incisive and firm and, while candidly meeting his correspondent on equal terms as a friend, brings him up to his own standards as writer. To some extent, also, Horace generalizes the opportunity given him by making the letter something of a document for every man, as he will do again in the *Art of Poetry*.

The second epistle is not an art of poetry but a messenger of poetry, and it rivals the best of Horace's hexameter work. Its structure is a marvel of co-ordination and continuity; its pure diction settles on the mind like snow, and its accumulating phrases shine and gleam like pristine drifts. Its variety of allusion, its alternations of tone, denote a versatile and apt artistic consciousness. Its doctrine is formed by two points of view, toward literature (the impetuous art) and toward human behavior (the gradual and growing concern of every man), which are balanced and joined and made interdependent and interinforming.

To begin, Horace waives the occasion momentarily, in favor of a Roman parable about the art of unloading merchandise. Advocating the "soft sell," he delights in reminding Florus of the minimum basis the young man has for complaining that he is being neglected by his senior. I told you I was lazy, he says at the end of the first anecdote; I told you not to expect any answers to your letters. And, incidentally, you complain that I don't send you any *poems?*

This is Horace's chance to apologize for poetry, to beg off

from the importunate reader on behalf of the poor pestered artist. He does so at once, with some lines of autobiography, some review of his lifework and description of his state of mind at this season, and some choice words on big city life—all topped off by a splendidly recorded interview between two "modern poets," who constitute the latest avant-garde Mutual Infatuation Society.

Having done this much, Horace proceeds to air a few complaints and to add a few comments of his own on the problem of the writer and the nature of the artistic experience—until with another parable he disposes of this subject by bidding farewell to his art and leaves the muse of meter, to go over to the muse of life.

The first 144 "valedictory" lines of the letter are easygoing and reflective, yet curiously and consistently to the point. The stories of the slave seller and of the soldier of Lucullus which inclose the initial apology are written with all the zest and deliberate joy (*curiosa felicitas*) at Horace's command. The apology then resumes, to become pro vita sua, and concludes with the assertion that poverty drove him to literature (quoted in General Introduction). Autobiographical candor then yields to a steady-handed, if good-natured, estimate of Horace's status *now*. He sees himself, on the threshold of fifty, as one who has earned the right to enjoy his leisure—he is in a position to sleep, not scribble. The predatory years have rolled by, robbing him of his familiar pleasures, one by one, and now are trying to wrench loose his grip on art:

> singula de nobis anni praedantur euntes;
> eripuere iocos, Venerem, convivia, ludum;
> tendunt extorquere poemata; quid faciam vis?[5]

[5] Lines 55–57. In line 56 we feel the rippling "series" effect of the predatory verb and its first object, the two plundered dactyls, and full stop on *ludum*, in 57, the heavy spondaic hand of time pressing down, twisting and wrenching Horace's poems away from him.

The practical question is, if he were to write now, what should it be? Horace points out that his own readers show different preferences, some for the lyrics, others for iambics (*Epodes*), others for satire. How can he be sure of pleasing every palate?

> carmine tu gaudes, hic delectatur iambis,
> ille Bioneis sermonibus et sale nigro.
> tres mihi convivae prope dissentire videntur,
> poscentes vario multum diversa palato.

And this practical concern leads Horace on to Rome itself, the infernal noise machine, whose sounds and jostling rhythms he records in a brief tone poem, "God made the country but man made the tune." Even in sympathetic Athens, life is not always easy for the withdrawn intellectual—at Rome he can't keep afloat. The lines have an Orphic clang, as Horace gives us himself, the little poet in the big city, peace of mind shattered, skills disconnected, dragged down and drowned in the metropolitan vortex. Of course, there is the compensation of fraternity, and, mindful of his fellow poets, Horace characterizes two modern masters bound each to the other in an ecstasy of mutual admiration, exchanging compliments like heroic Samnites trading blows in a daylong duel. It begins to seem as if one of the writer's heaviest burdens is other writers: *multa fero, ut placem genus irritabile vatum / cum scribo et supplex populis suffragia capto.* And Horace is rather glad to have resigned his membership in the fretful brotherhood.

Probably, reflects Horace as he begins to recapitulate the whole apology to Florus, there is too much writing going on anyway, geared to an uncritical sense of the spirit and purpose, of the *art* of literature. The truth is, judgment and criticism must be brought into play; like a censor, the writer must look over all the words on his list:

> at qui legitimum cupiet fecisse poema
> cum tabulis animum censoris sumet honesti.[6]

Infatuation with the sound of one's own words must give way
to the will to revise. The writer must chase even his most favored locutions out of the temple of art, no matter how appeal-
ingly they cling to the sanctum:

> audebit, quaecumque parum splendoris habebunt
> et sine pondere erunt et honore indigna ferentur,
> verba movere loco, quamvis invita recedant
> et versentur adhuc intra penetralia Vestae.

Furthermore, diction is the writer's sole treasure, so he must
be prepared to ransack his ancestral word palaces, to revive
good old words and win a new place for them; he must be
equally ready to exploit and manipulate the new vocabulary
which usage has fathered.

The good writer will flow like a river, strong and clear, and
he will bless and enrich the land with the wealth of his language.[7] He will learn to prune away excess, smooth out the

[6] Dr. Johnson took these lines as the motto for his *Dictionary*.

[7] Lines 120–21: vehemens et liquidus puroque simillimus amni
fundet opes Latiumque beabit divite lingua.

This is, I believe, the *locus classicus* of Denham's famous quatrain in *Cooper's
Hill*:
> "Oh could I flow like thee and make thy stream
> My great example, as it is my theme!
> Though deep, yet clear, though gentle, yet not dull;
> Strong without rage, without o'erflowing, full."

Denham's IMAGE of aesthetic doctrine (1642) had a pervasive influence on all
subsequent eighteenth-century style, as Pope's parody, at the other end of the
span (1728), wildly affirms:
> "Flow, Welsted, flow! like thine inspirer, Beer;
> Though stale, not ripe; though thin, yet never clear;

rough places, discard whatever is flaccid; he will appear to be doing all this in fun, when in fact, like a dancer, he is in agony. I myself, Horace adds, would rather be considered an awkward or compulsive writer, provided that my incompetent efforts pleased, or escaped, me, than be so acutely consciously of my failings as to be utterly miserable. Art was meant to bring pleasure into the world, and I don't want my illusions dispelled, any more than did the citizen of Argos who used to go to the empty theater and imagine he was listening to the best of all possible plays performed by the best of all living actors. The shock treatment may have brought the man back to his senses, but, as he himself said, it also deprived him of his faculty for delight.

Pivoting on this remarkable anecdote, which is somehow both appropriate and humane, Horace turns to the remaining subject of his letter to Florus. What he thinks about most these days, Horace resumes, is not art, but life. It is time, he imagines, to put aside childish things and live as a man, not play as a poet. It is even more appropriate to master the meter and rhythm of the good life than to compose the words best suited to the music of Latin. And the ethical precepts, the kinds of analysis and example which ensue, the point of view which emerges, in the last sixty-nine lines of the poem, constitute to a considerable extent a reprise of the two books of satire. The soliloquizing tone Horace adopts is distinctly

---

So sweetly mawkish, and so smoothly dull;
Heady, not strong; o'erflowing, though not full."

Dunciad, Book III, ll. 169–72

Eighteenth-century writers knew, loved, and used their Horace. After this, Tennyson's version seems rather watered-down:

"Clear and bright it should be ever,
Flowing like a crystal river."

"The Poet's Mind"

allied to that at the end of the fourth satire of Book I, where, we recall, Horace abandoned his defense of literature for a defense of the practical instruction in behavior he had received from his father. There too he took refuge in soliloquy and self-examination, saying to himself at the age of thirty: "I am, therefore I think." Life, he insisted, comes first—then, when I have time, I put something down on paper . . . *ubi quid datur oti / illudo chartis.* Here, some fifteen or more years later, he stands on the original proposition, stands by his views, and commands his consciousness to control the scene of his life. To us, his readers, it is by now a familiar moral landscape, its features having been made recognizable by representation of it throughout his artistic career. Money? Makes you richer, not better. Possessions? No one "owns" the things of this world. Luxury, a fastidious taste? As unstable as fashions, as variable as men. Of two young men, for instance, one would not take all the dates in the palm groves of Herod the Great in exchange for sports and free time; his brother *likes* to work. Each person has his Genius, and no two are the same.

Fortunately, Horace adds, I have enough, and I intend to use it as need requires. Not that the management of money isn't complicated—but the way you spend it and your motives also count for something. It makes a big difference whether you squander your goods or seize on the occasional chance in a holiday spirit, like a schoolboy at spring vacation, and find joy in the brief, fleeting hour:

> distat enim spargas tua prodigus an neque sumptum
> invitus facias neque plura parare labores,
> ac potius, puer ut festis Quinquatribus olim,
> exiguo gratoque fruaris tempore raptim.

Exiguo gratoque fruaris tempore raptim: here is a singularly familiar feature of the Horatian landscape, the *carpe diem,* the *ars fruendi.* Once he had confidently announced his intention to write *ubi quid datur oti.* In the letter to Florus he renounces his claims to literature but remains as firm in his allegiance to life as ever. He is, after all, he goes on to say, still the same passenger, whether the ship is large or small. And he hopes to come in, not first, not last, but simply last of the first and first of the last.

At the end of his career he thinks all the way back to its beginnings and mirrors in the ethical imagery of the letter to Florus elements from the first satire of Book I. The rapid series of "points" with which he quizzes the reader is very much like the debonair determination he showed in the first satire to examine life. Here too Horace, inquiring of his reader's moral health, concludes with some severity that unless Florus or any man cannot come up with some proper answers to the questions posed by his very condition as a moral being, he may deserve to lose his place at the banquet table of life:

> vivere si recte nescis, decede peritis.
> lusisti satis, edisti satis atque bibisti:
> tempus abire tibi est, ne potum largius aequo
> rideat et pulset lasciva decentius aetas.

Youth jostles age into the forcible recognition of certain facts: life may have been the scene of our lost opportunities; it may have been our mission to make life more enjoyable than we did; time may be about to thrust us aside.

Horace is no longer a man of letters. He is a mere advocate of truth. And so he takes a moment at the very end of his epistle to recall the grateful Epicurean image of the banquet, on which his first hexameter poem had ended. The feast is nearly over, and it's time for us older men to leave. The young people are here, and they will carry on better.

I would like in conclusion to make a few general observations on the *Art of Poetry*. Excellent detailed commentaries are available in the various editions of Horace, and the poem is among his best known and most often read; it has been used and judged in one way or another by most critics of literature. It is of course his longest work, but in many ways one of the most succinct, being clear and positive in its wording throughout, and there is little need of long explanation or complicated analysis. The fact that the work has invited so much discussion and has been so widely and consistently used indicates that it rewards serious consideration and is interesting to experience more than once. And for all the attention paid to it, for all the criticism and praise accorded it, the poem has stood up well. Far from being worn out, it is quite as new as it was when writers and critics first began to look on it as a handbook.

As early as Quintilian's time (A.D. 40–118), the poem was known by the conventional title, *Ars poetica*, although it is not a "poetics" or a primer of prosody or a manual of aesthetics. It is a letter, and fits naturally into the context of the great epistles of Book II. And although scholars have not as yet identified the actual members of the far-branching Piso family to whom the letter is addressed, Horace knew who they were and obviously levels his poem at the two young sons of a famous father, who are studying in Athens and thereby encountering the problems of writing in particular and of self-expression in general. He adopts the friendly colloquial tone and writes in the familiar straight-on-ahead style he has mastered by working in the genre of the *sermo*.

Like the *Satires*, the *Art of Poetry* moves on apace with its subjects in easygoing, sometimes rapid, sequence. Like the *Satires*, it teems with examples, that kind of rhetorical proof and evidence Horace steadily incorporated into his ideas: anecdote, analogy, metaphor, historical and literary allusions. The poem also deals with instances of excessive or deficient performance and delineates reductions *ad absurdum* or increases *ad optimum* of those elements which contribute to the formation of good taste and good sense.

Like the *Epistles*, the *Art of Poetry* concentrates on writing. When we recall Horace's decision, repeated with distressing frequency in the letters, to sever connections with the literary muse, it comes as something of a surprise to see how determined a writer he still is in the work traditionally placed at the end of the Horatian canon. Writing must have become like breathing to him—his lungs were still not just good but powerful. More specifically than young Florus, the young Pisos expect to be told how to write and what to look for in composition, and the characteristics of different genres. Horace expects them to be knowledgeable in the whole subject, willing to work at it in the way it demands. Criticism, self-criticism, judgment, desire, familiarity with the tradition and its various standards of excellence, all help supply matter for Horace's letter to the college students. It is significant that in the *Art of Poetry* the doctrine of the mean goes right out the window: men, gods, booksellers, consistently reject any compromise with poetic excellence, any apportioning of efforts or adjustment of aims:

mediocribus esse poetas
non homines, non di, non concessere columnae.

From the lyric and iambic modes much also carries over into Horace's literary manifesto: an animated yet precise form of utterance, a painstaking happiness in words (*curiosa felicitas*). Horace displays an exalted sense of the artist's role in civilized life when he writes of the poet's mission and work. When Orpheus "soothed lions and tigers," Horace says, what is meant is that the poet played a part in making man less savage and brutal. Amphion, "the sound of whose lyre moved stones," was, Horace deduces, a kind of builder and organizer. Early poets exerted a moral influence on their fellow men, and so the art and its artists won reverence and honor:

> sic honor et nomen divinis vatibus atque
> carminibus venit.

In addition to the scrupulous and heartfelt respect for art, the image-making power of the lyric poems is also felt in the letter. Horace's word-painting is versatile and winsome, his figures of speech familiar and strong. Often, in fact, he seems to be drawing a picture of the art of poetry for the two young *aficionados*. The much-labored maxim, *ut pictura poesis*, indicates this double interest in rendering as well as in design. The first lines of the poem reproduce a surrealist canvas whereon the artist *manqué* has turned his fair lady into a mermaid, a feathered Medusa, and a many-limbed futility goddess all at one and the same time. The painter, Horace argues, has gone awry by confusing the parts with the whole, in this case sacrificing feminine propriety to fish scales, feathers, and *collecta membra mundi*. Of course he is free to paint as he pleases, Horace admits; but if what he paints is to please us, a selective principle and canon of propriety must govern the whole result. Let him paint whatever things (and by implication, write whatever things)—the things must still go together, or the *work* will be, if not absolutely meaningless, positively preposterous.

So the poem begins literally in imagery. It ends, too, in caricature, with a figurative sketch of the poet *manqué*, his purpose awry, his art askew. The artist's compulsive claim to poetic license signifies a lack of control like that exploited by the surrealist painter. Empedocles on Etna is "free" to consider himself a god and in consequence leap nonchalantly into the flames. What better proof have we of the volcanic temperament of the artist than this total immersion in the spontaneous overflow of powerful feelings? Horace is surely striking a Cyclopean blow at art-as-neurosis here. The bad artist is the neurotic, Horace concludes—mad as a bear breaking loose from his cage, and as burly, and as relentless in pursuit of the reader. Because he can't write according to intelligible standards, he must compel the reader to listen, and so reads him to death, leeching on, getting under the skin. He may in fact have known rightly how to begin—like Empedocles (or even Homer!), he could plunge *in medias res*—but like the painter, he never found out how to stop. Art must not go on and on; it must go somewhere.

The ways of finding out what the work of art intends to do, where it means to go, constitute the main body of Horace's letter to the Pisos. Imagery again serves him well in this whole context, from the initial mermaid to the flamboyant figures of Empedocles and his brother bear of a bard at the end. A sinuous stream, cypress trees, an overly familiar "purple patch"; a milk-jug, a foaming boar at sea and a dolphin on land; bronze fingernails, bronze tresses—such things lead straight into Horace's doctrine of style, which is

that the whole is not the sum of, or greater than, its parts,
but their realization:

> infelix operis summa quia ponere totum
> nesciet.

Scholars and critics at large have often commented on the
unifying theme of the *Art of Poetry*, which is style rather
than subject matter, and Horace surely develops this theme
with remarkable ingenuity. All along we are being invited to
consider propriety and wholeness and the wedding of the old
to the new. Literature for him is the representation of truth,
not its embellishment, and poetic style is a real and active
energy, harnessed to this purpose. Eloquence and "order,"
for example, are secondary in Horace's consideration, whereas
the choice of a manageable subject is primary; he is convinced
that the means of execution will follow freely provided that
the artist has his whole end in view. *Le style c'est l'homme
même*, a conscious and knowing creature, a doer, not a
decorator:

> sumite materiam vestris, qui scribitis, aequam
> viribus, et versate diu, quid ferre recusent,
> quid valeant umeri, cui lecta potenter erit res,
> nec facundia deseret hunc nec lucidus ordo.
> ordinis haec virtus erit et venus, aut ego fallor,
> ut iam nunc dicat iam nunc debentia dici,
> pleraque differat et praesens in tempus omittat;
> hoc amet, hoc spernat promissi carminis auctor.

And I think most readers will agree that Horace's images
in the *Art of Poetry* manifest the propriety and sensuous
reality of his doctrine. Old words are seen as old leaves shed
by preceding generations, as a new vocabulary comes into
use. Traditions and genres are "well-marked differences and

shades of form and color." When a grandiose poet announces his grandiose intention, his mouth actually gapes open:

"fortunam Priami cantabo et nobile bellum."
quid dignum tanto feret hic promissor hiatu?

Or "the mountains will labor, and laughable mouse will be born"—delicately poised at the end on its own marvelously muscular monosyllable:

parturient montes, nascetur ridiculus mus.

Homer's words, immediately translated by Horace into comprehensive Latin hexameters, show no such ineptness: his plan promises light from smoke, not smoke from flames. Homer saw that, in order to arrive at Helen's Trojan transfiguration, it was not necessary to go all the way back to the twin egg:

nec gemino bellum Troianum orditur ab ovo.

Instead of glorying in eggshellsis, Homer *comes to the point, rushes* his reader away into the middle of things, *discards* what he can't use, *plots* and *contrives,* so that all the elements *join: semper ad eventum festinat et in medias res/. . . auditorem rapit . . . relinquit . . . mentitur . . . remiscet.* Horace's verbs exemplify Homer's style.

Horace's standard descriptions are perfectly serviceable:

scriptor honoratum si forte reponis Achillem,
impiger, iracundus, inexorabilis, acer,
iura neget sibi nata, nihil non arroget armis.
sit Medea ferox invictaque, flebilis Ino,
perfidus Ixion, Io vaga, tristis Orestes.

Or again, in the "ages of man" description of dramatic types which ends with the well-known sketch of the old-timer:

dilator, spe longus, iners, avidusque futuri,
difficilis, querulus, laudator temporis acti
se puero, castigator censorque minorum.

Horace's imagery and his word instinct never functioned better than they do in this "last" poem—which he says is of course a whetstone, not a "kervyng instrument." There are such minute and subtle touches as the line "not every critic discerns unmusical verses" (263), which is tricky to scan: *non quivis videt immodulata poemata iudex.* There are such succinct and telling phrases as *bonus dormitat Homerus,* in which the cadence seems to drop just where Homer nods. There is the fact that the writer is counseled to keep his work for at least nine years, reinforced by the fact that while he still has it he can still correct it, followed by the laconic truth: *nescit vox missa reverti.* There is the good dinner party, with the orchestra playing out of tune. To return for a moment to *ut pictura poesis,* it will be seen that the phrase is not a strict equation[8] but is introduced as a way of dealing with "perspective" and of suggesting the notion of permanent beauty. *Ut pictura poesis:* that is, Horace says, some pictures look better at a distance, others better close up. Some look better in the bright light of day, he continues; others are better when seen darkly. But the point is, he proceeds, that the best work stands up to close and repeated scrutiny, whereas the novel, the interesting flourish, pleased once and once only. The well-executed work that is all of a piece will be a joy forever; criticism, daylight, reviewing, will serve only to enhance it.

Horace's letter is firmly founded on style, at the same time that it is a trustworthy messenger of style. As for its many observations on the drama, these may be explained in several

[8] As it was for Shakespeare in the opening scene of *Timon of Athens.*

ways. In each letter of Book II Horace has showed genuine interest in the subject of dramatic poetry. It is probable that the young Pisos were directly interested in it. It is obvious that Horace appreciates to the full the impact of drama on the human mind and sees dramatic poetry as a major instance of literature at its most moving, vigorous, and appropriate strength, at the height of its power. Horace himself, I think, shared something of the comic spirit with his fellow writers and predecessors in the drama, more than an affinity for epic or tragedy. There are many comic materials in the hexameter poems—scenes, dialogue, remarks, antics—although these poems are of course discourses, not actions. Perhaps he was to some extent compensating for the lack of a directly productive faculty in the dramatic genre when in the verse essays he adopted dramatic examples to represent the principles of his critical doctrine.

For it is doctrine, this poem; it is a teaching and a persuasion. It says that the writer is neither an ancient nor a modern but a contemporary who models his work on the past, produces it in the present, and tries to make it good enough for the future. The writer is neither a wild native genius nor an expert technician: to the question what makes a work of art praiseworthy, nature or art, Horace simply says "Both":

> natura fieret laudabile carmen an arte
> quaesitum est: ego nec studium sine divite vena
> nec rude quid prosit video ingenium; alterius sic
> altera poscit opem res et coniurat amice.

Art, in Horace's eyes, is neither classical nor romantic. Feeling in fact comes first, in art as in life: desire, the will to create, the sensitive soul, impel man to art. It's just not enough, Horace reminds us, for poems to be *beautiful*—they have to be good poems, too! They have to do something to the reader. Responding to a work of art is like looking on the human countenance:

> non satis est pulchra esse poemata: dulcia sunto,
> et quocumque volent animum auditoris agunto.
> ut rídentibus arrident, ita flentibus adsunt
> humani vultus: si vis me flere, dolendum est
> primum ipsi tibi.

Horace was an honest enough romantic. Had he fallen on the thorns of life, he would have bled. But the classical sense of form, the Roman (and Greek) sense of purpose, the intellectual need for distinction, all give shape to the fundamental energy of self-expression and endow it with sensuous reality. Horace is keen on the subject of feeling; the inner changes of fortune that constitute the life of the soul he recognizes as primary. We are happy, depressed, or tortured, he writes, and we feel this first, before we are able to speak. But nature has made the tongue an interpreter of all the perpetual emotion contained in our lives:

> format enim natura prius nos intus ad omnem
> fortunarum habitum; iuvat aut impellit ad iram
> aut ad humum maerore gravi deducit et angit;
> post effert animi motus interprete lingua.

Classical utterance, distinct, appropriate, and formal, can assure the soul of reliable interpretation. In the *Art of Poetry* Horace clearly upholds classical standards as the primary means to a rational and interesting expression of the common life all men inherit and pass on. The romantic energy longs for the kind of expression that the classical discipline of art makes both possible and true.

Again and again, Horace shows that his attitude toward

art is neither radical nor reactionary. It is free and it is sensible because it is governed by an untiring interest in truth. His readers have often found, in one poem or another, or in the consistent development of his artistic genius, the truth, aptly recorded and beautifully designed. And he never abandoned his quest for knowledge. Writing for the benefit of the young Pisos, now studying in Athens, perhaps he is assuring them of what he had begun to learn in the same situation thirty years earlier:

> scribendi recte sapere est et principium et fons:
> rem tibi Socraticae poterunt ostendere chartae,
> verbaque provisam rem non invita sequentur. . . .
>
> respicere exemplar vitae morumque iubebo
> doctum imitatorem et vivas hinc ducere voces. . . .
>
> aut prodesse volunt aut delectare poetae,
> aut simul et iucunda et idonea dicere vitae. . . .
>
> omne tulit punctum qui miscuit utile dulci,
> lectorem delectando pariterque monendo. . . .

This whole passage (ll. 303–44), with its flashing wit, its composure and directness, its exactitude, is well deserving of the repeated hearings it has been given. For it tells us as nothing else can what Horace believes art can be. The art of poetry begins in wisdom and ends in delight. It looks to the example of life and draws forth living speech. It is bound to want either to please or to instruct, or to do both things together. The best will win most approval by making the truth not only known but attractive.

THE EPISTLE TO AUGUSTUS
The literary tradition, and the role of our Roman writers

Cum tot sustineas et tanta negotia solus

Since you alone have shouldered so many tremendous
Burdens of state, protecting our Italian nation
With strong defenses, restoring our high moral standards,
Reforming our laws, I offend against the public interest
If I waste your time with long-drawn-out conversation,
O Caesar Augustus.
　　　　　　　　　Romulus, good father Liber,
And Castor and Pollux, who after heroic feats
Were welcomed in the gods' own dwellings, protected the
　　　earth
And the peoples of earth—ending their violent wars,
Portioning out the land, establishing cities.
They complained, however, of not enjoying the favor
That their merit deserved while they were still living on
　　　earth.
Hercules clubbed the Hydra, crushed famous creatures
In labors he was fated to perform, but found out that envy
Could only be mastered by death. The brilliant performer
Dazzles the eyes of those he rises above
In exerting his powers; when his light goes out, he'll be
　　　loved.
But to honor you with timely regard, we have raised altars

Where oaths may be sworn by your Genius that no one like
    you
Has appeared before or is likely to appear again.
    And yet, these people of yours, discerning and fair
In rating you above all our leaders as well as the Greeks,
Fail to apply the same rule to most other things,
Favoring the old, despising the new, loathing all
That has not completed its time and vanished from earth.
Revering the past, they dote on the famous Twelve Tables,
The thou-shalt-not-sin's which ten men once put in writing;
On antique treaties our kings made on equal terms
With Gabii (on that occasion, you know,
They slew an ox to seal the event: on his hide
They traced in archaic script the terms of alliance)
Or with primitive Sabines; on sacred pontifical books
On yellowed Sibylline leaves; all inspired, they say,
By the muses on the Alban Mount in Very Old Latin.
    There's not much left to discuss, of course, if we hold
That because the best Greek authors are really the oldest
Roman writers can only be weighed on a similar scale.
Olives and nuts are both fruit, and therefore the olive
Has nothing hard inside, the nut nothing hard on the surface.
We've conquered the world and stand at the top of the
    heap,
So we paint, compose, and wrestle, with much more skill
Than the erudite race of well-lubricated Achaeans.
    If poems improve with age, like wine, then I wonder
How the vintage years work. What is the magic number?
A writer who fell a hundred years back comes under
The heading of Perfect Old Master? Or does he come under
The heading of New Stuff—No Good? Suppose we establish
A limit, to forestall dispute. "The old and approved

Has lasted a round hundred years." But what if he's short
A month, or a year? Where to place him? Alongside the
    ancients,
Or among those today and tomorrow regard with contempt?
"Well, a fellow who's short just a month, or as much as a
    year,
Is bound to assume his place with the ancient immortals."
I'll take your concession, and now let's pluck out one hair
From the horse's tail, then another, and then still another,
Or take one grain away from the heap, then another,
And your reasoning by years will collapse, as will your
    judgment
When it's based on dates, when you say that nothing is good
Till the goddess of funeral processions has made it divine.
    Ennius the wise and the brave, whom our critics have
    labeled
"The Other Homer," doesn't seem to care very much
What becomes of his "promise" or the dream Pythagoras
    sent
To inform him that Homer was living again within him:
Isn't Naevius being revived, and I mean REVIVED,
These days? All the rage? So SACRED IS EVERY OLD POEM.
Whenever the question comes up, which one of the two
Is finer, Pacuvius or Accius, the latter goes higher
By being so lofty, the former gets even more praise
For his erudition. Afranius' native *bel canto*
Is as neat as Menander's Greek. Plautus has *pace*,
Like his fast-flowing model, the slapstick Sicilian Epicharmus.
Caecilius? Excels in grandeur. Terence? In wit.
These are the writers great Rome is learning by heart;
These are the things she sees when she squeezes inside
Our packed theaters. And these are the names on her list

From Andronicus' day right down to our own.
   Sometimes the public see straight, sometimes they err.
If they admire and praise the old poets in such a way
As to put them above all else, and beyond compare,
They are wrong. If they find them to some extent
     old-fashioned,
Rather awkward and stiff in wording, and frequently flat,
They are right and support my view, which Jove will approve.
Now note, I'm not saying old Andronicus must go,
That the poems ought to be gutted, those lines I learned
When Orbilius pounded them into my head. I just wonder
When I hear them called flawless, little short of perfect,
     incomparable.
If a marvelous phrase gleams in their midst, for example,
Or a verse or two is turned rather more gracefully,
It carries along and sells the whole thing: that's not fair.
   I resent a work's being blamed, not for its grossness
Or awkward matters of style, but for being new,
When old things deserve not praises and prizes but excuses.
If I express a doubt as to whether old Atta's old play
Still stands up amid the saffron and flowers onstage,
Nearly all the old boys declare that modesty's dead
When I attempt to find some fault with *those* plays, the
     vehicles
For actors like dignified Aesop and talented Roscius.
Nothing is good unless they themselves have liked it;
Or perhaps they think it's a weakness to yield to your
     juniors,
To admit when you're old that what you learned while
     beardless
Was a loss. Whoever can praise the *Salian Motets* of Numa
And alone understand what is just as obscure to him

As it is to me, does not really favor the dead
And hail their genius, so much as flay *us* alive,
And everything we produce. If the Greeks had resisted
New works the way we do, what now would be left
For us to call old? What would the public now have
To thumb through again and again, *"Chaconne à son goût?"*
  When Greece laid down her arms, she started in trifling
And in prosperous times drifted into more decadent things.
An interest in athletes, an interest in horses, flared up;
She loved her sculptors in ivory, marble, and bronze;
Her eyes and her thoughts hung feasting on painted panels;
She reveled in flute music or swooned over tragedy.
Like a child bouncing round in play at the feet of her
        nurse,
What she wanted the most she eventually lost interest in.
You don't think our likes and dislikes DON'T tend to change?
But this was the peace and prosperity offered to Greece.
  At Rome it was long the accepted and enjoyable thing
To be up at dawn and open the door and lay down
The law to your clients, to lend money on good collateral,
To listen to your elders and give your juniors advice
About how to increase their estates or how to restrain
Some ruinous impulse or other. We were Practical People.
But now the lightheaded public have changed their mind.
Everyone's dying to write! The serious father,
The children, wear wreaths to dinner and dictate some lines.
Even I, who swear that I never compose any verses,
Lie worse than a Parthian: I get up at dawn
And call for my paper and pen and cases of books.
A man who can't navigate is afraid to go sailing;
You won't give wormwood infusions to a man who is sick
Unless you are sure you know just what they contain;

Doctors do doctors' work, and carpenters carpenters';
But we all write poems, whether we know how to do it or not.
   And yet this mistake has certain advantages to it;
This mild form of madness is not without method. For
      instance:
The bard is not mad for money; it's verse that he loves
And pursues alone; runaway slaves, or a fire,
A financial loss? He just laughs at them. He's not plotting
To cheat his partner or youthful ward. He subsists
On porridge and second-class bread. He's not a good soldier,
But he serves the state, if you're willing to grant that small
      things
Can contribute to broad objectives. The poet helps mold
The tender and lisping speech of the young, and diverts
The ear even then from coarse conversation; and soon
He can form the heart with his friendly advice, and expunge
Its rawness, its envy, its anger. Reciting great deeds,
He fits out the rising age with noble examples;
He comforts the sick at heart and holds up the helpless.
Where would the choir of innocent boys and young maidens
Learn to sing hymns if the muses hadn't offered a poet?
The chorus make known the gods' very presence, implore
Their help from on high, invoke the blessing of rain.
With the prayer the poet has taught them they make the
      gods smile
And ward off disease and danger and win for us peace
And a year of plentiful harvest. The gods on high
Find songs enchanting, as do the gods below.
   Our old-time farmers lived simple and steadfast lives,
Frugally wealthy. And after the harvest was stored,
They refreshed at holiday time both the body and the soul,
Which bore up under the strain by the hope for its end,

In the company of children, faithful wife, and the friends
Who shared in the work. They appeased the good earth with
      a pig,
Silvanus with milk, and each man's guardian spirit,
Who keeps track of the shortness of life, with flowers and
      wine.
Our licentious Fescennine verse came into being
By this tradition, when earthy invectives poured forth
From one side, then from the other. Delightfully free,
This sport was welcomed each time the season drew round,
Till the jokes became worse, and soon compulsively mean,
And savagely stalked through innocent homes, unpunished.
The slanderous tooth drew blood and the wounded wept;
Even those who escaped sensed its threat to the welfare
      of all.
And a law was proposed, with a penalty for libelous poems.
When the stick was brandished, writers soon changed their
      tune
And turned to more decorous ways of using their words.
    When Greece was captured, she herself made a slave
Of her savage subduer and introduced her fine arts
To the rustics of Rome. Our old Saturnian Meter
Went dry when fastidious minds suppressed so crude
A concoction. But many traces have lingered right on
From our uncouth past. Only quite late did the Roman
Apply his mind to the study of good Greek models.
After the Punic Wars, he had leisure to ask
What Sophocles, Thespis, Aeschylus, might have to offer.
He tried to translate (and transfer right onto his stage)
In a comparable style, and was pleased to find he could do it.
By temperament being a high-minded, vigorous fellow,
He came by the tragic art naturally enough,

Succeeded quite well, except for the fact that he feared
To erase, wrongly considering that a disgrace.
   Comedy is sometimes thought to be easier to write,
Based as it is on ordinary life, which is what
Actually makes it much harder: you can't fool the audience!
Plautus can barely sustain the roles of the young-man-
In-love, the watchful father, the devious pander.
He poses his Burlesque Sweeney among nightingales;
He just slaps the whole thing together without taking pains,
Being anxious to hear the money go clink in the box,
And doesn't care whether the play stands straight on its feet
And succeeds or whether it fails and flops.
                                    A writer
Propelled onstage by a chariot named Gloria (not Pecunia)
Has his wind taken out if the spectators sit on their hands,
But swells way up if they cheer him. It's a many-slandered
      thing,
This grease-paint world that breaks or makes a man happy
On a steady diet of superlatives and diminutives.
If the comic stage sends me back home hollow and thin,
With a *succès d'estime* (the kind of success nobody
Gets steamed up about except you), or sends me back home
Nice and fat, with a hit, I say to it: "Hell and farewell!"
   A confident poet will often be put in a panic
And fright when the cheapseats, so stupid, so stolid, so
      superior
In numbers, inferior in taste and good sense, and quite ready
To fight if the knights demur, call out for a bear
Or a prize fight in the middle of the play. Those roly-prolies!
They came here to SEE something! But so does everyone
      else
Who goes to the *theater* today, including the knights.

Pleasure has switched her allegiance from the ear to the eye.
It gets more and more spectacular: the curtain stays up
Four or five hours, while the troops dash by, the cavalry,
Then the infantry (obscene, these mob scenes). Kings are
    dragged in,
Their hands bound behind them (so high a peripeteia).
Chariots, carts, wagons, and boats go whooshing
Across the stage, closely followed by captured statues,
Ivory or Corinthian bronze. Democritus *laughed?*
Were he still in earth, he'd have enough reason for mirth
Just watching the people gape at their favorite new monster,
A giraffe or a nice white elephant; he'd look at the
    audience,
Rather than the play, as a much more interesting spectacle.
He'd probably think the writers were telling their stories
To a donkey (the latter has pretty big ears, I admit,
But he doesn't use them for listening). What voice could
    conquer
The sounds that rebound from our theater walls? Garganian
Oak trees lashed by the wind, the sea up in arms?
No, there's a new play on, with lots of new gadgets
And imported costumes, dressed to the eyebrows with which
The actor has just made his entrance. Those sound waves
    you hear
Are right hands colliding with left hands, right by your ear.
"Has he said anything?" "Not a word." "What's all the
    noise for?"
"Just look at that robe: it's the new shade, poison-purple-
    pellon."
    But please don't think that I'm unwilling to praise
Well-written plays, even though I don't write them myself.
The dramatist walks on a tightrope, it seems to me,

Making me catch my breath and clutch at my heart
With his words, mere words, making me glad or sad,
Filling me full of false fears, whisking me off
To Thebes or Athens at will: the illusion is magic.
   But, Augustus, you may be willing to turn your attention
To writers who'd rather resign themselves to the hands
Of a reader than risk the scorn of a hardhearted viewer.
You may want to add good books to your gift to Apollo,
And stimulate writers as well, to work all the harder,
And frequent the fair precincts of green Helicon.
   We poets can bring a bad name on ourselves, quite often
(Let me chop down my own cherry tree for a moment), by
      offering
A book when you're worried or weary; when our feelings
      are hurt
If a friend has ventured to challenge one single verse;
When, reading aloud, we go back and read once more
Something we weren't asked to repeat; or when we complain
That our labor's lost sight of—the platinum shred
Of our wit overlooked; when our hope leads us to assume
That the minute you know we're hard at work on a poem
You'll naturally send for us and strictly refuse us to be
In need of a thing, and insist that we keep right on writing.
Still, it's worth your while to take cognizance of those
Who minister unto your merit at home and abroad,
And not to intrust your fame to an unworthy servant.
Old Choerilus (his verse was certainly querulous and
      garrulous)
Must have been a real favorite with Alexander the Great,
To get paid for what he composed—and in solid sovereigns.
But ink will sometimes leave a stain on the fingers,
And poor writers smudge fine deeds with inadequate words.

The same king who paid on the line for a really bad poem
Forbade by law anyone but Apelles to paint him,
Any sculptor except Lysippus to model in bronze
The living likeness of Alexander the Brave.
If you applied this power of subtle judgment in art
To books and the gifts their muses require, you would swear
The man had been born in the dull lowlands of Boeotia.
   Those poets beloved by you, your Varius, your Vergil,
Don't disgrace your judgment of them, or your gifts,
Which reflect great credit on the donor. A likeness in
     bronze
Is no more true an expression of the subject's features
Than a poet's account of the deeds, characters, and minds
Of illustrious men. As for me, I wouldn't prefer
My "little conversations" that creep along close to the
     ground
To epic narrations—of faraway lands and streams,
Of forts flung high in the hills, of barbarous realms,
Of wars over all the world brought to final conclusion
By you, of the gates of Janus at last swinging shut
And keeping the peace, of that Rome the Parthians fear
With you as its prince—if my powers but matched my
     desires.
Your majestic achievement cannot be aptly encompassed
In makeshift song; my modest attainments preclude
Attempting a work that lies outside of my range.
Fools rush in and embarrass a prince with their praise,
Even more so if what they say has meter and form.
We learn more quickly and bring back to mind more readily
The things we laugh at than those we respect and revere.
I don't want myself weighed down by fulsome attentions,
My caricature in wax put up for sale;

I don't want my praises sounded in ill-tempered lines,
Or to turn red myself at receiving the fatuous gift,
And be carried stiff in my coffin alongside my poet
Down Stinky Street, where they sell that too frank incense,
The praise that nauseates me, and where shopkeepers caper,
Selling pepper and spice DONE UP IN OLD SHEETS OF PAPER!

TO JULIUS FLORUS, STILL
CAMPAIGNING WITH TIBERIUS
Literary ambitions, and how to survive them

Flore, bono claroque fidelis amice Neroni

Florus, trustworthy friend to Tiberius the noble
And true, suppose a merchant were trying to sell you
A slave boy born in Tivoli or Gabii,
And described the commodity as follows: "A fine lad he is,
Handsome from head to foot; he's yours, to have
And to hold, for exactly five hundred dollars. At a nod
This houseboy flies right to work. He's well trained,
Knows a little Greek, will do any job you assign him.
The clay is still damp: you can form it just as you wish.
His voice, though untrained, will sweeten your hours of
          drinking.
Too many promises may make the buyer suspicious
When a seller who wants to unload his goods builds them up
Way over their merits. I don't have to sell you this fellow—
I'm not in a jam. I may not be rich, of course,
But I'm not in debt. There's hardly another manmonger
Who'd make you an offer like this; there's hardly another
Buyer I'd make it to. He ducked out of work
One day and hid underneath the stairs, as a kid
Will do who's afraid of the whip that hangs in the hall,
But that's about all. I've told you the worst." Now, if that
Didn't faze you, you'd hand him the cash and call it a deal.

Flore, bono claroque fidelis amice Neroni

I imagine he'd get his price and keep himself clear
Of charges of misrepresenting. You bought his goods,
Including their faults, with your eyes wide open; you heard
The bill of sale read out loud. You're not chasing after
The seller and trying to sue, when you don't stand a chance?
Now, I told you how lazy I was, the day you departed;
I told you how virtually crippled I was for such tasks
As writing dutiful letters, to head off your scolding
And deep-felt disgust when nary a letter from me
Came back in answer to yours. But what was the use,
Even though the law's on my side, if you keep right on firing?
You even complain in addition to this that I lied
When I said I'd send on the poems you're still waiting for.
  One of Lucullus' soldiers had saved up his pay,
And one night, while he was snoozing away dog-tired,
Every last cent was stolen. In his ravening rage
The soldier grew fierce as a wolf, mad at himself
For losing the money and mad at the rascal who stole it.
They say that he knocked out a fortress high in the hills,
A royal stronghold, loaded with money and jewels.
He got some medals for this brave feat, and was decorated
With a cash reward of some eight hundred dollars as well.
It just so happened that about the same time, his colonel
Was itching to take some castle or other by storm
And began to harangue our hero in the sort of language
That would put the heart back in a coward. "On your way,
    man!
Godspeed your flying feet where courage now calls you:
You'll win the fine prize you deserve. Why do you *stand*
    there?"
The soldier, a plain country fellow, but quick as a cat,
Replied, "Ask someone who's just had his money belt stolen:

261

He'll be glad to go on your mission."

                                  I had the good luck
To be educated at Rome, to learn "O Muse,
Of the wrath of Achilles that brought such ruin on the
       Greeks."
Amiable Athens carried me further along,
So that soon I was anxious to draw the lines marking off
The straight from the crooked, to continue my search for
       truth
In the groves of Academe. But hard times forced me
From that pleasant spot, a civil war tide swept me off
Quite unprepared, to confront the superior strength
Of Caesar Augustus. Philippi clipped my wings,
Relieved me of military service and my father's estate,
Displaced me from house and home, and MERCILESS POVERTY
DROVE ME TO POETRY. Now that I'm quite well fixed,
It would take a lot more than a shock infusion of hemlock
To cure me of thinking how much better off I am sleeping
Than writing.

                 Our pleasures steal off, one by one, with the
       years,
Which have already snatched my zest for laughter and love,
For playing and feasting. And now they're trying to twist
The poems loose from my hand. What can I do?
Not all men admire or desire quite the same things:
You find pleasure in lyrics and rejoice in my odes;
Another man likes the bittersweet style of iambics,
The epodes I write; while still another likes SALT,
Still black from the dactylic mines of a Greek
       "conversationalist,"
Like Bion, which I sprinkle around quite a bit in my satires.
To me these requests look a lot like three dinner guests

Who don't agree in their tastes, and keep right on asking
For totally different courses. What shall I serve them?
What shall I not bring in? He orders something:
You send it back. What you want is unappetizing
And tastes, of course, sour to the others.

                            Besides, do you think
I can turn out poems in Rome, what with everything else
I have to worry about and keep up with? I'm wanted at court
To vouch for a friend; another expects me to drop
Whatever I'm doing and come and hear him read
Some new stuff he's written; this man lies sick in bed
At home on the Quirinal Hill; this one is flat
On his back at the other extreme—on the Aventine;
I mean at home on that hill—and both must be seen:
And it's certainly a case of wide open space in between
Those two places! "Oh sure, but the streets are clear—
Didn't I just hear you say it was clear across town from the
      one
To the other? Nothing to bother your thinking en route."
A building contractor bustles along with his mules
And manhandlers; gigantic derricks, lifting and swinging
Blocks of stone or heavy wood beams into place;
Melancholy funeral processions jockeying for position
With great big wooden four-(unoiled)wheeled wagons;
A mad dog races his shadow down one gutter;
A fat, mud-spattered sow rolls down the other.
Trudge forward, poet—think out melodious lines
En route. The chorus of writers, one and entire,
Detests the town and yearns for the sacred grove,
Duly rejoicing, as clients of Bacchus, in sleep
And shadowy peace. Surrounded by noise night and day,
You expect me to sing, to follow the narrow little track

Blazed by the bards? Even a man of some genius,
Who has chosen to live in the quiet surroundings of Athens,
Has given a good seven years of his life to research,
Grown gray over books and ideas, turns out to be
More taciturn than a statue, striking the people
At large as something to laugh at. And what about me,
Making my home here at Rome, in the midst of the strife,
On the stormy waves of big city life? Is it proper
To weave a design of words to awaken the lyre?

    Remember the two famous brothers, both lawyers in Rome,
The one a consulting, the other a trial, attorney?
They weren't just brothers-in-law, they were brothers-in-love,
A Gracchus, as it were, to a Mucius, who never would speak
Of each other except in terms of unqualified praise.
Does any less wild a current dance through our poets
With their very high frequency waves of mutual praise?
I write my odes, a friend of mine his elegies:
"Good gracious!" says Propertius, "how perfectly propitious
That piece of yours is! What a WORK OF ART! How
    auspicious!
ALL Nine must have helped with the carving!" "Oh, it's not
    so deserving
As that last thing of yours, which is *nescio quid maius new,*
Et tout ce qu'il y en a de plus!" Watch us for a moment,
Standing in front of the new library of Apollo
Just built by Augustus and OPEN TO ALL OUR POETS
AT ALL HOURS: notice the pride in our eyes, the MON-
YOU-MENTAL importance we attach to all that we do.
And now, if you're free for another moment or two,
Follow along, tune in on our talk, keep in view
How each one addresses the other, or makes a beret
Of the words that apply to himself he finds fit to say.

Like heroic Samnites, we stand there and slug away
Until evening at last puts an end to the mutual fray.
In *his* judgment *I* go down as a new Alcaeus,
And *my* view of *him?* As one clearly destined to free us
Of Callimachus' being unique. If this is too weak
And he wants something stronger, I argue that now no longer
Will Mimnermus be thought of alone as completely above
All others who take as their subject the pleasures of love
And nurse their "ellergy" for fair Aphrodite's haunts:
I name him Mimnermus, and that seems to be what he wants.

    I have to put up with a lot, so long as I write
To please the NEVER UNRUFFLED RANKS OF THE POETS,
So long as I beg on my knees for public approval.
Now that my studies are over, my sanity restored,
I can safely close my ears when they start to recite.

    Poets who write bad verses are laughed at, but *they*
Like what they write and set themselves up as good models;
If *you* can't find a word to say on the subject,
They can, and do, and are pleased to hear themselves praised.
But the man with the nerve to have written legitimate verse,
Will correctly assume the role of the sensible critic:
He will dare strike out the words, exiling them,
As it were, from the precincts of Vesta, even though they
Still want to hang around home—as soon as he finds
Them lacking in dignity, gravity, good solid sense.
He will bring once again to the light, make known to his
      people
What has long lain hidden in darkness but deserves
      reviewing:
The splendid language and style of oldsters like Cato
Or Cethegus, at present kept out of sight and disfigured
By sheer neglect, or silted over by age.

The true poet makes good use of the new inventions
In language and style—their usefulness brought them to
    birth
And kept them alive, after all. The strong, clear stream of his
    verse
Flows evenly, purely along. He will pour out his wealth
And fertilize the Latian land with his richness of speech.
He will prune back the overthick growth, keep cultivating
The rough spots, applying his instinct for order and neatness,
Uproot the things that lack native strength. He will TWIST
AND TURN AND MANEUVER, but LOOK LIKE HE'S PLAYING,
As a dancer who foots the soft "Afternoon of a Faun"
Can change the beat and clomp on the boards like a Cyclops.
    I suppose that as long as my poor little things pleased
    others,
Or at least fooled me, I'd prefer to be thought of as offbeat,
With an obvious case of write's disease—the trembling,
Misguided fingers, the mind as white as a sheet—
And not be wise to myself and curl back my lips
And snarl at the world from the doghouse of my discontent.
A legendary citizen of Argos—you know the story—
Sat happily alone applauding, though the playhouse was
    empty,
Convinced he was hearing a first-rate tragic performance.
A model of sense and deportment in all other things,
Exemplary neighbor, congenial host, attentive
To his wife, perfectly capable of pardoning his slaves,
Of not flying into a rage if the seal on a wine jar
Was broken, of not walking over a cliff or stepping
Off into an open well. Thanks to the effort
And interest of relatives, he finally found himself cured.
But as soon as the bilious disease was sent on its way

Flore, bono claroque fidelis amice Neroni

By a full-strength infusion of glucose, and he came to himself,
"Holy smoke, my friends!" he exclaimed, "you haven't _cured_
    me,
You've _killed_ me, robbing my mind of its principal pleasure,
Denying the illusion that was its most valuable treasure!"
    Of course, the best use to make of your life is to GROW UP
IN WISDOM, when it's time, to put aside childish toys,
To think as a man and leave the games to the boys,
Not searching for words that blend with the Latin Lyre,
But learning the rhythms of life you need to acquire,
The meter, the pulse, of that music. And so I fall silent,
Inwardly speaking the words that wisely inspire:

> You'd go tell the doctor if you kept craving something
>   to drink
> And no amount of water could slake your thirst. Won't
>   you think
> Of confessing the truth to a soul, when the more you
>   acquire,
> The more increasing seems to be your desire?
> If your wound wouldn't heal when the herb the doctor
>   prescribed
> Didn't work, would you trust the powers the doctor
>   ascribed
> To a treatment like this, which they clearly do not
>   deserve?
> Had you heard that those whom the gods most want to
>   preserve
> They first make rich? Being richer, but not at all wiser,
> Would you still make use of the words of the same
>   adviser?

If wealth had the power to make you wise, or less fearful
Or greedy, then surely you'd blush if a single man lived
Who was more avaricious. But look at the practical side
Of the question before us: what *constitutes* possession?
You *own* what you bought with the brass piece you clinked
    on the scale
(To cymbalize the sale) and, in legal terms, are now free
Or "Mancipated" to USE it. But possession itself
Is nearly ten-tenths of the law. The land, for instance,
Which supports you, is actually yours to have and to hold;
Orbius' steward, who reaps the crops that are destined
To furnish you grain, feels the weight of *your* ownership,
And this is "Usucaption," not "Mancipation."
The point is: you pay out money and get back some grapes,
Poultry, eggs, a good cask of mead; and so, LITTLE
BY LITTLE, please notice, in this way you're buying the farm
Someone has already paid fifteen thousand dollars,
Or perhaps even more, to POSSESS. You put up the cash
Or pay on the instalment plan for whatever you USE.
The man who has bought a farm in Aricia or Veii
To raise his home-grown supplies, dines on boughten goods,
Whether he thinks so or not; he bought the logs that heat
The kettle that boils his water in the chill of the evening.
He calls all that land his own, right up to those poplars
Planted along the boundary line to end all dispute
As to where his property begins; as though *anything*
Were our *own* which can change its owners and transfer its
    rights
To some other hands, in a moment of time, by petition,
By purchase, by confiscation; at last, by death.
Since "perpetual use" is actually granted to none,
And one heir comes swiftly along in the wake of another,

Flore, bono claroque fidelis amice Neroni

As a wave washes over another, what is the good
Of estates or granaries? Why merge Lucanian uplands
With Calabrian uplands, when Death, who cannot be bribed,
Will reap all the profits and people both large and small?
    Jewels, ivory, marble, old Etruscan bronzes,
Paintings, the family silver, an expensive wardrobe
Dyed African purple: there are some who don't have these
      things,
And others who don't even want them! Of any two brothers,
One will prefer to the wealth Herod's palm groves convey
Loafing and playing and oiling his body all day.
The other—hard-working, wealthy—from dawn to night
Is clearing his woods with fire and axe, all his might.
And why this happens only that Genius can know
Who guides our star at birth, our Comrade in Life,
The mortal god of our human nature, whose aspect
Changes for each single person, who is both good and bad.
I intend to use what I need of the small pile I have,
And not worry over my heir's opinion of me
When he finds no more than what I myself have been given.
And yet I would like to know just how to distinguish
The frankly generous soul from the spendthrift, the frugal
From the miser. It makes some difference whether you throw
Your money away or whether (while neither refusing
To spend on occasion nor simply slaving away
To make even more) you enjoy the pleasurable hour,
Though fleeting and brief, like a schoolboy at spring holiday.
    So long as sordid need keeps clear of my cabin,
Whether the ship that has me aboard is large or small,
I'll still be the same. I am not always borne along
Under full sail, with the north wind smack behind me,
Nor yet is my life a constant veering and tacking

269

In the teeth of the hostile south. In this "human race,"
Where position and wealth and physical strength and good
     looks
And talent and mental accomplishments all have their place,
I come in last of the first and first of the last.
    And you're no miser? Good show! The rest of your faults
Have gone off with what one? You're devoid of empty
     ambition?
You're minus all fear and fury at the prospect of death?
You just laugh at dreams, at magical horrors, at "wonders,"
At night-flying spooks; you think of Thessalian "portents"
And of fortunetellers as fraught with poetic fallacies?
Well, how are you on your birthdays? Grateful or hateful?
Do you always forgive your friends? And improve with the
     years,
A better and gentler person as old age comes on?
Is it quite to the purpose to pluck out the single thorn
Where so many flourish? Does it really lighten the load?

    If you don't know how to live, get off the road:
    Make way for the people who do. You've had your fling.
    You've had dinner, and drinks; it's time to GET GOING.
    If you stay on and drink any more, the young people left
    Will mock you and rock you: as partygoers they're more
     deft.

THE ART OF POETRY

Humano capiti cervicem pictor equinam

Suppose you'd been asked to come for a private view
Of a painting wherein the artist had chosen to join
To a human head the neck of a horse, and gone on
To collect some odds and ends of arms and legs
And plaster the surface with feathers of differing colors,
So that what began as a lovely woman at the top
Tapered off into a slimy, discolored fish—
Could you keep from laughing, my friends? Believe me, dear
    Pisos,
Paintings like these look a lot like the book of a writer
Whose weird conceptions are just like a sick man's dreams,
So that neither the head nor the foot can be made to apply
To a single uniform shape. "But painters and poets
Have always been equally free to try anything."
We writers know that, and insist that such license be ours,
And in turn extend it to others—but not to the extent
Of mating the mild with the wild, so that snakes are paired
With birds, and tigers with lambs.
                To works that begin
On a stately note and promise more grandeur to come
A couple of colorful patches are artfully stitched
To shimmer and shine, some sequins like these, for instance,
When the altar or grove of Diana, or perhaps it's a rainbow,
Or the Rhine is being described: "The sinuous stream

271

Rustles daintily, tastefully, on midst the sylvan scene."
But you put it in just the wrong place! You draw cypress
    trees
Particularly well? But you're paid to hit off the likeness
Of the desperate sailor swimming away from his shipwreck!
This thing began as a wine jar: how come it comes
Off the wheel at last as a milk jug? Make what you want,
So long as it's one and the same, complete and entire.
    O father, and sons who deserve a father like yours,
We poets are too often tricked into trying to achieve
A particular kind of perfection: I studiously try
To be brief, and become obscure; I try to be smooth,
And my vigor and force disappear; another assures us
Of something big which turns out to be merely pompous.
Another one crawls on the ground because he's too safe,
Too much afraid of the storm. The poet who strives
To vary his single subject in wonderful ways
Paints dolphins in woods and foaming boars on the waves.
Avoiding mistakes, if awkwardly done, leads to error.
Nearby the gladiators' school there's a craftsman who molds
In bronze with special skill the lifelike shapes
Of fingernails and straying strands of hair,
But the whole result of his work is much less happy:
He can't represent the figure complete and entire.
If I were to try to cast a good piece of writing,
I'd no more prefer to be like this fellow than live
With my nose at an angle, no matter how much admired
I was for my coal-black hair and coal-black eyes.
    Take up a subject equal to your strength, O writers,
And mull over well what loads your shoulders will bear,
And what they will not. The man who chooses a subject
He can really manage won't be at a loss for the words

Or the logical order they go in. As for order itself,
Its power and charm consist, if I'm not mistaken,
In saying just then what ought to be said at that point,
Putting some things off, leaving others out, for the present:
The author of the promised work must choose and discard.
   In weaving your words, make use of care and good taste:
You've done it right, if a clever connection of phrases
Makes a good old word look new. If you have to display
Some recondite matter in brand-new terms, you can forge
Words never heard in the pre-tunic days of Cethegus;
License is given, on condition that you use it with care.
New-fashioned words, just coined, will soon gain currency,
If derived from a Grecian source, *and* in small amounts.
Will the Roman refuse the license to Vergil and Varius
And grant it to Plautus and Caecilius? And why should I
Be refused the right to put in my bit, if I can,
When the language of Ennius and Cato enriched the speech
Of our native land and produced some new terms for things?
It has always been granted, and always will be, to produce
Words stamped with the date of the present. As trees change
     their leaves
When each year comes to its end, and the first fall first,
So the oldest words die first and the newborn thrive
In the manner of youth, and enjoy life. All that we are
And have is in debt to death, as are all our projects:
The Portus Julius where Neptune is at home on the land
And protects our ships from his storms—a princely
     achievement;
The Pontine marshes, inhabitable only for boats
And plagues in the past, but now a food-bearing land
That feels the weight of the plow and feeds nearby towns;
The straightening-out of the Tiber that used to wreak havoc

On fields of grain but has now learned to mend its ways—
All these projects, whatever men make, will perish,
And the fame and dignity of speech are equally mortal.
Much that has once dropped out will be born again,
And much of our language now held in high repute
Will fall to the ground if UTILITY so decrees,
With which rests the final decision, the ultimate standard,
The legal existence, of speech.
                      Homer has showed us
The meter to use to describe sad wars and great deeds
Of kings and princes. The uneven couplet that joined
One verse to another was first adapted to grief,
But elegy easily turned into epigrammatic
Couplets expressive of thanks for prayers answered.
Who wrote these first little couplets? The critics are STILL
Disputing the subject; the case is still on the books.
Fury equipped Archilochus with his iambics:
The foot slipped into the comic sock as neatly
As into the tragic boot, so dramatists used it
To make their dialogue heard, even over the noise
The audience was making—the rhythm of purposeful action.
The muse intrusted to lyric verse the accounts
Of gods and the children of gods, of a winning boxer,
Of a prize-winning race horse, the laments of young lads in
      love,
The intoxicating freedom of wine. If I can't observe
These distinctions of form and tone, do I really deserve
To be hailed as a poet? Why, from a false sense of shame,
Do I prefer being ignorant to learning? A good comic
      sequence
Just won't submit to treatment in the meters of tragedy.
Likewise, Thyestes' feast resents being told

In strains more nearly like those that comedy needs
In the vein of everyday life. Let each of the styles
Be assigned to the places most proper for it to maintain.
Of course, now and then even comedy raises her voice:
Angry old Chremes swells up like a supersorehead;
And the Tragedy of Telephus, the Plight of Peleus, stoop
To the muse of prose for words of grief when, poor
Or exiled, either hero discards the bombast
That jars on our ears and his wordsafootandahalflong,
To let his lament wing its way to the hearer's heart.
   It isn't enough for poems to be things of beauty:
Let them STUN the hearer and lead his heart where they will.
A man's face is wreathed in smiles when he sees someone
     smile;
It twists when he sees someone cry; if you expect *me*
To burst into tears, you have to feel sorrow yourself.
Then your woes will fasten on me, O Telephus, Peleus;
If you speak incongruous lines, I'll snooze or I'll giggle.
Touching words most become the sorrowful countenance,
Blistering threats the enraged, playful remarks
The cheerful, suitably dignified speech the severe.
For nature first forms us, deep in our hearts, to respond
To the changing guise of our fortunes; she makes us take
     heart
Or drives us wild or bends us down to the ground
And lets us writhe over inconsolable grief;
Then she brings these emotions out by using the tongue
To interpret them. If a speaker's words don't accord
With his fortunes, the Roman knights and those wretched
     wights
Who bought only standing room will both rock the house

With uproarious laughter. It will make a great deal of
    difference
Who's speaking: a god or a hero, a wise old man,
Or a fervent fellow in the flower of youth, or a matron,
A *powerful* matron, a busy old nurse, or a merchant,
A wandering merchant, or a man who farms the green field,
Or the Colchian or Assyrian type, or a man bred at Thebes,
A man bred at Argos.
                You should either stick to tradition
Or invent a consistent plot. If you bring back Achilles,
Have him say how laws don't apply to him, have prowess
Prevail over status, make him ruthless, impatient and fierce,
And ANGRY! Let Medea be wild, inconquerably so,
Ino tearful, Io "lost"; let Ixion
Go back on his word; let Orestes be sadly depressed.
If it's something as yet untried you put on the stage
And you dare construct a new character, you must keep
To the end the same sort of person you started out with,
And make your portrayal consistent.
                     It's hard to write
Of familiar concerns in a new and original way.
You're better off telling the story of Troy in five acts
Than being the first to foist something new and untried
On the world. In the public domain you'll have private rights
If you keep from loitering around the most common places
And from dawdling on the easiest path, and take pains to
    refrain
From translating faithfully word for word, and don't leap
Right down the close-scooped well of the source you draw on,
Precluded by shame or the laws of your task from lifting
Your foot up over the edge. And don't begin
As the Cyclic poet once did: "And now I shall sing

Of the fortune of Priam and famous war of that king."
What could issue from the mouth that made such an
    opening?
Mountains will labor, a funny little mouse will be born.
To take on less is a much more sensible labor:

"Tell me, O Muse, of the man who, after Troy fell,
    Came to know well all manner of cities and men."

This writer plans to send up not smoke from the flames
But light from the smoke, to deliver some marvelous events:
Antiphates' giants, Scylla, Charybdis, the Cyclops.
Diomedes' return is not traced back to begin
With Meleager's death. The Trojan War doesn't start
With the egg of the twins. He is eager to get to the point
And hurries the reader along to the middle of things,
As if they were already known, and simply leaves out
Whatever he thinks he can't bring off shining and clear,
And devises so well, intermingling the true and the false,
That the middle part fits with the first, the last with the
    middle.
    Now hear what I and the rest of your listeners expect
If you want them to sit there and wait till the curtain comes
    down
And the cantor intones *"vos plaudite . . .* now is the time."
Make careful note of the way each age group behaves,
And apply the right tone to their changeable natures and
    years.
The child who by now knows how to reel off his words,
And plant his feet squarely beneath him, likes most of all
To play with his friends; he flies into rage like a flash
And forgets it equally fast, and changes every hour.
The beardless youth, finally free of his guardian,

Rejoices in horses and hounds and the sun-drenched grass
Of the Campus Martius: he is putty in your hands to mold
To evil courses, resentful of warning advisers;
Slow to provide for his needs but recklessly fast
To spend his money, enthusiastic, intense,
But quick to transfer his affections. As his interests change,
The man is seen in the manly style of his life:
He looks for wealth and for friends, is a slave to success,
Is wary of making a move he will soon be concerned
To undo. A great many troubles harass the old man,
Either because he keeps on trying for gain
And yet won't touch what he has, worried and afraid
To use it, or perhaps because in all that he does
He's slow and phlegmatic, and keeps postponing his
      pleasures,
Conscious of the rainy days he should be prepared for,
"Difficult," always complaining, ready to praise
The good old days when he was a boy and reprove
And disapprove of the young. As the years come along,
They bring along much that is fine; as they disappear,
They take many fine things away. In portraying our roles,
We will dwell on the matters best suited and best attached
To the age in question, and not let the old men's parts
Be assigned to a youth or the manly parts to a boy.

    The events are either enacted on stage or described
As having occurred. But things intrusted to the ear
Impress our minds less vividly than what is exposed
To our trustworthy eyes so that a viewer informs himself
Of precisely what happened. Still, you are not to show
On stage what ought to take place backstage: remove
From our eyes the substance of things an eloquent messenger
Will soon be ready to state in person. Medea

Must not butcher her boys in front of the people;
Unspeakable Atreus should not cook up human flesh
Before our eyes, nor should Procne change into a bird,
Or Cadmus into a snake. Whatsoever such stuff
You *show* me, I won't believe it, I'll simply detest it.

    The play that expects to be asked for another performance
Once it's been given, should be just five acts long,
No more, no less. A god must not intervene
Unless the action tangles itself in such knots
That only a divine deliverer can work the denouement;
A fourth actor should not try to come forward to speak.

    The chorus should be handled as one of the actors and play
An important part, singing between episodes
What advances the plot and fits in well with the action.
Let it favor the good and offer them friendly advice,
Control the wrathful and develop a fondness for soothing
With quiet words the fearful in heart. Let it praise plain
      living,
The blessings of justice, the laws, and the doors left open
By Peace. Let the chorus respect the secrets it's told.
Let it pray to the gods, devoutly imploring that fortune
Return to the unhappy low and depart from the proud.

    The present-day brass-bound flute produces a tone
That rivals the trumpet's, unlike the primitive pipe,
With its thin, clear tone and one or two stops, warbling
      woodnotes
To give the chorus the pitch, and provide an
      accompaniment—
A sound that could nevertheless carry in the uncrowded halls
When virtuous, decent, well-behaved folk came together.
But after a victorious people began to acquire
More land, and surround their cities with larger walls,

And drink to the Genius in broad daylight without shame,
More license entered the rhythms and modes of the music.
How could these rough country types be expected to judge,
Just off from work, mixed in with the city crowd,
The uncouth sitting next to the wealthy? And so the flute
    player
Added movement and gesture to the primitive style
And fluttered his robe as he strutted around the stage.
New notes increased the restricted range of the lyre,
And unrestrained wit produced a new form of eloquence,
So that even the thought, which had been such a fine
    detective
Of useful clues and prophet of future events,
Now resembled the unclear, ambiguous dictates of Delphi.
    The writer who vied for the paltry prize of a goat
With tragic song, soon bared shaggy satyrs to view
On the stage, coarsely probing for laughs without losing
    dignity—
Some pleasant device and novel attraction like this
Being all that could make the spectator stay on and watch
After having fulfilled the ritual rites of the occasion,
And drunk a good bit, and been freed from the normal
    restraints.
But those laughing, bantering satyrs will have to be told
To transform the mood from the grave to the gay with
    some care
And not let a god or a hero, previously seen
Coming out from his palace clad in royal crimson and gold,
Move into a dingy shack and a low way of talking
Or, avoiding the depths, climb too fantastically high.
For tragedy, not condescending to mouth low lines,
Joins the satyrs but briefly, and not without some hesitation,

Like a matron commanded to dance on a festive occasion.
I assure you, good Pisos, if I write a satyr play,
I will not use only commonplace nouns and verbs
Or "plain words," nor try to depart from the tragic tone
To the point where it makes no difference whether Davus is
     speaking
With maudlin Pythias (who's just swiped some dough from
     old Simo)
Or Silenus, tutor and guide to his heavenly ward.
I shall set my sights on familiar things: anyone
Will think he can do as well but will soon find he can't
When he tries it and sweats and strains to bring it off.
The order and inner coherence and careful connection
Are what make your writing take hold: your major success
Consists in mastering the language that is common to all.
I incline to believe that when fauns trot in from the woods,
They ought not to act as if they were reared in the gutter
And virtually lived in the Forum, with citified ways
And prettified lays like those of young-bloods-about-town,
Or resort to indecent remarks and crack dirty jokes.
The better-class patrons may take offense (the freeborn,
The knights, the wealthy) and refuse to award the crown,
As it were, unwilling to see in a favorable light
What the roast-beans-and-chestnuts crowd find so
     entertaining.
    A short syllable followed by a long is of course an iambus.
It moves along fast, so a verse consisting of six
Full-fledged iambic stresses has come to be known
As iambic trimeter. But recently, to come to our ears
More slowly and solemnly, father Iambus adopted
A firm-footed son, the spondee. Affable and kind
Though he was, the iambus did not admit the young man

On equal terms into this partnership, but reserved
The second and fourth foot all for himself. This iambus
Appears but rarely in the "fine old" trimeters of Accius,
And the spondaic stress in the lines which Ennius heavily
Launched on the stage is a sign of hasty production
Or a fault to be chalked up to careless ignorance of style.
Not every critic can spot the lines that don't quite scan
    right,
And Roman poets have been granted too much indulgence.
Shall I therefore run wild and write without any
    restrictions
Or consider that everyone is bound to see my mistakes
And cautiously keep well within the bounds of indulgence?
I may have avoided the fault without rating praise.
Thumb through your Greek examples by day and by night!
Your ancestors praised both the wit and rhythms of
    Plautus?
For admiring both of these things they were *too* tolerant,
Not to say dense, if you and I can distinguish
A crudeness in phrasing from lapidary strength of wit,
And catch the legitimate beat with our fingers and ears.
    Thespis is said to have discovered the unknown style
Of the tragic muse, and to have carted his plays about,
With actors singing the lines and performing the parts,
Their faces smeared with a paste concocted from wine lees—
So they trudged around in road shows, reveling in tragedy.
Aeschylus thought up the masks and distinctive costumes;
He built the first stage on a platform of several small
    boards
And taught his actors a lofty manner of speech
And a stately, high-booted stride. These tragic arts
Were succeeded by Old Comedy, whose many good points

Humano capiti cervicem pictor equinam

Should be noted. From freedom that form declined into
    license
And fell upon violent ways that required regulation.
The law was obeyed and the chorus then lapsed into silence,
Deprived of its right to insult and abuse its victims.
  Our Roman poets have left no style untried
And have not been the least deserving when they have dared
To desert the traces of Greece and dwell on affairs
Originating here among us, on our native designs,
Whether tragic or comic. Latium would be as triumphant
In language as in character and military might
If a single one of her poets could endure the effort
And time-consuming, slow discipline of the file.
Oh, descendants of Numa, turn your backs on the poem
Which many a day and many a diligent erasure
Have not corrected, which a sensitive, newly-pared nail
Has not run over and checked, at the least, ten times.
  Because Democritus held that *genius was all*
And the miserable practice of art far inferior to it,
And denied that sensible poets rated a place
On Helicon's heights, most poets neglect their appearance—
They won't cut their nails or their beards, they won't take a
    bath,
They wander off somewhere alone. For surely the name
And the fame of the poet will attach itself to that dome
Which has never intrusted itself to the shears of Licinus,
Which trips for treatment to three times as many
    psychiatrists
As even Switzerland harbors have failed to set straight.
What a fool am I to purge myself of my bile
Seasonably, every spring! If I'd only refrained,
I'd be unsurpassed as a poet. But perhaps it's not worth it

To lose your head and then write verses instead,
So I'll play the whetstone's part, giving edge to the steel,
Without being able to cut. And though I write nothing,
I'll point out the writer's mission and function and show
Him where his best material lies and what
Nurtures and shapes the poet, what best accords
With his role, what worst, where the right path goes, and
    the wrong.
    The principal source of all good writing is wisdom.
The Socratic pages will offer you ample material,
And with the matter in hand, the words will be quick to
    follow.
A man who has learned what is owing to country and friends,
The love that is due a parent, a brother, a guest,
What the role of a judge or senator chiefly requires,
What part is played by the general sent off to war,
Will surely know how to write the appropriate lines
For each of his players. I will bid the intelligent student
Of the imitative art to look to the model of life
And see how men act, to bring his speeches alive.
At times a play of no particular merit,
Artistically lacking in strength and smoothness of finish
But with vivid examples of character drawn true to life,
Will please the audience and hold their attention better
Than tuneful trifles and verses empty of thought.
    To the Greeks the muse gave genius, the Greeks she
        endowed
With eloquent speech and greed for nothing but praise.
Our Roman lads learn arithmetic and divide
The unit into its hundreds. "The Son of Albinus—
You here today? All right, your turn to recite!
Subtract a twelfth from five-twelfths, and what have you left?

Come on, Albinus Minus—don't think so hard!"
"One-third, Sir." "Fine! You'll keep track of your money,
    you will.
Now take that original sum and add on a twelfth.
How much?" "One-half." When once the corrosive concern
For petty cash has tainted our minds, can we hope to write
    poems
To be oiled with cedar and kept in smooth cypress cases?
   Poets would either delight or enlighten the reader,
Or say what is both amusing and really worth using.
But when you instruct, be brief, so the mind can clearly
Perceive and firmly retain. When the mind is full,
Everything else that you say just trickles away.
Fictions that border on truth will generate pleasure,
So your play is not to expect automatic assent
To whatever comes into its head, nor to draw forth a child
Still alive from Lamia's stomach after she's dined.
Our elders will chase off the stage what is merely delightful;
Our young bloods will pass up the works that merely make
    sense.
He wins every vote who combines the sweet and the useful,
Charming the reader and warning him equally well.
This book will bring in money for Sosius and Son,
Booksellers, travel across the sea, and extend
Its author's fame a long distance into the future.
   There still may be some oversights, and we may be willing
To overlook them, for the string won't always play back
What the hand had in mind: quite often you ask for a flat
And get back a sharp. You brandish your bow at the target,
But the arrow won't always fly home. If happy effects
Figure more, I won't take offense at the few bad spots
Which either carelessness let slip onto the page

Or human nature took too little pains to avert.
And what's the truth here? If a slave who copies out books
Keeps making the same mistake no matter how often
He's warned, he can't be excused; if a harpist keeps striking
The same wrong note, he'll be laughed at. I would reserve
The role of Choerilus for poets who strike something *good*
Two or three times in the course of a largely flawed work,
Which makes me laugh as a matter of sheer amazement.
Good Homer sometimes nods, which gives me a jerk—
But sleep may well worm its way into any long work!

A poem is much like a painting: one will please more
If you see it close up, another if seen from a distance;
One prefers being viewed in the shade, while the other
Prefers being seen in broad daylight and doesn't shrink back
From the piercing glance of the critic. One pleased once;
The other will always please, though it's called for ten times.

Let me say to the older of you two boys, and remind
You to take it to heart, no matter how wise you may be
And well directed to the right by your father's voice:
The doctrine of the mean does not correctly apply
To all things, but rather to a few quite definite matters.
The average lawyer, consultant or trial attorney,
May lack Messalla's delivery, may not know as much
As Aulus Cascellius, and still be of no little worth.
But men and gods and booksellers WON'T PUT UP
WITH SECOND-RATE POETS. If the orchestra playing at dinner
Is all out of tune, if the ointment offered each guest
Is lumpy, if sour Sardinian honey is served
With the poppy seeds, the party is spoiled all the more;
It could have gone on perfectly, simply without them.
So a poem, designed and destined to afford the soul
Genuine pleasure, if it falls somewhat short of the top,

Sinks right down to the bottom. If a man can't play,
He avoids the weapons drill going on in the Campus.
And if he can't handle the ball or discus or hoop,
He stands off, lest he provoke the justified laughter
Of spectators crowded around and forming the circle.
But someone who doesn't know how dares fashion verses.
Why not? He's free, freeborn, in fact, and his income
Is rated at a knightly sum, has a fine reputation.
    But you, my dear fellow, will refrain from speaking or
        acting
Without Minerva's consent? That shows good judgment
And a sound attitude. If you ever do write something,
        though,
Be sure to expose it to such ears as Tarpa the Censor's,
And your father's, and mine. Then put the parchment away
For a good nine years! What you haven't yet published
You can always destroy, but once a word is let go,
It can't be called back.
                   When primitive men roamed the forests,
Orpheus, the sacred interpreter of heavenly will,
Turned them away from killing and living like beasts
And hence is said to have tamed wild lions and tigers.
Amphion is said, as founder of the city of Thebes,
To have moved the stones and led them wherever he wished
By the sound of his lyre and the winning appeal of his voice.
This was the wisdom of former times: to distinguish
Public from private concerns and sacred from common,
To forbid impromptu liaisons and makes rules for marriage,
To build towns and carve out the laws on pillars of wood.
The poets who taught by expressing these things were
        acclaimed:
They and their works were considered divine. After them,

Tyrtaeus and Homer won wide renown by sharpening
Masculine minds to a warlike pitch with their poems.
Oracles were uttered in song, and a way of life
Pointed out, along gnomic lines. The favor of kings
Was courted in verse, and festival joy was found
As the suitable end to periods of long, hard work—
Lest you make excuses for Apollo, the god of song,
Or the muse so skilled with the lyre.

                       The question is raised
Whether nature or art makes a poem deserving of praise.
I fail to see what good either learning can be
Which is not veined with natural wealth or primitive genius.
Each needs the other's help and friendly alliance.
The racer who wants to win has learned, as a boy,
To strain and train, shiver and sweat, stay away
From women and wine. The flute player who gets to play
At the Pythian games has long since studied and shuddered
In the presence of his teacher. Today, it's enough just to
    say:
"I PEN these marvelous POEMS—I'm a Creative Person.
The last one's a dirty shirt. I won't get left back,
Admitting I just don't know what I've never yet learned."
    Like the auctioneer who collects a crowd for a sale,
The poet with property or money put out in loans
Is ordering flatterers to make a profit from him.
But when he can serve a nice little dinner for friends,
Or put up the bail for a poor man who's not a good risk,
Or rescue one held in the gloomy grip of the law,
I'll marvel if the lucky man can always distin-
Guish the false friend from the true.

                      And if you have given,
Or intend to give, a present to someone, don't take him

To hear, still glowing with joy, some verses you've written.
He'll shout out "Fine! Oh, *excellent!* How superb!"
Go pale at the sombre parts, even squeeze out a drop
Of dew from his friendly eyes, and pound on the ground
With his foot to keep time, and dance a bit for sheer joy.
Just as hired mourners often behave much better at funerals
Than those sincerely bereaved, so the man who pretends
Makes more perpetual emotion than your honest admirer.
Kings are said to ply with drink after drink
And put through the ordeal by wine the man they would test
As worthy of the royal friendship. And if you would write,
Don't ever forget: there's a motive concealed in the fox.

    If you read something out to Quintilius, he'd usually say,
"You could straighten out *this*, or *that*." And if, after trying
Two or three times with no luck, you'd said you could *not*
Improve on the passage, he'd tell you to strike it right out
And hand back to the anvil those verses that came out so
        bent,
To be hammered into shape once again. Then, if you
        preferred
Standing by your mistake to changing it, he'd waste not a
        word
Or an ounce of energy more, and not interfere
With your loving, alone and unrivaled, yourself and your
        work.
The fair-minded, thoughtful man will reproach the verses
That come out spineless and flat, find fault with the clumsy
And rhythmically harsh; with a straight black stroke of
        the pen
He will line out disorganized parts; your elegant effects
He will simply cut out; he will force you to let in more light
On the dark passages, point out ambiguous phrasing,

And note what ought to be changed, a real Richard Bentley,
Who won't stop to say, "But why should I harass a friend
With these minor repairs?" These minor repairs will create
A major disaster, once that friend is exposed
To a hostile reception and unfriendly jeers in public.
   The mad poet only makes sensible people avoid him
And fear to touch him, as if he were plagued by the itch
Or the royal disease of jaundice (yellow as gold
And worth a king's ransom to cure) or St. Vitus' dance
Or lunatic frenzy. Kids chase after and taunt him.
With his head held high, he strolls off belching his lines,
And then if he falls down a well or into a pit—
Like a fowler whose eyes are steadily trained on the merles—
He may yell long and loud for help: "To the rescue! This
     way,
Fellow citizens!" None will care to come pull him out.
And if someone *should have* the urge to lend him a hand
And let down a rope, I will say, "But how do you *know*
He hasn't intentionally thrown himself in and *doesn't*
Want to be saved?" and then I will tell of the death
Of the Sicilian poet. Because Empedocles wished
To be thought an immortal god, he leaped into Etna,
This cool customer, to his fiery fate. We are left
To conclude that poetic justice or poetic license
Includes suicide. To save some person from death
Against his will is just as wrong as to kill him.
This isn't the first time it's happened, and if he's pulled out,
He will not necessarily be made over into a man
And put aside his desire for a memorable end.
   It's not quite clear what drove him to write, in the
     first place—
Did he sprinkle his well-wrought urine on ancestral ashes?

Or blasphemously joggle the ground at some sacred spot?
At any rate, he's got it bad; and, bold as a bear,
If he's strong enough to have smashed in the fretwork of bars
That kept him confined to his cage, he's on a rampage,
Stampeding unlearned and learned alike, in his rage
To recite. Once he's caught you, he'll hang on with all his
      might;
The leech just clings to your skin and never gives in
Until bloated with blood; *he'll* never run out of breath
But will read you and read you and read you and read you
      to death.

NOTES

P. 33   MAECENAS: Gaius Cilnius Maecenas (died 8 B.C.), the aristocratic descendant of an old Etruscan family. Friend, confidential adviser, and diplomatic agent of Augustus. Friend and patron of Horace, who "dedicates" the work to him by addressing him in the first poem, as in the *Epodes*, the first three books of *Odes*, and the *Epistles*.

FABIUS: Fabius Maximus of Narbo, a typical Stoic essayist.

P. 35   THE MAN OF ATHENS: Supposed by some to refer to Timon of Athens.

P. 37   UMMIDIUS: This name, like many in the *Satires*, may derive from a character in Lucilius.

NAEVIUS (in some manuscripts "Maenius"), NOMENTANUS: Typical spendthrifts.

TANAIS: A eunuch, perhaps a freedman of Maecenas.

THE FATHER-IN-LAW OF VISELLIUS: Called *herniosus* by Porphyrion (scholar of the third century A.D., whose commentary on Horace is still extant, though not in its original form), who also quotes, with reference to this line, the Greek saying "either a eunuch or ruptured."

P. 38   CRISPINUS CONJUNCTIVITIS: Plotius Crispinus, a Stoic versifier and moralizer. Horace calls him *lippus*, in allusion to the eyestrain resulting from constant reading which makes the eyes red and watery. Horace himself also had this ailment, as he says, for instance, in *Sermones* I. 5. 30–31: *Hic oculis ego nigra meis collyria lippus illinere.*

P. 39   THE SYRIAN SOCIETY . . . : Horace begins the satire with a string of the decidedly fringe professions whose members mourn the passing of their benefactor Tigellius, who was apparently a soft touch for any fellow entertainer: (1) *Ambubaiarum collegia*, the "society" of feminine flute players from Syria; (2) *pharmacopolae*, quacks who hawked their drugs about the markets; (3) *mendici*, beggars, especially begging priests of Isis and Cybele, the latter known as "collectors for the Great Mother"; (4) *mimae,* actresses, "starlets," or "models"; (5) *balatrones,* "fast talkers," open-air confidence men.

THE DEATH OF TIGELLIUS: The Hermogenes Tigellius referred to here and at the beginning of the third satire of Book One is the *Sardinian* popular entertainer of previous years, known to Julius Caesar and Cicero. There is another man named Hermogenes Tigellius, referred to elsewhere by Horace as still alive and flourishing, a competent musician, on whom Horace is much harder than he is on the Sardinian songster of the earlier generation. The *second* Tigellius, whom Horace ribs mercilessly, is referred to at *Serm.* 1. 3, 129; 4. 72; 9. 25; 10. 18, 80, 90.

P. 40 FUFIDIUS: The name of an unidentified individual like many others mentioned in this satire: Rufillus, Gargonius, Cupiennius (possibly Gaius Cupiennius Libo, a friend of Augustus, but more probably "a certain Mr. Desirous"), Marsaeus, Cerinthus, Hypsaea, Catia.
TERENCE'S PLAY: *The Self-Tormentor*
CATO: Marcus Porcius Cato, "Cato the Censor" (234–149 B.C.).
IT IS WELL WORTH WHILE . . . : A parody of Ennius, with an emphatic insertion of NON:

> Audire est operae pretium, procedere recte
> qui moechis non voltis . . . [Horace].

> Audire est operae pretium procedere recte
> qui rem Romanam Latiumque augescere voltis
> [Ennius].

P. 41 GALBA: Sometimes identified with a prominent jurist.
SALLUSTIUS: Not the historian, Gaius Sallustius Crispus; perhaps his nephew, although Horace addresses a friendly Ode to the latter (*Carm.* ii. 2).
ORIGO: An actress of Cicero's day.

FAUSTA: The daughter of Sulla (Lucius Sulla Felix, 138–78 B.C.) and wife of the Milo who was accused of the murder of Clodius at Bovillae, January 20, 52 B.C. Although defended by Cicero, Milo was condemned to exile and finally returned from Marseilles only in 48 B.C., when he met his death in Italy.

VILLIUS: One of Fausta's lovers and therefore called "the son-in-law of Sulla," *Sullae gener*.

LONGARENUS: Another of Fausta's lovers.

P. 42 LYNCEUS: The keen-eyed Argonaut.

P. 43 OUR BIRD-WATCHER CAROLS . . . : Horace's three and a half lines in the Latin text constitute a clever paraphrase of a six-line epigram by Callimachus (*Anthologia Palatina*, xii. 102).

P. 44 TO DISTINGUISH BETWEEN . . . : Horace says, "to distinguish between the solid and the void" (*inane abscindere soldo*), with reference to Epicurean physics, where the atoms or matter (*solidum*) move in the void or empty space (*inane*).

TO QUOTE PHILODEMUS . . . : Horace here alludes to an epigram of Philodemus, a celebrated Greek Epicurean philosopher and writer of erotic epigrams (*ca.* 110—*ca.* 40–35 B.C.).

ILIA: The mother of Romulus.

EGERIA: Tutelary nymph and consort of Numa.

P. 46 TIGELLIUS: The Sardinian singer.

HIS FATHER'S: Julius Caesar, the adoptive father of Octavian.

P. 47 MAENIUS: Name of an unidentifiable individual, like others in this satire, Novius, Balbinus, Hagna, Ruso, Labeo, whose conduct typifies their excesses.

P. 48 THE DWARF SISYPHUS: An amusing freak, not quite two feet tall, kept by Mark Antony and given this overwhelming mythological nickname.

P. 51   IF THE . . . PHILOSOPHER ALONE IS KING: In Stoic doctrine
the *sapiens* was everywhere the perfect master of himself,
"king of kings," etc. A Lucilian fragment, quoted by
Porphyrion, rehearses the formula which Horace evidently
imitates here: *Non dum etiam qui haec omnia habebit,
Formosus dives liber rex solu' vocetur.* The subject of the
Sixth Stoic Paradox treated by Cicero is: *solum sapientem
esse divitem.*
CHRYSIPPUS: The chief Stoic philosopher (280–207 B.C.),
who succeeded Cleanthes as head of the Stoic sect.
ALFENUS: Alfenus Varus, a shoemaker from Cremona, who
came to Rome and had a brilliant career as a jurist, at-
tained the consulship (39 B.C.), and was accorded a public
funeral. He is also referred to by Vergil in the Ninth
Eclogue.

P. 52   THE POETS: The three most important writers of the Old
Comedy, of whose works only the eleven plays of Aristophanes (444–388 B.C.) are extant.
LUCILIUS: Gaius Lucilius (180–102 B.C.), a Roman knight
of good family and fortune, who served under Scipio
Aemilianus "Numantinus" (*ca.* 185–129 B.C.) in the
Numantine War, was a friend of Scipo and Laelius and
a member of the brilliant "Scipionic Circle." Lucilius
wrote some thirty books of satires, the majority in hexameters, of which we still have about 1,300 lines or parts
of lines. His work exerted an obviously great influence on
Horace and Juvenal.
THAT LUCKY STIFF, FANNIUS: *beatus Fannius,* a "lucky"
writer, to have so many readers. Like other names in this
satire, otherwise unidentifiable: Albius, Pomponius, Sulcius, Caprius, Caelius, Birrius, Rufillus, and Gargonius
(again, from Satire Two), Baius, Scetanus, Trebonius.

P. 55   PETILLIUS CAPITOLINUS: Accused of peculation, tried and
acquitted, although the evidence was strongly against him.

P. 57   LIKE THE JEWS: For the proselytizing spirit of the Jews,
         see also Matt. 23:15: "Woe unto you, scribes and Phar-
         isees, hypocrites! for ye compass sea and land to make one
         proselyte, and when he is made, ye make him twofold
         more the child of hell than yourselves"; also Cicero *Pro
         L. Flacco* 28: *scis quanta sit (Iudaeorum) manus, quanta
         concordia, quantum valeant in concionibus;* also Horace's
         phrase near the end of the next satire.

P. 58   Horace's trip to Brindisi, a seventeen-day journey cover-
         ing some 360 Roman miles, is easy to trace on a map of
         modern Italy (see map). Its occasion was the mission of

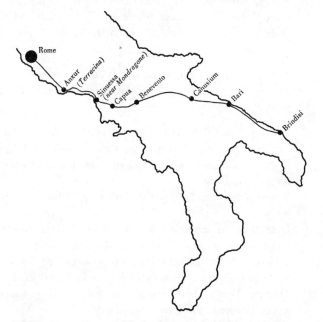

Maecenas to meet Mark Antony at Athens in the autumn
of 38 B.C., in an attempt to negotiate the growing differences between Antony and Octavian. Horace started

out with Heliodorus (otherwise unidentified) and met
Maecenas, L. Cocceius Nerva, and Fonteius Capito at
Anxur (modern Terracina). They were joined by Vergil,
Plotius Tucca, and Varius at Sinuessa. On arriving at
Brindisi, Maecenas, Cocceius (friendly to Antony), and
Capito (presumably uncommitted) embarked for Athens,
leaving Horace, Vergil, and Tucca to return to Rome.
Varius left the party at Canusium (modern Canosa).

The poem appears to be a rather close imitation of
Lucilius' description of his journey from Rome to Capua
and from there to the straits of Messina. For example,
Horace parodies lines of Lucilius when he mentions the
town "whose name just won't scan" (*mansuri oppidulo
quod versu dicere non est*). Scholars have not yet named
this *oppidulum*.

P. 62   LET APELLA THE JEW BELIEVE IT: *credat Iudaeus Apella /
non ego*, referring to the Roman opinion that the Jews
were extraordinarily superstitious.

P. 63   FELLOW-ETRUSCANS, OF LYDIAN STOCK: There was the
tradition that the Etruscan nobility was descended from
Lydian colonists, as the Roman aristocracy claimed de-
scent from Troy.
SERVIUS: Servius Tullius, the sixth king of Rome (578–535
B.C.).
LAEVINUS: An otherwise unknown descendant of the Va-
lerian *gens*, one of the great Roman families. Marcus
Valerius Poplicola helped Brutus in expelling Tarquinius
Superbus, the seventh king of Rome, banished in 510 B.C.
DECIUS: Decius Mus, consul 340 B.C., the first consul of
his family and therefore a *novus homo*.
APPIUS THE CENSOR: Probably Appius Claudius Caecus,
censor in 312 B.C., rather than Appius Clodius Pulcher,
censor in 50 B.C.

P. 67   NATTA: Otherwise unknown; by using lamp oil to rub himself with, he cheats his own lamps.

P. 68   RUPILIUS REX: P. Rupilius Rex of Praeneste (modern Palestrina), elected praetor in 43 B.C.; proscribed by the triumvirs, he fled to Brutus in Asia.

HALF-BREED PERSIUS: *hybrida . . . Persius,* perhaps the son of a Greek father and Roman mother.

LIKE A WHITE HORSE: *ut equis praecurreret albis;* white horses were regarded as the fastest.

P. 69   SO BRUTAL TO KINGS: Marcus Brutus had slain only one who could be called a king, Caesar, but he claimed descent from L. Junius Brutus, who drove Tarquinius Superbus into exile.

P. 70   PRIAPUS: In this melodramatic monologue the statue of Priapus speaks, describing the weird work of the two hags Canidia and Sagana, padding spookily around their haunts, "the Gardens of Maecenas." The area referred to on the Esquiline Hill had been a potter's field, but was acquired, cleared, and improved by Maecenas, like the Borghese Park or others in Rome today. Made handsome and habitable, the region included a section of the *agger* or embankment of Servius (the "Servian Wall"). In Horace's poem the scene still shows traces of the earlier funereal character of the district.

H. M. H. N. S.: *Hoc monumentum heredes non sequitur,* the usual inscription or a marker defining the dimensions of a plot of ground assigned for burial purposes.

None of the names in this satire can be accurately identified.

P. 73   THE SACRED WAY: *Via Sacra,* the oldest and most famous street in Rome, running through the Forum and along the foot of the Palatine, called *sacra* because of the shrines along the way.

BOLANUS: Unknown.

TRASTEVERE . . . VILLA AURELIA: *trans Tiberim . . . prope Caesaris hortos*, "gardens" left by Julius Caesar to the people of Rome.

P. 74   VISCUS: The two Visci (both mentioned in the next satire) were the sons of Vibius Vuscus, a Roman knight, literary men, and intimate friends of Horace.

P. 75   ARISTIUS FUSCUS: Intimate friend of Horace, to whom he addresses the Integer Vitae Ode (*Carm.* i. 22) and the tenth epistle of Book I.

P. 77   CATULLUS AND CALVUS: Gaius Valerius Catullus (87–?54 B.C.) and Gaius Licinius Calvus (82–47 B.C.), friends and contemporaries, writers of avant-garde lyric poetry; "modern poets."

P. 78   PITHOLAUS: A writer of epigrams, about whom little is known.

THE PECULATION OF PETILLIUS: Referred to earlier in the fourth satire of Book I.

CORVINUS: M. Valerius Mesalla Corvinus (64 B.C.–A.D. 8), the friend of Tibullus, and distinguished orator of the Augustan age.

PEDIUS PUBLICOLA: Also spelled Poplicola; not clearly identifiable, but obviously a type of eloquent, conscientious lawyer.

FURIUS THE FRENZIED: *Turgidus Alpinus iugulat dum Memnona dumque defingit Rheni luteum caput . . .* This "turgid Alpinist" had written an *Aethiopis* in which he introduced the slaying of Memnon by Achilles, as well as a poem on Caesar's Gallic Wars in which occurred the bombastic line *Iuppiter hibernas cana nive conspuit Alpes.* In the fifth satire of Book II, Horace "quotes" this line but substitutes "Furius" for "Iuppiter." Many editors follow Porphyrion in identifying the "Furius" alluded to in both passages as M. Furius Bibaculus, but as C. Nipperdey pointed out long ago (Jena, 1858) this identification is not tenable.

TARPA: Sp. Maecius Tarpa, a public licenser of plays.

FUNDANIUS: Otherwise unknown, but referred to again by Horace in *Serm.* ii. 8.

P. 79 DAVUS . . . CHREMES: Stock characters in Roman comedy.

POLLIO: Gaius Asinius Pollio (76 B.C.–A.D. 4), distinguished statesman, orator, poet, and historian. In 39 B.C. Pollio founded the first public library in Rome.

VARRO ATACINUS: P. Terentius Varro (82–*ca.* 35 B.C.), surnamed "Atacinus," not to be confused with the famous long-lived polymath, M. Terentius Varro, "Reatinus."

CASSIUS: Cassius Etruscus, otherwise unknown.

P. 80 ARBUSCULA: A famous mima, or actress, of some twenty years earlier.

PANTILIUS, DEMETRIUS, FANNIUS, HERMOGENES ("Homogenes"): Artists' of notoriously low tastes, contrasted with the select group of the poet's friends: Plotius (Plotius Tucca); Valgius (Gaius Valgius Rufus); Octavius (Octavius Musa, the poet and historian); Bibulus (L. Calpurnius Bibulus, comrade of Horace's student days); Servius (perhaps Servius Sulpicius Rufus the younger); Furnius (Caius Furnius, a distinguished orator).

HERE BOY: Addressed to the slave who was acting as Horace's secretary.

P. 99 TREBATIUS: Gaius Trebatius Testa, a friend of Cicero and prominent jurist; an "elder statesman."

P. 100 I COME FROM FRONTIER STOCK: The colony at Venusia (Horace's birthplace) was founded in 291 B.C. during the Third Samnite War. It borders on the provinces of Apulia and Lucania.

P. 101 CERVIUS: An informer, like Caprius and Sulcius of *Serm.* i. 4.

ALBUCIUS: Otherwise unknown; according to Porphyrion, he poisoned his mother.

TURIUS: A corrupt judge of Cicero's day.

SCAEVA: Otherwise unknown.

P. 102 LAELIUS: Gaius Laelius Sapiens, consul in 140 B.C., patron of Terence and principal speaker in Cicero's *Laelius* (or *De Amicitia*).

METELLUS: Q. Caecilius Metellus Macedonicus, consul in 143 B.C., a political opponent of Scipio but on friendly terms with him.

LUPUS: L. Cornelius Lupus, consul in 156 B.C.

WHO WRITES EVIL THINGS: *si mala condiderit in quem quis carmina.* The Twelve Tables, as quoted by Cicero and Pliny, prescribed capital punishment for *mala carmina,* i.e., slander. Horace takes the *mala* to mean "of bad quality."

P. 104 OFELLUS: A farmer of the old style whose land had been taken from him and assigned by Octavian to one of his veterans named Umbrenus (ll. 114 and 133). He probably was a neighbor of Horace near Venusia, one of the towns whose lands were taken for the reward of soldiers after the Battle of Philippi in 42 B.C.

P. 106 GALLONIUS: An auctioneer, satirized by Lucilius.

RUFUS: Impossible to identify certainly.

AVIDIENUS ... DOG: A notorious miser, nicknamed "Dog" in reference to the Cynics.

ALBUCIUS ... NAEVIUS ... TRAUSIUS ... UMBRENUS: Otherwise unknown.

P. 110 DAMASIPPUS: A bankrupt speculator, recently converted to Stoicism.

TO THE FARM: Horace's Sabine Farm.

PLATO: Perhaps the writer of Middle Comedy (428–389 B.C.).

MENANDER: Chief poet of New Comedy (342–291 B.C.).

ARCHILOCHUS: The early Greek satirist (714–676 B.C.).

EUPOLIS: A writer of Old Comedy (*ca.* 446–411 B.C.), mentioned along with Cratinus and Aristophanes in *Serm.* i. 4.

P. 111 ON THE STREET: *Ianum / ad medium,* "the middle Janus," at the central arch, a quarter in the Forum where most of the business in lending and investing money was transacted.

THE SLY OLD SISYPHUS: *vafer . . . Sisyphus,* proverbially the cunningest of men (Homer *Iliad* vi. 153). Corinthian bronze was famous from early times; Sisyphus was the mythological king of Corinth, and one of his bronze possessions would be a genuine antique, no "authentic reproduction." Cf. also Aeschylus, *Sisyphus,* frag. 229: "a bronze pan mounted on a lion."

MERCURY THE METTLESOME: *Mercuriale . . . cognomen,* "Mercury's favorite," as one protected by the god of commerce and gain.

P. 112 STERTINIUS: An oracle among Stoics, but otherwise unknown.

THE BRIDGE: The Fabrician Bridge, built in 62 B.C.

P. 113 FUFIUS . . . ILIONA: With reference to a performance of Pacuvius' play *Ilione.*

NERIUS: A banker.

CICUTA: "Hemlock," a moneylender.

P. 114 PERELLIUS: The creditor's name.

ANTICYRA: Greek town on the Gulf of Corinth, best source of hellebore, which was regarded as a cure for insanity.

STABERIUS: Unknown.

ARRIUS: Quintus Arrius, who gave a funeral feast in honor of his father at which several thousand guests were present.

P. 115 ARISTIPPUS: A disciple of Socrates and founder of the Cyrenaic School of philosophical hedonism (*fl.* 370 B.C.).

P. 117 OPIMIUS IMPOVERISHED: *Pauper Opimius*, i.e., "poor Mr. Welloff."

P. 118 CRATERUS: A celebrated physician of Cicero's day.

P. 122 PRODIGAL SON OF AESOP: Palmer's note on this passage is worth quoting at length: "Aesopus, the famous tragic actor, contemporary of Roscius, the famous comic actor, and friend of Cicero, left an enormous fortune to his prodigal son, of whom Cicero writes, *Att.* xi. 15. 3: *filius Aesopi me excruciat.* . . . He carried on an amour with Metella, a notorious adulteress, wife of P. Cornelius Spinther. Dolabella, Cicero's son-in-law, husband of his only daughter Tullia, had become entangled by the same woman: Cicero's 'torture' was probably caused by some circumstances connected with these intrigues. It is curious that Horace, in speaking of this hare-brained spendthrift, uses the same words, *filius Aesopi,* the expression used by Cicero. This looks as if Horace was fresh from a study of Cicero's letters, a conclusion which is to be drawn from many passages beside this." (Arthur Palmer, *The Satires of Horace* [London, 1901].)

POLEMON . . . XENOCRATES' VOICE: Polemon, an Athenian roustabout, returning home from a spree, heard the voice of Xenocrates expounding the philosophy of the Academic School (396–314 B.C.). He entered the room, was immediately converted by the doctrine, and afterward became the successor of Xenocrates as head of the school.

EXCLUDED LOVER: *amator / exclusus.* The next lines, 262–71, constitute a transposition into dactylic hexameters of lines from the opening of Terence's play *The Eunuch.*

P. 124 MARIUS . . . HELEN: A reference to the principals in a sensational murder-suicide case apparently much discussed at the time.

P. 125 THE DAY THOU SETTEST: *dies Jovis,* our Thursday. There was no Roman week, but here is a trace of the Eastern week, as well as a reference to ceremonial bathing in the morning, an Eastern, not a Roman, custom.

AGAVE: In the *Bacchae* of Euripides.

TURBO: A small but stalwart gladiator.

P. 127 CATIUS: Otherwise unknown; perhaps an Epicurean philosopher or a writer on baking.

P. 128 AUFIDIUS: Otherwise unknown.

P. 131 TO DRINK DEEP: *fontis ut adire remotos atque haurire queam vitae praecepta beatae;* a parody of Lucretius, *De Rerum Natura* i. 927 and iv. 2: *iuvat integros accedere fontis atque haurire.*

P. 132 TEIRESIAS: This satire is a burlesque continuation of the scene in *Odyssey* xi. 90 ff., where Ulysses in the lower world learns from Teiresias that he will return home safely but reduced to poverty.

P. 133 SPORCA MISERIA: "some filthy Dama," a common slave-name, as in *Serm.* i. 6 and elsewhere.

P. 134 THE MODERN POET FURIUS: For the verse of "Furius," *Iuppiter hibernas cana nive conspuit Alpes,* Horace writes here: *Furius hibernas cana nive conspuet Alpes.*

P. 135 NASICA . . . CORANUS: Roman names otherwise unknown. Like the Roman terms *scriba* and *quinquevir,* they do not perplex Ulysses and Teiresias.

A FINE YOUNG HERO: A reference to Octavian, at this time a little over thirty.

P. 138 THIS WAS WHAT I HAD PRAYED FOR: A SMALL PIECE OF LAND: *Hoc erat in votis: modus agri, non ita magnus*—i.e., Horace's Sabine Farm.

SON OF MAIA: Mercury, the god of gain (and of poets, having invented the lyre).

THANKS TO HERCULES: In the story here alluded to (and

told by Porphyrion in his commentary), Mercury is appealed to by Hercules and reveals the treasure at his request. Hercules was the Italic god, sometimes associated with Silvanus. He came to be connected with treasure-trove, and a tenth of the find was donated to him.

P. 139 FUNERAL HALLS: A reference to Venus Libitina, ancient Italic goddess of funerals.

MONARCH / OF MORNING: *Matutine pater;* Matutinus was an ancient Italic god of the early morning, here identified with Janus, god of good beginnings.

P. 140 WHAT'S UP IN THE BALKANS?: The Dacians had gone over to Antony's side; in 31 B.C. an invasion was feared, and in 30 war was declared against them.

P. 141 LEPOS: A dancer of the day, "Mr. Charming."

CERVIUS: A country neighbor of Horace, perhaps the proverbial Deer Old Fellow, because the deer was said to live to a great age (*cervina senectus,* Juvenal xiv. 251).

ARELLIUS: Another neighbor, rich but apparently miserly, "Mr. Driedup."

P. 144 THE FREEDOM TRADITIONALLY YOURS: *libertate Decembri;* at the feast of the Saturnalia (December 17 to 24) slaves were given considerable liberty of speech and action, in memory of the Golden Age in which there were no masters and slaves.

VOLANERIUS: Unknown.

P. 145 MULVIUS & Co.: Unidentified diners-out.

P. 148 PAUSIAS: Of Sicyon, famous Greek painter (*fl. ca.* 370 B.C.).

ATHLETES: Horace names Fulvius and Rutuba, probably two contemporary gladiators, and Pacideianus, a gladiator mentioned by Lucilius and Cicero.

P. 150 THE DINNER: The guest list: Fundanius, Viscus, Servilius Balatro, Vibidius, Varius, Maecenas, Nomentanus, Nasidienus, Porcius.

HYDASPES: An Indian slave, a rare luxury.

P. 151 ALCON: Another slave.

"SHADES": *umbrae,* uninvited guests, left to a guest to bring with him.

P. 165 HERCULES' DOORS: That is, on one of the columns before the entrance to the temple of Hercules, the patron of gladiators.

P. 166 TO THE OPPOSITE SIDE: *in Aristippi furtim praecepta relabor* ("I slip back quietly into the teachings of Aristippus"), i.e., into the doctrine of hedonism.

GLYCON: A famous contemporary athlete.

P. 167 "YOU WILL . . . BE KING": Transposition into dactylic hexameter of a jingle in trochaic tetrameter: *rex eris si recte facies si non facies non eris.*

THE ROSCIAN LAW: L. Roscius Otho, when tribune of the people in 68 B.C., passed a law that the fourteen rows of seats at the theater just above the orchestra should be assigned to the *equites.*

P. 168 CURIUS / CAMILLUS: Solid old Romans.

PUPIUS: A writer of tragedy, otherwise unknown.

BAIAE: A favorite seashore resort of Romans.

P. 169 TEANO: Teanum Sidicinum, an inland resort town of Campania.

P. 170 LOLLIUS MAXIMUS: Addressed again in the eighteenth epistle of this book, where it appears that he had served as a soldier in the war against the Cantabri in the north of Spain (25–24 B.C.). Otherwise unknown, but perhaps a relative of the distinguished M. Lollius to whom *Carm.* iv. 9 is addressed.

P. 171 UNSINKABLE: *immersabilis.*

P. 174 JULIUS FLORUS: Little is known about him except for Horace's reference here to the mission to Armenia in 20 B.C. Porphyrion says that he wrote satires adapted from Ennius, Lucilius, and Varro.

TIBERIUS: Tiberius Claudius Nero, son of Tiberius Claudius Nero and Livia, the wife of Augustus. He was adopted by Augustus in A.D. 3, after the death of Gaius and Lucius Caesar, and of course eventually became the emperor "Tiberius" (Tiberius Julius Caesar Augustus) who succeeded Augustus and ruled A.D. 14–37.

TITIUS: Otherwise unknown.

CELSUS: Celsus Albinovanus, to whom the eighth epistle of this book is addressed.

PALATINE LIBRARY: The public library founded by Octavian in 28 B.C. in the temple of Apollo on the Palatine Hill.

P. 175 MUNATIUS: Probably the son of Lucius Munatius Plancus to whom *Carm*. i. 7 is addressed.

P. 176 TIBULLUS: Albius Tibullus, the elegiac poet (48?–19 B.C.).

CASSIUS OF PARMA: One of the assassins of Caesar, but called *Parmensis* to distinguish him from the more famous leader of the conspiracy Gaius Cassius Longinus. Cassius Parmensis was put to death on orders from Octavian after the battle of Actium. He was obviously, in Horace's opinion, a rather good poet.

P. 177 TORQUATUS: Otherwise unknown.

ARCHIAS: According to Porphyrion, a maker of unpretentious furniture.

SECOND CONSULATE TAURIAN: That is, in the second consulship of T. Statilius Taurus, 26 B.C.

MOSCHUS: A rhetorician of Pergamum, accused of poisoning and defended by Torquatus and Asinius Pollio. Seneca says (*Contr*. ii. 151. 13) that he was found guilty and went into exile at Marseilles, where he taught rhetoric.

CAESAR'S BIRTHDAY: Augustus' birthday, September 23, celebrated by the Roman knights on two successive days.

P. 178 SEPTICIUS, BUTRA, SABINUS: Otherwise unknown.

P. 179 NIL ADMIRARI: "to marvel at nothing," as in Cicero's

phrase and in Pythagoras' proverbial *mēden thaumazein.*

P. 180 MUTUS: Otherwise unknown.

AGRIPPA'S ARCADE: *porticus Agrippae,* a portico near the Pantheon built by Agrippa (M. Vipsanius Agrippa, 63 B.C.–A.D. 12, the able general and right-hand man of Augustus), one of the most popular lounging places in Rome. Also called from its frescoes representing the voyage of the Argonauts, the *porticus Argonauticarum.*

CIBYRA: A commercial city of Phrygia.

BITHYNIA: A province of Asia Minor north of Phrygia, bordering on the Black Sea.

P. 181 THE KING OF CAPPADOCIA: Ariobarzanes III (52–42 B.C.).

LUCULLUS: L. Licinius Lucullus (*ca.* 117–56 B.C.), famous for luxurious living at the end of a long public career. Horace's story is repeated by Plutarch, who also moralizes on the career of the general as follows: "And indeed, Lucullus' life, like the Old Comedy, presents us at the commencement with acts of policy and of war, at the end offering nothing but good eating and drinking, feastings and revelings, and mere play."

FABIANS . . . VELINES: Names of tribes, denoting typical voting districts.

P. 182 GARGILIUS: Otherwise unknown.

MIMNERMUS: Greek elegiac poet of Colophon (*fl.* 632–629 B.C.).

P. 184 OR DEPLORING THE FLIGHT OF CINARA (UNDER WHOSE REIGN I WAS NOT AS I AM): *fugam Cinarae maerere protervae;* I quote in the parenthesis lines 3 and 4 from *Carm.* iv. 1: *non sum qualis eram bonae sub regno Cinarae.* Horace also refers to Cinara in *Carm.* iv. 13. 21 and *Epistles* i. 14. 33.

P. 185 REPLY TELEMACHUS GAVE: Cf. *Odyssey* iv. 601 ff.

PHILIPPUS: L. Marcus Philippus, a famous Roman orator, consul in 91 B.C., distinguished for his energy and wit.

CARINAE: A fashionable quarter of Rome, so called because some of the buildings on it resembled the hulls of ships. It was on the western slope of the southern spur of the Esquiline Hill, where the church of S. Pietro in Vincoli now stands. It was not far from the Forum, but the approach is steep and Philippus was old.

VULTEIUS MENA (Or Volteius); the name shows that he was a freedman of Greek birth and that his *patronus* was a Volteius.

P. 186 LATIN HOLIDAYS: *indictis* (*sc. feriis*) *Latinis*, i.e., *feriae Latinae,* vacations declared on a date not fixed but appointed and announced each year, usually at the end of April or beginning of May.

P. 188 CELSUS: Celsus Albinovanus, mentioned earlier in the third epistle.

P. 190 SEPTIMIUS: Probably the friend addressed in *Carm.* ii. 6.

P. 191 FUSCUS: Aristius Fuscus, Horace's close friend, mentioned in *Serm.* i. 9, 10, and the person to whom the *Integer vitae* Ode (*Carm.* i. 22) is addressed.

THE DOG-STAR'S FURY: The sun enters the constellation of the Lion on July 23, and the Dogstar rises about the same time.

P. 192 THE MOSS OF AQUINUM: From lichens found at Aquinum in Latium, a dye was made which imitated the Tyrian purple but which was of course less valuable.

P. 193 THE SHRINE OF OUR LADY OF VACUITY: *fanum . . . Vacunae.* Vacuna was a Sabine goddess. The modern title I give her is taken from Gilbert Highet's chapter on Horace in *Poets in a Landscape* (New York, 1957).

P. 194 BULLATIUS: Otherwise unknown.

LEBEDUS: A small town on the coast between Smyrna and Colophon.

GABII / OR FIDENAE: Important places in early times, these towns, like *Ulubrae* at the end of the letter ("Frogville"), had become deserted villages.

P. 196 ICCIUS: Unknown except for this reference and *Carm.* i. 29.

P. 197 POMPEIUS GROSPHUS: Also mentioned in *Carm.* ii. 16.

CANTABRIANS: Eventually conquered by Agrippa in 19 B.C.

ARMENIANS: Submitted to Tiberius without resistance after King Artaxias had been murdered by his subjects.

CRASSUS' BANNERS: Phraates, the Parthian king, restored the Roman standards taken long before from Crassus at Carrhae (53 B.C.).

PROSPERITY FLOWS: *aurea fruges Italiae pleno defudit Copia cornu.*

P. 198 VINIUS: His cognomen, as Horace says in lines 8 and 9, was Asina; both Asina and Asellus were Roman cognomina. Asina does the donkey work of delivering the three books of Odes to Augustus. Augustus' reply to this letter is partially preserved in the Suetonian *Vita:* "Onysius (Monsieur L'Âne) has brought me your little volume, and I accept it, small as it is, in good part, as an apology. But you seem to me to be afraid that your books may be bigger than you are yourself; but it is only stature that you lack, not girth. So you may write on a pint pot, that the circumference of your volume may be well rounded out, like that of your own belly."

PYRRIA: The name of a maid in a play of Titinius, who stole a ball of wool but, being drunk, carried it so clumsily that she was caught.

P. 199 BE OFF . . . : A tripping last line: *vade vale cave ne titubes mandataque frangas.*

P. 200 VARIA: Modern Vico Varo, a small town on the Anio; the nearest market town.

LAMIA: L. Aelius Lamia, also referred to in *Carm.* iii. 17. Though not famous in the age of the Republic, the Lamiae were a prominent family under the Empire.

P. 202 THE OX WISHES HE WERE CAPARISONED . . . : *optat ephippia bos, piger optat arare caballus.*

P. 203 VALA: Numonius Vala, otherwise unknown.

VELIA: A town in Lucania twenty-four miles south of Paestum.

ANTONIUS MUSA: A freedman and physician of Augustus, whom he had cured of a serious illness in 23 B.C. by the cold-water treatment.

CLUSIUM: A town in Etruria; or perhaps the reference is to some baths twelve miles south of Clusium, at modern S. Casciano di Bagni.

P. 204 STRANGER TO ELEA: Velia was the Latin name for Elea, the colony famous in early days as the site of the Eleatic School of philosophy founded by Xenophanes in 540 B.C. Among its eminent philosophers were Parmenides, Zeno, and Melissus. A "Stranger from Elea" is one of the interlocutors in two dialogues of Plato, the *Sophist* and the *Statesman*.

MAENIUS: A typical spendthrift.

P. 206 QUINCTIUS: Otherwise unknown, but possibly the Quinctius Hirpinus to whom *Carm.* ii. 11 is addressed.

P. 207 JUPITER ALONE . . . : These lines are said to be from a panegyric of Augustus by Lucius Varius.

P. 209 DIONYSUS . . . PENTHEUS: A paraphrase of Euripides, *Bacchae*, lines 492–98.

P. 210 LEFTY: *Scaeva*, i.e., "Monsieur Gauche."

P. 211 CAN'T WIND UP EVENTUALLY AT CORINTH: A proverbial Greek expression: "Not every man may go to Corinth."

P. 214 LOLLIUS: The Lollius Maximus of the second epistle.

P. 215 WHETHER LONG JOHN: Reading *Castor sciat an Dolichos*.

MINUCIAN WAY: Mentioned only here and in Cicero, *Ad Att.* ix. 6. 1; perhaps the road from Beneventum through Canusium to Brundisium which Horace took on his journey to Brundisium. It was shorter but rougher than the Via Appia to Brundisium by way of Tarentum, later put in good order by Trajan.

EUTRAPELUS: Publius Volumnius Eutrapelus, who received his cognomen on account of his wit (*eutrapelia*).

P. 216 SPANISH CAMPAIGN: The campaign against the Cantabrians, under the lead of Augustus himself, 27–25 B.C.

P. 218 THEON THE VENOMOUS: A proverbial calumniator.

LICENZA: The modern name of the river Digentia near Horace's Sabine Farm.

CANTALUPO: Cantalupo Bardello, modern name of Mandela, the village near Horace's farm.

P. 220 CRATINUS: The poet, famous for his conviviality.

A CAREER IN BUSINESS: *Forum putealque Libonis:* the *puteal Libonis* was a place in the Forum, which had been struck by lightning and surrounded by a low wall or curbing like that of a well (*puteus*). The praetor held court there, and the stalls of the money-changers were close by.

CATO: Probably Cato Uticensis (95–46 B.C.).

IARBITAS . . . TIMAGENES: Iarbitas was an imitator of Timagenes, a Greek rhetorician of Alexandria (*fl.* 55 B.C.) who was later brought to Rome; he had a reputation for wit, eloquence, and bitterness.

P. 222 AND THAT'S WHY THEY CRY AND COMPLAIN: *hinc illae lacrimae,* a proverbial saying, from Terence's play *The Woman of Andros,* line 126.

P. 223   VERTUMNUM IANUMQUE, LIBER, SPECTARE VIDERIS
   SCILICET UT PROSTES SOSIORUM PUMICE MUNDUS.

The first two lines picture the book as ready to saunter forth on the *vicus Tuscus,* where the bookstalls were. The Sosii brothers had a shop there, near a statue of Vertumnus-Janus, i.e., the god of change and exchange; and the region was a "red-light" district as well.

P. 224 UTICA . . . VILLAGE IN SPAIN: Utica in North Africa (near Carthage) and Ilerda in Spain, representing the provinces generally, where books that had lost their popularity at Rome might still find a sale.

LOLLIUS . . . LEPIDUS: 21 B.C.: M. Lollius was elected without a colleague, because the other consulship was intended for Augustus. When Augustus declined the position, Lollius took Lepidus as his colleague.

DECEMBER: The Suetonian vita says, *sexto idus Decembris,* i.e., December 8 (65 B.C.).

P. 248 LIBER: Bacchus.

P. 249 THE FAMOUS TWELVE TABLES: The XII Tables, a collection of the principal rules of the oldest Roman law originating in ancient customs (*mos maiorum*); in early times used as schoolbooks.

ANTIQUE TREATIES: A copy of the treaty made by Tarquinius Superbus with Gabii was extant in Horace's time. It was written on bull's hide.

PONTIFICAL BOOKS: The books containing the directions for rituals and the annals of the pontiffs.

YELLOWED SIBYLLINE LEAVES: *annosa volumina vatum* ("moldy scrolls of seers").

ALBAN MOUNT: As on a Roman Parnassus.

P. 250 AFRANIUS: Lucius Afranius, born in 154 B.C. A writer of *togatae,* comedies based on Italian life.

EPICHARMUS: A writer of the so-called Sicilian Comedy (540–450 B.C.).

CAECILIUS: A Roman comic writer, author of *palliatae* (adaptations of the New Comedy style), died 168 B.C.

P. 251 ANDRONICUS: Livius Andronicus' first play was produced in 240 B.C.

ORBILIUS: Lucius Orbilius Pupillus, a native of Beneventum, migrated to Rome at age fifty (63 B.C.); here immortalized by Horace as *plagosus,* "the flogger."

ATTA: A writer of *togatae,* contemporary with Afranius.

SALIAN MOTETS: *Saliare . . . carmen:* the hymns of the Salii, a priesthood said to have been instituted by Numa. The hymns were virtually unintelligible in later times.

P. 253 WHERE WOULD THE CHOIR: With reference to Horace's own *Carmen Saeculare*.

P. 257 CHOERILUS: An epic poet of Iasos who wrote a poor poem on the exploits of Alexander and was rewarded for it.

P. 258 LYSIPPUS: One of the most famous Greek sculptors.
BOEOTIA: Boeotians were proverbially stupid.

P. 259 STINKY STREET: The *vicus Tuscus*, also with a pun on *tus* ("incense"); cf. also Epistle 20, Book I.

P. 260 FLORUS: The Julius Florus to whom Epistle 3 of Book I is addressed.

P. 261 ONE OF LUCULLUS' soldiers: Lucullus commanded the Romans in the war against Mithridates, 74–67 B.C.

P. 262 LIKE BION: Bion the Borysthenite, notorious for his wit and cynicism, taught philosophy at Athens early in the third century B.C.

P. 264 PROPERTIUS: *Carmina compono, hic elegos:* I take *hic* here as a reference to Propertius (Sextus Aurelius Propertius, the elegist, born 51 B.C.).
CATO / OR CETHEGUS: Cato the Censor, and Cethegus (consul in 204 B.C.).

P. 269 HEROD'S PALM GROVES: *Herodis palmetis pinguibus:* the date-palm groves at Jericho, i.e., the "wealth" of Herod the Great, King of Judaea 39–4 B.C.

P. 271 Perhaps Gn. Calpurnius Piso (consul in 23 B.C.) and his two sons.

P. 272 GLADIATOR'S SCHOOL: *Aemilium . . . ludum,* a gladiatorial training school near the Circus Maximus (erected by Aemilius Lepidus). There were shops on the outside, opening on the street, the last one in the row or arcade being the craftsman's workshop mentioned here.

P. 273 ALL OUR PROJECTS: Constructions begun by Julius Caesar but continued and completed only by his successors. (1) The Portus Julius: the cutting-in of a channel to connect the Lucrine Lake with the Lake of Avernus; (2) the draining of the Pontine Marshes; (3) the straightening of the course of the Tiber to prevent flooding and to protect farm lands.

P. 275 THE ROMAN KNIGHTS AND THOSE WRETCHED WIGHTS: The whole audience: the *equites* had the choice seats.

P. 277 TELL ME, O MUSE: A paraphrase of the opening lines of the *Odyssey*.
ANTIPHATES: King of the Laestrygonians, *Odyssey* x. 100 ff.

P. 285 LAMIA: A female monster used to frighten Roman children.
SOSIUS AND SON: As in *Epistles* i. 20: a famous bookdealer.

P. 286 MESSALLA: The lawyer mentioned in *Serm* i. 10.
AULUS CASCELLIUS: A distinguished jurist, contemporary with Trebatius.

P. 289 QUINTILIUS: Quintilius Varus, whose death in 23 B.C. Horace laments in *Carm*. i. 24.

P. 290 RICHARD BENTLEY: *fiet Aristarchus* ("will prove to be an Aristarchus"): Aristarchus was the famous Alexandrian Homeric scholar of the second century B.C. (*ca*. 217–143 B.C.), thought of proverbially as the keen, searching critic.